state
of the
nation

Other Potomac Associates Books

HOPES AND FEARS OF THE AMERICAN PEOPLE

THE LIMITS TO GROWTH

A NEW ISOLATIONISM: THREAT OR PROMISE?

U.S. HEALTH CARE: WHAT'S WRONG AND WHAT'S RIGHT

POTOMAC ASSOCIATES is a nonpartisan research and analysis organization which seeks to encourage lively inquiry into critical issues of public policy. Its purpose is to heighten public understanding and improve public discourse on significant contemporary problems, national and international.

POTOMAC ASSOCIATES provides a forum for distinctive points of view through publication of timely studies and occasional papers by outstanding authorities in the United States and abroad. Although publication implies belief by Potomac Associates in the basic importance and validity of each study, views expressed are those of the author.

POTOMAC ASSOCIATES is a non-tax-exempt firm located at 1707 L Street, NW, Washington, D.C. 20036.

A POTOMAC ASSOCIATES BOOK

state of the nation

edited by
William Watts and
Lloyd A. Free

Universe Books
New York

Published in the United States of America in 1973 by Universe Books,
381 Park Avenue South, New York, N.Y. 10016

© 1973 by Potomac Associates

Library of Congress Catalog Card Number: 72-92491
Cloth edition: ISBN 0-87663-178-2
Paperback edition: ISBN 0-87663-904-X

Printed in the United States of America

Contents

PREFACE   *page 11*

ACKNOWLEDGMENTS   *page 15*

I   PROGRESS OR DECLINE: THE PUBLIC'S EVALUATION   *page 19*

II   WORRIES AND CONCERNS   *page 33*

III   SOCIAL CHANGE: THE YOUNG, THE OLD, THE WOMEN   *page 42*

IV   URBAN AFFAIRS   *page 64*

V   MINORITY GROUPS   *page 84*

VI   JUSTICE, CRIME, AND LAW   *page 104*

VII   HEALTH CARE   *page 121*

VIII   THE ENVIRONMENT   *page 135*

IX   ECONOMIC AFFAIRS   *page 155*

X   INTERNATIONAL AFFAIRS   *page 179*

XI   DEFENSE AND AID   *page 205*

XII   GOVERNMENTAL REFORM AND REORGANIZATION   *page 223*

XIII   AMERICANS' VALUES, ASPIRATIONS, AND
       FEARS   *page 249*

XIV   STATE OF THE NATION   *page 264*

       AFTERWORD   *page 270*

       APPENDIX 1: Questions and Overall Results   *page 274*

       APPENDIX 2: Tables Giving Demographic Breakdowns
       page 302

       APPENDIX 3: Computing Personal and National
       Ladder Ratings   *page 352*

       APPENDIX 4: International Patterns   *page 353*

       APPENDIX 5: Computing Composite Scores   *page 355*

       APPENDIX 6: Design and Composition of the Sample
       page 358

Tables

TABLE   1   Major National Issues and Degrees of Public Concern   *page 35*

TABLE   2   Concern with International Threats   *page 39*

TABLE   3   Personal Ladder Ratings of Women and Men   *page 62*

TABLE   4   Present Place and Preferred Place of Residence   *page 82*

TABLE   5   Price and Wage Changes, February 1971-May 1972   *page 161*

TABLE   6   Internationalists and Isolationists   *page 203*

TABLE   7   Support for Governmental Spending on Major National Issues   *page 252*

TABLE   8   National Hopes   *page 257*

TABLE   9   National Fears   *page 258*

TABLE   10   Personal Hopes   *page 259*

TABLE   11   Personal Fears   *page 260*

TABLE   A-1   Average Personal Ladder Ratings   *page 304*

TABLE   A-2   Average National Ladder Ratings   *page 307*

TABLE   A-3   Worries and Concerns: International (composite scores)   *page 310*

TABLE   A-4   Worries and Concerns: Domestic (composite scores)   *page 313*

TABLE   A-5   International Patterns   *page 316*

TABLE   A-6   Governmental Spending: International and Defense (composite scores)   *page 318*

TABLE   A-7   Governmental Spending: Domestic (composite scores)   *page 320*

TABLE   A-8   Trust and Confidence (composite scores)   *page 323*

TABLE   A-9   Evaluations of Governmental System (composite scores)   *page 326*

TABLE A-10   Need for Change in Governmental System   *page 328*

TABLE A-11   Progress: International Problem Areas (composite scores)   *page 330*

TABLE A-12   Progress: Foreign Policy Matters in General   *page 332*

TABLE A-13   Progress: Domestic Problem Areas (composite scores)   *page 334*

TABLE A-14   Progress: Domestic Problems in General   *page 337*

TABLE A-15   Progress: Overall Situation at Home and Abroad   *page 339*

TABLE A-16   Concerns and Governmental Spending (overall composite scores)   *page 341*

TABLE A-17   Progress and Confidence (overall composite scores)   *page 343*

TABLE A-18   Evaluation of International Situation in General   *page 346*

TABLE A-19   Evaluation of Domestic Situation in General   *page 348*

TABLE A-20   Evaluation of Overall State of the Nation   *page 350*

TABLE A-21   Composition of the Sample   *page 360*

Preface

Where do we stand as a nation today? How far have we come in the past few years? The past year? Where are we going? How do we think things are being handled in this country? How are we doing abroad?

What objectively *is* the state of the nation? And what psychologically is the mood of the American people?

How do Americans view and understand the realities of the worlds—local, national, international—in which they live? What are the assumptions, values, aspirations, and fears that motivate them? How do the perceptions of Americans accord with the facts?

These questions are large and difficult to deal with. Yet they are questions that all of us, at one time or another, ponder and worry about. In a land as vast and varied as ours, with a citizenry of so many backgrounds, races, outlooks, and shades of opinion, it is no wonder that reliable answers are extraordinarily hard to come by. The current proliferation of study projects, both governmental and private, aimed at measuring the quality of life in the United States is direct testimonial to the importance attached to finding such answers. For on those answers can, and should, hinge national decisions that will affect the lives of us all.

STATE OF THE NATION

State of the Nation represents an attempt to take the composite temperature and pulse of the American body politic. It is an effort we intend to repeat at least every two years. Because of its very breadth and scope, we recognize that this first effort is bound to have flaws. But we hope our study will contribute to the great

11

and continuing discussion of national needs and national purpose.

Just what is the nature of the project?

In brief, we have tried to combine a succinct unbiased over-view of the major events of the past year with an unusually sensitive measurement of public attitudes toward these events and toward national trends and developments as a whole. (Just how we went about measuring those attitudes is spelled out in Chapter I.) By juxtaposing an objective, factual review of the past year's highlights in a number of key policy areas with an analysis of the subjective views of the citizens at large about those same policy areas, we have attempted to develop a unique portrait of America and Americans today.

This portrait is intended to help every concerned citizen—from White House official and member of Congress to the average man or woman on the street—understand better the interplay between events and the way in which those events are viewed by the public at large. Through such an understanding, we hope to clarify constraints and opportunities for policymakers, define more sharply the aspirations of our citizens, and illuminate paths for leadership.

Any survey of this kind must, of course, set limits on both the issues examined and the time span covered.

We found considerable guidance in selecting the most important issues for citizens of this country by reviewing the findings of the first Potomac Associates book, *Hopes and Fears of the American People.** That study was based in part on a sampling technique identical to the one employed in this book, a technique by which concerns and aspirations of Americans for their own lives and for the nation as a whole can be determined. Beyond that, naturally, we consulted informed individuals, newspapers, other opinion samples and annual reviews, and our own judgments to assemble our list of subject areas. The fields of concern we chose do not constitute a fixed agenda for future volumes in this series. Quite to the contrary, we foresee a revised table of contents with each subsequent edition, to take account of refinements in our technique, the changing course of events, and shifts in citizens' concerns.

The question of an appropriate time span presented another

---

* Albert H. Cantril and Charles W. Roll, Jr., *Hopes and Fears of the American People* (New York: Universe Books, 1971).

kind of problem. The calendar year seemed the appropriate choice at the outset, particularly with a presidential election year ahead. Sample opinion at the beginning of 1972, cover the year 1971, write the book, and release the results in mid-1972, in time to influence electoral thinking—the logic for this approach seemed unassailable.

But further reflection and the unpredictable course of public events moved us in another direction. First of all, the announcements in 1971 of President Richard M. Nixon's planned trips to Peking and Moscow in the first half of 1972 meant that any opinion sampling in advance of those journeys, and any historical review that did not include them in its perspective, would quite simply be guilty of an omission of critical, perhaps fatal, magnitude. Beyond that, there was the problem of obtaining the most current governmental statistics for this survey, in which the federal role is of prime importance. In many instances, the most important data do not appear until the end of the federal fiscal year, June 30, when final tallies and reports are completed.

As we began to settle on a mid-year cutoff point, other considerations appeared to support this approach. As an election year moves on into summer—particularly a presidential election year —the views and opinions of citizens inevitably become more focused. The issues are discussed and debated in a more highly charged political atmosphere. And new trends are more likely to emerge as the public concentrates on broad national concerns.

Finally, and decisively for us, we kept returning to the question, What is the purpose of the book? Did we want to publish a document in the middle of an electoral campaign, with the goal of influencing the course of that campaign by providing observer and practitioner alike with a combined polling guide and briefing yearbook? Or did we want to wait and publish after the elections, hoping instead that our findings would help explain what had just happened and would assist those charged with leadership—in and out of government, at every level of our society—in charting new paths and assignments ahead?

As our deliberations progressed, the decision all but made itself. The federal fiscal year it should be. The survey year for this book therefore covers the period from July 1971 through June 1972, although, when appropriate, references are made to events and studies outside that time frame.

The opinion sampling for the book was commissioned by Potomac Associates and conducted exclusively through The Gallup Organization. Field questioning was carried out during and between the first two weekends in June 1972, just at the end of our survey year. A somewhat larger-than-average national sample, 1,802 individuals, was polled. To give greater statistical reliability to analyses relating to black Americans, the number of cases in this population group was specially augmented. The composition of the sample and an explanation of how it was drawn are contained in Appendix 6. The questionnaire itself, a summary of all answers, and selected tables showing detailed demographic responses are set forth in Appendixes 1 and 2.

So there we are. In the pages that follow we hope readers will find a useful, informative, and instructive picture of contemporary America.

In those pages the record of the past year speaks.

The people themselves also speak, often in their own words, frequently in direct and poignant phrases.

We believe there is much to be learned from what they say.

Acknowledgments

State of the Nation was well over a year in the making. Its genesis, in a sense, dated from a luncheon gathering in April 1971, when Lloyd Free talked about plans he was working on for a project that would combine the subjective evaluation of the American public as to the country's situation with objective reviews of developments at home and abroad during the preceding year. This project was to include an in-depth survey and analysis of the public mood—a study that would build upon the techniques pioneered by Lloyd and his late colleague, Hadley Cantril, techniques employed in the first Potomac Associates book, *Hopes and Fears of the American People*. What Lloyd had in mind went well beyond that earlier effort and coincided perfectly with our own desire to undertake a more comprehensive examination of public opinion within the perspective of the past year's trends in a number of policy areas.

It is with genuine respect and admiration that I acknowledge the fundamental contribution Lloyd Free has made to this endeavor. The design of the questions used—so critical to any successful polling effort—was almost entirely his own handiwork, as was most of the interpretation and write-up of the data collected by The Gallup Organization.

This book was not, to be sure, just a one- or two-man effort. In putting together the historical record and interpretation of the survey year (which comprises the first parts of Chapters III–XII), we drew on the wisdom and expertise of a remarkable team of writers. Each contributor worked under an unusually difficult time schedule, yet still was able to bring together in brief synthesis a look at the factual record combined with telling insights and perspectives.

For their role in this enterprise, then, I am enormously indebted to: Jack Rosenthal, the *New York Times;* John Herbers, the *New York Times;* Harold Fleming, president, Potomac Institute; Ronald J. Ostrow, the *Los Angeles Times;* Stephen P. Strickland, director, Washington office of the Health Policy Center–University of California, San Francisco; Rice Odell, editor, *CF Letter* (a publication of the Conservation Foundation); Elizabeth W. King, economic consultant to Potomac Associates; Robert W. Tucker, professor of political science at The Johns Hopkins University and consultant to Potomac Associates; Francis E. Rourke, professor of political science at The Johns Hopkins University.

Finally, I wish to express my deep gratitude to all my Potomac Associates colleagues, who labored so hard in so many different ways to make this first *State of the Nation* possible—and in particular to Don Lesh, for his tireless assistance and encouragement in the editorial review process, and Inette Lipkin, for her unstinting efforts in typing, retyping, and organizing the hundreds of pages of manuscript.

W.W.

There are so many to whom I could acknowledge my debt in connection with the sections on public opinion in this book that it is hard to know where to start—or stop. In broader range, I shall first mention those who through the years have helped me most in perfecting my talents, such as they are: Paul Lazarsfeld, who taught me most of what I know about the rudiments of social science research; Archibald Crossley, who, in the course of our collaboration, inducted me into the practical skills of the polling art; George Gallup, whose organization has so satisfactorily carried out assignments for me through the years; and especially my late partner Hadley Cantril, who set my feet upon the path of public opinion research and indoctrinated me into the system of transactional psychology that provided the systematic base for my work.

In a more immediate time frame, I am immensely indebted to, and admiring of, Bill Watts of Potomac Associates, who had the vision and imagination to see the importance and potential of the *State of the Nation* project when we discussed it a year ago. He backed this study to the hilt, not only financially, but also in terms of his own time, effort, lively intelligence, excellent judgment, and diligent editorial skill, without which this book would not be what it is.

Then there is my son, Peter Free, a trained computer programmer, among other things, who exhibited unbelievable diligence and skill in pulling the thousands of figures that spewed out of the computer into meaningful tabular form—a function without which my contribution to this book literally would have been impossible.

Also to be mentioned is Ellen Yunger, who typed so many windy words that wended wearily from my wide-ranging wisdom that she literally wore out an IBM electric typewriter ribbon every day during the height of our activity.

I was also assisted in the framing of our complicated questionnaires by Albert H. Cantril and Charles W. Roll, Jr., coauthors of *Hopes and Fears of the American People*. Charlie Roll, in his position with The Gallup Organization, also oversaw the interviewing and tabulating phases of our project, and Tad Cantril provided several basic insights.

Finally, I wish to thank Josephine Favali, who so beautifully composed (in the printing sense of the term) the tables in the appendixes of this book.

L.A.F.

I.
Progress or Decline: The Public's Evaluation

Things aren't much better than they were five years ago. Not enough progress has been made to amount to anything.
> an equipment operator in Florida

I like it the way it is now. Even though it's not perfect, it's pretty good.
> a retired New England school teacher

The government is in chaos. There are many problems we U.S. citizens face with no answers, now or in the future.
> a General Motors employee in a large eastern city

Things are better than my parents had them.
> an executive's wife in a New York suburb

The country is going to hell. The administration is throwing away money. The President doesn't stay on the job. . . . I don't think this country has any future the way things are going now.
> a retired worker in the Southwest

The U.S. isn't looked up to as it used to be. We are kind of a Lone Ranger in the United Nations.
> a factory engineer in Ohio

Our prestige abroad has been upheld because of the way the president has handled the war in Vietnam and his visits to other countries. I think most countries appreciate us and feel that we are doing the right thing.
> a grocery store manager in a northern California suburb

Most people seem to have more money than they ever have had before. They seem to be on a spending spree.
> A retired Ford Motor Company worker in Dallas, Texas

19

A good many reports in recent times have given the impression that the American public is largely composed of frustrated, unhappy individuals fed up with the circumstances of their lives. If, through public opinion polls, the people are allowed to speak for themselves, however, the majority view suggests a different, less simplistic story.

In February 1972, a Gallup poll found that 74 percent of Americans were satisfied with their housing situation, 78 percent with their standard of living, and no less than 84 percent with the work they do. This hardly sounds like a discontented people. True, the level of satisfaction among black Americans was considerably lower in each category than among whites. But trends over the last two decades show that, in their overall outlook on life, the gap between the two races has been narrowing as well.

Notwithstanding the prevailing satisfaction of our citizenry with the "here and now" aspects of their lives, an air of unease is abroad in the land.

The same Gallup poll showed that, while 58 percent of Americans were satisfied with the future they and their families anticipated, 30 percent felt the opposite. In traditionally optimistic America, there was apparently a significant lack of assurance about the future. This sense of disquiet was demonstrated, too, by the fact that, in that February poll, only 37 percent of the American public said they approved of the way the nation was being governed, with more than one-half (54 percent) expressing outright dissatisfaction.

The Institute for Social Research at the University of Michigan reported in the spring of 1972 "a widespread feeling that the quality of life in this country has been deteriorating. Americans can give considerably more examples of ways that life in this country is getting worse than ways it is getting better." According to the Institute's director, Angus Campbell: "Most prominent of their criticisms is the belief that economic conditions have worsened, with inflation and taxation most frequently mentioned. Crime, drug use, declining morality, public protests and disorders, and various aspects of environmental pollution are cited by significant numbers of people as evidence of 'things getting worse'." *

A Harris Survey released in June 1972 bore a comparably nega-

---

* "Quality of Life Getting Worse for Many Americans," *ISR Newsletter*, Spring 1972.

tive headline: "Feelings of Alienation Up Sharply in Past Year." It showed, among other things, that 68 percent of the public agreed with the statement, "the rich get richer and the poor get poorer;" 53 percent with "what you think doesn't count very much;" and 50 percent with "the people running the country don't really care what happens to people like yourself."

This discrepancy between the evaluations people made of the conditions of their own lives on the one hand and of the general social situation on the other points up what some other societies would consider a curious divorcement in the thinking of Americans. In the United States, the country of individualism *par excellence,* there is a sharp distinction in people's minds between their own personal lives and national life. Believing that individuals not only should but can take care of themselves and stand on their own two feet, Americans appear not to make a direct connection between their individual situations and the conditions of the nation —except in the case of war or severe national calamity. As a result, they find it possible to feel that they as individuals can fare well, even though they perceive the country to be faring poorly.

This situation was dramatically demonstrated in the public opinion survey described in *Hopes and Fears of the American People.* The survey upon which that book was based utilized a particular polling technique called the "self-anchoring striving scale," a device previously administered by the Institute for International Social Research to cross sections in the United States and many other countries representative of more than one-third of the world's population.*

In this unique system, people are asked first about the wishes and hopes embodied in their own concept of the best possible life for themselves, and then about the fears and worries characterizing their concept of the worst possible life. In this way, each respondent defines his own scale of values from best to worst (hence the designation "self-anchoring"). He is then shown a picture of a ladder, symbolizing the "ladder of life," with steps numbered from zero at the bottom (representing the worst pos-

---

* See Hadley Cantril, *The Pattern of Human Concerns* (Rutgers University Press, 1965); Lloyd A. Free and Hadley Cantril, *The Political Beliefs of Americans* (Rutgers University Press, 1967; paperback edition, Simon and Schuster, 1968); and F. P. Kilpatrick and Hadley Cantril, "Self-Anchoring Striving Scale: A Measure of Individuals' Unique Reality Worlds," *Journal of Individual Psychology,* XVI (November 1960).

sible life) to ten at the top (representing the best possible life). In the light of his own values, he then indicates on which step of the ladder he feels he stands at the present time, where he thinks he stood five years before, and where he expects to stand five years in the future (hence "striving scale").

A similar series of questions is then asked about the respondent's hopes and fears for his country: what he thinks would be the best possible state of affairs, what he thinks would be the worst; where he thinks the nation stands on the ladder at the present time, where he believes it stood five years before, and where he feels it will stand five years in the future.

The hopes and fears elicited by this approach obviously reveal a good deal about the values members of a society use to assess their own lives and the state of their nation. A comparison between ladder ratings for the present and the past indicates whether respondents sense progress, personal and national, or the reverse. The relationship between the ratings for the future and for the present shows whether people are generally optimistic or pessimistic about their own and their country's future.

The startling situation in January 1971, described in *Hopes and Fears of the American People,* was this: the great majority of Americans had a healthy sense of personal progress and were distinctly optimistic about their own futures. Rather than exhibiting the sense of national progress revealed in earlier surveys, however, the public clearly felt that the nation had lost ground over the preceding five years, and their optimism about the country's future was decidedly restrained.

What we wanted to know was whether this bifurcated mood of personal progress but national doubt had persisted during the year and a half that separated the *Hopes and Fears* study of January 1971 and our present survey conducted in June 1972.*

RATING PERSONAL WELL-BEING

In January 1971, the American people gave their personal lives ratings on the imaginary "ladder of life" that looked like this: **

---

* Since both polls were carried out by The Gallup Organization by exactly the same methodology, the results of the surveys are strictly comparable.
** The method used in calculating ladder ratings is described in detail in Appendix 3. In judging these ratings it must be borne in mind that the highest possible score is a theoretical 10 and the lowest is zero. A change of 0.6 of a step is considered statistically significant.

Past   5.8
Present   6.6
Future   7.5

The rating for the present, it should be noted, was 0.8 of a step higher than that for the past, indicating a sense of personal progress. Similarly, the future rating was 0.9 of a step above that for the present, denoting considerable optimism.

The fact that people did not give themselves a present rating nearer the top of the ladder indicates, of course, that they were not euphoric. Nevertheless, the average rating they assigned themselves in the present was exactly the same as the rating they had given in response to the same question asked in 1958 by the Institute for International Social Research, before the alleged mood of personal discontent discerned by so many current commentators had set in.

A year and a half later, in the survey we conducted in June 1972, average personal ladder ratings came out like this:

Past   5.5
Present   6.4
Future   7.6

The same feelings of personal progress and optimism delineated in the *Hopes and Fears* survey had obviously continued into mid-1972. Again, there was an upward shift from past to present, in this case, 0.9 of a step, and a further escalation from present to future of no less than 1.2 steps. In other words, the American people tended to be even more optimistic about their personal futures in mid-1972 than they had been a year and a half before. These findings clearly call into question the picture drawn by some observers of Americans dissatisfied with their personal lives and jaundiced in their outlooks for the future.

A close examination of personal ladder ratings reveals relatively few statistically significant differences in the ratings given by different subgroups of the population.* In predictable fashion, the average ratings for the present given by whites and by families with incomes of $15,000 per year or more were higher than those given by blacks and families with incomes of less than

* Variations in personal ladder ratings among demographic subgroups are given in Table A-1 in Appendix 2. (All demographic tables with the prefix "A" appear in Appendix 2.) A change of 0.6 of a step or more in a ladder rating is considered statistically significant.

$5,000 per year. Correspondingly, business and professional people considered themselves better off than manual workers.

The highest proportion of satisfied Americans was to be found among the well-educated, whites, and professional and business elements in the upper-income bracket. Least satisfied were the poor and the blacks, who are clearly aware that their lives leave a good deal to be desired when judged according to prevailing American values, with their emphasis on material well-being. In the United States it seems to be particularly difficult to consider yourself poor but happy, especially if you happen to be black.

In fact, blacks at every income level rated the present condition of their lives lower than whites at corresponding income levels, as shown below:

Family Income	Whites	Blacks
$15,000 plus	7.1	6.2
$10,000–$14,999	6.9	5.8
$7,000–$9,999	6.2	5.9
$5,000–$6,999	6.0	5.6
Under $5,000	6.1	5.1

This difference is most significant among those blacks with family incomes above $10,000 or below $5,000 per year.

In shifts in personal ladder ratings from past to present, indicative of one's relative sense of progress, there were also a few significant variations among demographic groups. Among those exhibiting the greatest feelings of progress were the college-educated, the well-to-do, and those who called themselves suburbanites.* The optimism of these three groups was matched by that of the young (eighteen to twenty-nine), who gave themselves a lower absolute rating in the present but felt, nonetheless, that they had come a long way from their level of five years before.

In contrast, there were no statistically significant upswings from past to present among those with grade school educations or less and those with family incomes under $5,000 a year. Nor was any measurable sense of progress evident among older people (fifty and over) or, in a related category, among the so-called nonlabor group made up predominantly of households headed by

---

* The method used for classifying people by place of residence is described in Appendix 2.

retired people. It may be that the lives of older people have become so stable that for them "progress" is a relatively meaningless concept.

In looking at shifts in ladder ratings from present to future, a measurement of optimism, these older groups also showed little expectation of betterment; the upward shifts that did occur were not statistically significant. Nor did those with only grade school educations or less expect much positive change in their futures. Young people, on the other hand, quite understandably exhibited the highest level of optimism—understandably, because their confidence in the future had not yet been tested.

A special word about black Americans is in order. As mentioned earlier, the present ladder ratings they assigned themselves were significantly lower than those of whites. Blacks revealed just about as much sense of progress from past to present as whites, however, and were significantly *more* optimistic about their personal futures. The comparative figures are:

	Blacks	Whites
Past	4.8	5.6
Present	5.5	6.5
Future	7.3	7.6
Shift from Past to Present	+0.7	+0.9
Shift from Present to Future	+1.8	+1.1

In the face of such feelings of progress and optimism, it would seem an exaggeration to claim that members of the black community today display overall frustration or hopelessness in their perceptions of personal opportunity.

A ONE-YEAR EVALUATION

The generally positive picture we have just described was buttressed by the responses we received to an additional question that narrowed the past-to-present time span from five years to one year.

We asked: *Now let's consider just the past 12 months. In terms of your own personal happiness and satisfaction, would you say that today, as compared to* one year ago, *you are better off, about the same, or worse off?*

Better off	46 percent
About the same	41
Worse off	12
Don't know	1
	100 percent

Personal progress clearly seemed very real to almost one-half of the American public, with only a bit more than one in ten feeling they had retrogressed. And the figures for blacks tend to confirm our earlier findings, as illustrated below:

Better off	41 percent
About the same	45
Worse off	12
Don't know	2
	100 percent

Three out of ten of the older people, the poor, and those with grade school educations said they were better off than a year earlier, with half or more feeling that they had at least held their own.

In sum, then, with slight qualification for the generally disadvantaged groups mentioned, the American people continued to exhibit a sense of satisfaction about their personal lives in mid-1972, just as they had in the *Hopes and Fears* survey a year and a half before.

RATING THE NATION

As described in *Hopes and Fears of the American People,* the public's assessment of the national situation in January 1971 was spectacularly different from their evaluation of trends in their personal lives. The average ladder ratings for the nation at that time were:

Past	6.2
Present	5.4
Future	6.2

Unlike the readings at the personal level, the average rating for the nation in early 1971 was actually *lower* than that for five years before—an unprecedented drop of 0.8 of a step on the ladder.* Instead of a sense of national progress from past to present, the public indicated their belief that the national situation had actually deteriorated over the preceding five years. And, while the shift from present to future amounted to an affirmative 0.8 of a step, this sense of optimism was so restrained that the most that people hoped for after five years was that the country would be back where it had been ten years before!

The people's assessment of the state of the nation in 1971 was unquestionably the most pessimistic recorded since the introduction of public opinion polling almost four decades ago, in the midst of the great depression of the 1930s. In fact, the public mood recorded in the 1971 survey might well be designated the "great mental depression" of the early 1970s, a characterization supported by studies of college students conducted in 1970 by Daniel Yankelovich, Inc., which showed that a "mood of personal despair and depression" existed even among the young at that time.**

The crucial question for this study was, of course, Did that mood of national depression and sense of deterioration persist a year and a half later, or had the public's perception of national affairs improved? The answer we got was enigmatic. The national ladder ratings given by the American people in mid-1972 were:

Past   5.6
Present   5.5
Future   6.2

The rating for the present appears a shade below the rating for the past, but the difference is not statistically significant. The present average national rating in mid-1972 was, then, essentially the same as that given for five years earlier, with no measurable shift to be seen.

The sense of national deterioration evident in early 1971 had

---

* Only once before, in the Philippines in 1959, had a country surveyed by this technique shown an absolute past-to-present decline. That case, and several other cases in which both past and present ratings were extraordinarily low, are described in Hadley Cantril's *The Pattern of Human Concerns.*

** *The Changing Values on Campus: Political and Personal Attitudes of Today's College Students,* a survey conducted for the JDR III Fund by Daniel Yankelovich, Inc. (N.Y.: Washington Square Press, 1972).

indeed diminished, if not disappeared. The public no longer thought that the country had lost ground. But neither did it perceive improvement over the preceding half decade. Rather, the public seemed to sense that the national progress made in the intervening year and a half since January 1971 had served to restore the country to its equilibrium and that America was now holding its own.

Another important development was also evident from the figures. In the 1971 survey, the public thought that the country would be better off in the future than it was in the present, but the progress expected over the ensuing five years would simply bring the country back to where it had been ten years before. In other words, the fact that the past and future ladder ratings were exactly the same (6.2) showed that no overall progress was anticipated over the total ten-year span. In the mid-1972 survey, on the other hand, the future rating (6.2) was significantly higher than both the present rating (5.5) and the past rating (5.6). By mid-1972 the American people were counting on the nation's making substantial progress within the ten-year period they had been asked to consider.

The demographic subgroups of the population were remarkably uniform in their judgments on national progress. (See Table A-2.) There were no statistically significant variations among the groups in the rating they assigned their country for the present.

Nor did a single demographic group exhibit a statistically significant shift, either up or down, between past and present ratings. Every population group agreed that in mid-1972 the country stood just about where it had five years earlier.

Finally, when it came to differences between present and future ratings, the degrees of optimism indicated were also remarkably uniform. The only groups that stood out at all were those more optimistic than average—white collar workers and the handful of respondents who characterized themselves as very liberal.

PROGRESS ON THE INTERNATIONAL FRONT

To give additional depth to the overall measurements of national progress or decline, we included in the questionnaire a number of follow-up questions. The first had to do with international affairs.

We asked: *Considering the international situation overall, do you think that in handling foreign policy problems in general during the last 12 months the U.S. has made much progress, some progress, stood still, lost some ground, or lost much ground?*

Made much progress	8	percent
Made some progress	56	
Stood still	17	
Lost some ground	9	
Lost much ground	2	
Don't know	8	
	100	percent

If the top two percentages are combined, it appears that close to two-thirds of the American people believed that the U.S. had moved on the international front during the year ending in mid-1972; but the consensus was that it had made "some," not "much," progress.

Demographic breakdowns are particularly difficult to compare, when, as in this case, they involve complicated sets of percentages, each including four, five, or six figures. To arrive at meaningful comparisons, we devised a "composite score" system yielding one overall figure that represents all answers to a particular question.* For example, we scored "made much progress" at 100 points; "made some progress" at 75; "stood still" at 50; lost some ground" at 25; and "lost much ground" at zero. The median of the scoring range is 50, representing in this case the "stood still" point.

The overall composite number on the question of progress or decline in the international field was 66. Well above the median of 50 and well below the maximum of 100, this score indicates a preponderant opinion, fully consonant with the results above, that the nation had made some, but not much, progress internationally.

---

* The method used in computing composite scores is explained in Appendix 5.

Scores for the various population subgroups showed impressive unanimity in evaluating the nation's international performance. The only deviations of any significance from the overall score of 66 were to be found among professional and business people and Republicans (both of whose composite scores were somewhat above average) and among blacks and families in the lowest income bracket (both of whose composite scores were lower than average but still well above the "stood still" point). (Demographic breakdowns on this question are given in Table A-12.)

PROGRESS ON THE DOMESTIC FRONT

In looking at affairs at home, the American people were not quite as sanguine. Very few, indeed, thought the country had made "much" progress in the past year, but a majority saw at least some forward movement.

The question we asked was: *Summing up the overall domestic situation here in the U.S. today, do you think that in handling domestic problems generally we as a nation have made much progress, some progress, stood still, lost some ground, or lost much ground during the last 12 months?*

Made much progress	4 percent
Made some progress	54
Stood still	22
Lost some ground	12
Lost much ground	3
Don't know	5
	100 percent

The overall composite score on this question was 62, slightly lower than the international score of 66. Once again, there was a high degree of uniformity in the opinions of population subgroups. (See Table A-14.) Only two groups deviated significantly from the average. Republicans, exhibiting solidarity with a Republican president, came up with a composite score of 66. The college-educated and those who characterized themselves as very liberal, groups which tend to follow public affairs developments more closely than the citizenry as a whole, had composite scores of 57 and 54 respectively.

THE CONSENSUS IS PROGRESS

At the end of each interview, when, after a battery of questions on domestic and international issues, the respondent had the nation's situation well in mind, we sought an overall assessment of the country's progress.

We asked: *Now that you have had a chance to review our overall situation today at home and abroad, is it your considered opinion that, in general, we as a nation have made much progress, some progress, stood still, lost some ground, or lost much ground during the last 12 months?*

Made much progress	7 percent
Made some progress	60
Stood still	17
Lost some ground	10
Lost much ground	2
Don't know	4
	100 percent

One aspect of these findings might seem at first glance rather surprising: the combined total of respondents who thought that the country had made either much or some progress (67 percent) was actually higher than the number who saw progress either on the international front (64 percent) or in the domestic arena (58 percent). The explanation for this apparent discrepancy, we have concluded, lies in the process of education our respondents went through in the course of their interviews. The questions we asked apparently reminded them of all aspects of national life and led them to an enhanced final assessment of overall progress.

The overall composite score for this last question was 66. Once again, evaluations were impressively uniform among the different population groups. (See Table A-15.) Somewhat higher ratings were given by Republicans, as well as by residents of communities with populations ranging from 2,500 to 50,000. Less positive than average were the college-educated, labor union households, political Independents, and those who classified themselves as very liberal and very conservative. Moderates, in short, were happier about the overall situation than those inclined toward either side of the ideological spectrum.

Despite these slight deviations from the norm, it is apparent that the American people judged that their nation had made progress —some at home, even more abroad—between early 1971 and mid-1972. If they sensed progress overall, what then were their concerns? How deeply did those concerns go? And how much relative weight was given each of these concerns in assessments of domestic and international affairs, and, finally, of the national situation as a whole?

II.
Worries and Concerns

The price of food and clothing has gone up out of all reason.
    a North Carolina farmer

I'm afraid of race wars with people killing each other. More riots and killings.
    the wife of an executive in New York State

I hope my children won't get involved with narcotics.
    a janitor in rural Mississippi

I fear rising crime among the blacks, especially street crimes. We are afraid to go out on the streets. One of my friends was even attacked and beaten up on her own front lawn.
    a retired woman in Baltimore

I hope the Vietnam War will end so I won't have to worry about my boys dying anymore.
    an Indiana housewife

I am concerned about pollution. I'm afraid of suffocating: unclean air, unclean water, and unclean food.
    a black woman in the deep South

I live alone so I hope I won't get sick and bedridden and have to depend on others.
    a retired man in Philadelphia

I think it's terrible that so many people graduate from high school and then can't find jobs.
    a maid in a Brooklyn hotel

I hope someday I can build a new home.
    the wife of an aircraft worker in Illinois

To get at the problems that most worried Americans, we included in our survey a battery of questions asking respondents to describe the level of their apprehension over various domestic and international problems facing the country. For twenty-seven areas, we asked the people to tell us whether they were concerned about the issue mentioned a great deal, a fair amount, not very much, or not at all. We again used a system of composite scores to permit ranking of the subjects in order of degree of concern. Weights were assigned to the various categories of answers, ranging from 100 in the case of "a great deal" to zero for "not at all." * The results of this ranking appear in Table 1.

The ranking of public concerns in 1972 proved vastly different from the listing that emerged in 1964 when the Institute for International Social Research began a series of similar surveys. The top five items in the initial survey eight years ago were all related to international affairs or defense:

1. Keeping the country out of war
2. Combating world communism
3. Keeping our military defense strong
4. Controlling the use of nuclear weapons
5. Maintaining respect for the United States in other countries

Only in sixth place did a domestic item surface: maintaining law and order.

With the sole exception of Vietnam, in mid-1972 international and defense subjects, including even the danger of war and the threat of communism, had dropped out of the top third of the list. This shift in people's priorities was not sudden. As early as 1968 the Institute for International Social Research had found that concern about domestic matters, compared with earlier assessments, had increased substantially. Several exclusively domestic issues had moved into the upper bracket, previously the reserve of international matters: first, a number of interrelated items having to do with maintaining law and order (crime and juvenile delinquency, rioting in the cities, drugs and drug addicts); and then, inflation and the cost of living.

By 1972, as Table 1 shows, mounting concern about these

---

* The method used in computing composite scores is explained in Appendix 5.

TABLE 1   MAJOR NATIONAL ISSUES AND DEGREES OF
             PUBLIC CONCERN
             composite scores

Rising prices and the cost of living	90
The amount of violence in American life	90
The problem of drug addicts and narcotic drugs	89
Crime in this country	89
The problem of Vietnam	88
Cleaning up our waterways and reducing water pollution	84
Reducing air pollution	83
Insuring that Americans in general, including the poor and the elderly, get adequate medical and health care	83
Protecting consumers against misleading advertising, dangerous products, and unsafe foods and drugs	82
Collecting and disposing of garbage, trash, and other solid wastes	80
The problems of the elderly	78
Unemployment in this country	77
Reducing poverty in this country	77
Improving our educational system	77
Keeping our military and defense forces strong	77
Maintaining respect for the U.S. in other countries	76
Maintaining close relations with our allies and keeping our military alliances strong	75
Rebuilding run-down sections of our cities	72
Economic and business conditions generally	71
The problems of our cities in general	71
Providing adequate housing for all the people	69
The threat of communism at home and abroad	69
The danger of a major war breaking out in the near future	66
The problem of black Americans	65
The problem of Communist China	61
The problem of Soviet Russia	61
Improving mass transportation systems, such as buses, trains, and, in some cities, subways	56

domestic problems moved them to the very top of the list, higher even than Vietnam. Several other domestic items made their way into the top bracket as well: the amount of violence in American life (the score for which was almost certainly augmented by the shooting of Governor George C. Wallace of Alabama shortly before our interviewing began), water and air pollution, health care, consumer protection, solid waste disposal, and problems of the elderly.

Only after these concerns does the first internationally related item apart from Vietnam appear: keeping our military and defense forces strong. And this item, which occupied third place in 1964, ranked in mid-1972 at the same level as such domestic problems as unemployment, poverty, and education.

Nothing could better document the startling shift in priorities in the minds of the American people away from problems abroad to those here at home.

We can only surmise about the causes of the change in emphasis. Some of the domestic problems cited as chief concerns have, no doubt, grown worse during the years since 1964. Crime, drug use, air and water pollution, and solid waste disposal all come to mind. But many, perhaps most, have not. The current rate of inflation, for example, is considerably lower than it was during several periods in the recent past. There is nothing unusual about violence in American life: witness the 1964 riots in our cities. The medical care available to the majority of Americans today is certainly no worse and probably a good deal better than it was in 1964. Consumers needed protection in the past every bit as much as they do now. The elderly are more adequately cared for through social security and medicare today than they have ever been in American history. And the proportion of the population classified as poor is no greater now than in the recent past.

The reassessment that has taken place, then, must be attributable at least as much to psychological as to objective factors. A combination of increased awareness of the domestic issues and rising expectations, as well as a growing disillusionment with the Vietnam War, and, by association, with most international activities, could explain in large measure the greater public concern with the domestic scene.

PATTERNS OF DOMESTIC CONCERN

The domestic problems of highest concern—inflation, violence, crime, drug use, water and air pollution, medical care, consumer protection, solid waste disposal, and problems of the elderly—are those which affect Americans regardless of class, race, age, or location. It is no accident that the composite scores of population subgroups reflect considerable unanimity on these subjects. (See Table A-4.) Only a few exceptions stand out: the well-to-do were more worried about drugs and air pollution and less worried about inflation than average; the very poor were more concerned about problems of the elderly, no doubt because such a large proportion of those with family incomes under $5,000 per year are oldsters; the young appeared less concerned about the drug problem than their elders; and people in the West were worried about air and water pollution even more than those living on the eastern seaboard or in other regions of the country, possibly because of the rapidity with which these problems are growing along with the population of the western states.

This unanimity of concern disappeared, however, on problems more socially and ideologically controversial. This was especially true for problems identified with large cities: housing, education, poverty, unemployment, urban renewal, mass transportation, and the problems of black Americans.

On these issues, the following general picture emerged: on the side of higher-than-average concern were, naturally, the big-city dwellers themselves, sometimes joined by the suburbanites; the young, frequently expressing themselves as a more socially conscious group than their elders; the blacks; and those who characterized themselves as liberals. Also deeply concerned about education, the problems of black Americans, and urban problems in general were those with annual incomes of $15,000 and over. Showing far less than average concern about most of these big-city problems were people living in towns, villages, and rural areas, those who called themselves conservatives, and Republicans.

PATTERNS OF INTERNATIONAL CONCERN

The composite scores for different population subgroups on international issues show only minor variations. (See Table A-3.) In most cases, the differences are not statistically significant although the patterns that emerge are suggestive. Nevertheless, we have confined our attention throughout the book to the genuinely significant (and therefore more telling) variations.

The young, as expected, were highly concerned about Vietnam. They were, however, significantly less worried than those in the oldest age bracket about the strength of our national defense, actions of the two major communist powers, and the threat of communism in general. Joining the young in these attitudes were the well-to-do and the college-educated. These latter two groups were also less concerned about the danger of a major war erupting than those with less income and less education.

Manual workers, perhaps justifying in part their "hard hat" reputation, saw eye to eye with older people (fifty and over) in their above-average concern about national defense, Communist China and the Soviet Union, and the threat of communism in general, combined as well with a strong preoccupation over maintaining respect for the U.S. abroad.

There was one other differentiation of note: women tended to be much more preoccupied with the danger of war and the potential threats of China, the Soviet Union, and communism than did men.

LESSENED INTERNATIONAL CONCERN

We noted earlier the striking and continuing shift of emphasis among Americans from international to domestic issues. There were actually two dynamics at work here. Concern about domestic problems has, indeed, burgeoned. But, concurrently, a sequence of developments on the world scene, highlighted by clearly popular presidential summitry, caused the level of most international concerns to drop dramatically in both a relative and an absolute sense.

Table 2 forcefully illustrates this second point. Composite scores indicating degrees of concern about international issues derived in our 1972 study have been compared with those obtained by the Institute for International Social Research in 1964 and 1968. Concern with Vietnam and our military alliances remained relatively stable between 1968 and 1972. Concern with maintaining respect for the U.S. abroad lessened. And the level of public worry about war and peace, national defense, Communist China, the Soviet Union, and the threat of communism in general dropped very much lower than in earlier years.

TABLE 2 CONCERN WITH INTERNATIONAL THREATS
composite scores

	1964	1968	1972
The danger of war	90	83	66
The threat of communism	86	79	69
Keeping our military defense strong	74	81	61
Maintaining respect for the U.S. abroad	81	82	76
Soviet Russia	75	73	61
Communist China	83	88	77
Vietnam	71	91	88
Keeping our military alliances strong	68	75	75

The reassuring impact of the presidential visits to mainland China and the Soviet Union in the spring of 1972, we have concluded, reinforced the public's estimate that international tensions have eased, that there is no longer so much need to worry about external dangers as in past years. This feeling no doubt has contributed to the growing tendency of the American people to look inward.

Another factor in this diminishing level of international concern, we suspect, has been the growing disillusionment with the frustrating, and at times humiliating, results of America's activist role abroad, epitomized by our experience in Vietnam. The spectacle of the world's greatest power apparently unable to "win" against a small communist adversary has not been easy for Americans to face.

OVERALL PATTERNS

Before probing public opinion on specific issues, we sought to identify overall patterns in the concerns of different subgroups of our citizenry.

To do so, we derived average across-the-board scores for the international and domestic subjects, respectively, on which degrees of concern were elicited. For international matters as a whole, the average of composite scores was 72. For domestic problems, it was a significantly higher 78, another expression of stronger public concern for domestic rather than international affairs.

There are some interesting variations among demographic groups in these overall scores. (See Table A-16.) Women, for example, tended to be more concerned on both international and domestic counts than men, while young people (eighteen to twenty-nine) were noticeably less disturbed about international problems than those fifty and above. In contrast, persons with only a grade school education ranked far above the norm in their concern over international affairs (with a score of 77), perhaps because they did not share the sense of relaxation and reduction of tensions felt by others in a year of diplomatic spectaculars. Almost as concerned about international matters were manual workers in general and labor union households in particular, along with southerners (who in polling results through the years have consistently shown themselves to be the most nationalistic of all regional groups in their outlook on the world).

Joining the young in less-than-average concern for the international situation were several groups that tend to follow the news more closely than their counterparts and, hence, were presumably more impressed with recent developments indicating a relaxation in international tensions: the college-educated, families in the top income bracket, those in white collar and the professional and business categories, city dwellers in general and residents of our largest metropolitan areas in particular. In a fuzzing of the traditional ideological spectrum, this grouping also included both Republicans and those who classified themselves as liberals.

More-than-average worry about domestic affairs as a whole was expressed by individuals in the top family-income bracket, city dwellers in general and residents of our largest metropolises in particular, manual workers (especially labor union members and their spouses), Catholics, Democrats, and self-designated liberals—most of whom consistently in public opinion surveys have tended to be more liberally oriented than is the norm. Not surprisingly, the highest overall score of any group on domestic concerns was registered by black Americans, who turned in a whopping 85 as compared to the national average of 78. Significantly below average were several more traditionally conservative groups: people living in small towns and rural areas, those who identified themselves as moderately conservative, and Republicans.

The most concerned groups overall, as indicated by higher-than-average scores in both their international and domestic outlooks, were manual workers and labor union families. Least concerned, with substantially lower scores on both international and domestic problems, were Republicans.

We turn now to an examination of contemporary America through an analysis of events and opinion in specific problem areas. In each case, we first let the objective record speak and then let the people speak. The broad patterns of opinion and concern we have described here appear again and again as the American people express themselves on contemporary issues.

III.
Social Change:
The Young. The Old.
The Women

The freedom given to young people today! Dope, tolerance, rape!
    a female hairdresser in a middle-sized eastern city

My greatest fear is to lose my niece. That would be awful. I'd lose my home. I'd be a homeless old man.
    an eighty-eight-year-old man in a small eastern city

My goal is developing myself the way I would want to rather than the way I am forced to. My husband goes off to work every day and chooses his profession; but I'm left at home as a housewife. I'm just not happy being me.
    the twenty-six-year-old wife of a pharmacist in a large eastern city

The Record Speaks

Pluralism—the interaction of political blocs—has been a staple of American society and politics for so long that there is scarcely room left in the Washington alphabet soup for the abbreviated names of more special interest groups. They range from the AAA, ABA, ACA, and ADA all the way to ZPG.* These are, for the most part, groups representing traditional economic and professional interests—the so-called Establishment. But in the

---

* American Automobile Association, American Bar Association, Americans for Constitutional Action, Americans for Democratic Action, and Zero Population Growth, respectively.

42

last year or so, a whole new pluralistic wave has washed across the country. What might now be called "public pluralism" became rampant in 1972.

Women were organized into bodies such as NOW, the National Organization of Women. Fearful of hijacking and other violence, airline pilots formed a lobby of their own. Poor black women marched under the banner of the National Welfare Rights Organization. The already familiar cry of "black power" has now been supplemented; Puerto Rican and Mexican-Americans struggled to forge a National Spanish-Speaking Coalition to promote "brown power." Domestics, median age forty-six, established a National Committee on Household Employment. In January 1972, even the wives of our diplomats won a ruling that they were no longer required to fix cucumber sandwiches, or knit afghans, at the whim of the ambassador's lady. And homosexuals paraded in peace marches, with signs such as "Bring the Boys Back Home, (signed) The Gay Liberation Front."

This public pluralism, this effort to organize against perceived injustice, has many causes. Some are rooted in the history of labor, or the civil rights tide of the 1960s. But other causes are still more profound.

Families have come unraveled in a phenomenon demographers already have a label for: "uncoupling." Not many years ago, for unmarried young people to move out of their parents' homes was near scandalous. For older adults to live with their children and grandchildren was expected. No longer. In the 1960s, the Census Bureau has reported, there was a 133 percent increase in the number of persons under twenty-five living alone and a 51 percent increase among persons over sixty-five. The total number of one-person households jumped during that decade from 6.9 to 10.7 million.

As families have decentralized, so have cities. Indeed, the very word "city," unmodified, has lost its meaning with the proliferation of urban functions in the suburbs. The total urban settlement, what Secretary of Housing and Urban Development George Romney calls "the real city," is now more fragmented and stratified than the neighborhoods of old central cities ever were. There are whole suburbs—"leisure worlds"—for the elderly. There are areas where apartments and bars cater to the young and single, as in suburban Schaumburg, Illinois, 30 miles northwest of Chicago.

There are manorial suburbs, industrial suburbs, even town-house suburbs. They may be only a few miles apart, but the gulf is as wide as it used to be between Atlanta and Seattle.

It is as if American society were disassembling itself and then, almost simultaneously, reorganizing into a new form. A nation that once was divided by family, geography, and private interest now is being redefined by age, class, and public interest. And now this sea change is being quickened by two rising social forces—the power of youth and the power of women.

Some dismiss these not as forces but as fragile fads, the product of the nation's insatiable appetite for shock and novelty. On the contrary, their strength is as entrenched as the Constitution itself, as the newly ratified Twenty-sixth and soon-to-be ratified Twenty-seventh amendments attest. Taken together, organized youth and organized women already are strongly shaping a new character for all of American life.

THE PIG AND THE PYTHON

The growing force of youth arises from what, in biology, is called "peristalsis." That is what happens when the pig is swallowed by the python. It passes down the length of the serpent, a moving bulge, until digested. There is an analogous social process, one which might be called "population peristalsis." Birth rates, which often fluctuate wildly from decade to decade, produce steep bulges and contractions in the serpentine profile of the population. But a process which, in the python, produces digestion, in society creates a fundamental form of indigestion. A sharp rise in the number of older adults means a soaring demand for doctors; a sharp drop in the number of first and second graders throws thousands of teachers out of work. There are a host of forces for change in society—affluence, migration, revolutionary change in communication and transportation. But none is more important than the very composition of that society.

The pig in our particular python is the baby boom that followed World War II. It produced an enormous bulge indeed. For decades, the number of births in the United States rarely varied more than 100,000 a year. But then, like a thunderclap, came the boom. Total births in 1947 were 3.5 million—a jump of 800,000 in one year. Each year the number went up until, in the peak year of 1960, there were 4.3 million births. When you recognize that there were 2.2 million births in 1934, the magnitude of the baby boom comes into perspective: there now are *twice as many* Americans age twelve as there are age thirty-eight.

Because of the size of the youth culture, its restless twists and turns have become magnified. Events that once might have been laughed off as sophomoric hijinks now become the milestones of social history: flower children, drugs, war protest, reversion to beatific or supernatural visions. Like other recent years, 1972 encouraged the thought that, as youth goes, so goes the nation.

A dominant concern was the course of American education, whose costs have risen proportionately to the baby boom bulge. The financial distress of Roman Catholic parochial schools grew increasingly severe. Enrollment continued to drop, to 4.2 million in 1971, down from a 1965 peak of 5.6 million. But parental demands for higher quality accelerated. The need to extend to the suburbs increased. And the number of low-paid nun teachers continued to plunge.

In January 1972 New York Governor Nelson A. Rockefeller pledged to find a constitutional way to provide $33 million in "parochiaid." In April, confronted with a hostile Supreme Court ruling on the subject, President Nixon told a Catholic audience in Philadelphia: "I am irrevocably committed to these propositions: [that] America needs her nonpublic schools; that those nonpublic schools need help. Therefore we must and will find ways to provide help."

Financial burdens weighed just as heavily on public schools. City after city rejected school bond measures, even in places that have traditionally been proud of their school systems, such as Portland, Oregon, where the schools were forced to close in early May. One remedy sprang up almost simultaneously in every corner of the country. Courts in California, Texas, Minnesota, and New Jersey struck down the present heavy reliance on the property tax to finance education. There were proposals, consequently, for a new form of national sales tax, revised state income taxes, or state equalization programs, all designed to reduce the property tax and provide an alternate, fairer source of funding for education.

Increasingly, the pivotal point for the youth bulge in the population is in the college years. And the most prevalent form of higher education finally began to win public attention: the community or junior college. Once scorned as "high schools with ashtrays," these institutions have in recent years exploded into a major social force. In February 1972 the Census Bureau reported that, while total university enrollment doubled in the 1960s, junior college enrollment *quadrupled*. There now are 2.5 million junior college students. By 1975, experts estimate, the number will double yet again, reaching 5 million.

College campuses during the 1971–72 school year appeared considerably more subdued than in previous years; youthful passions and interests fragmented. There were waves of protest demonstrations in the wake of the president's decision to intensify pressure on North Vietnam in May. But even these were short-lived. One factor in this "cooling of the campuses" was the draft; the new lottery system among nineteen-year-olds and a sharp drop in draft calls combined to ease some of the pressure underlying past war protests. A second factor was less tangible but just as strong; across the country, the rebelliousness of youth appeared to be waning. "The youth revolution has turned sour," Gerald Peary, a bearded twenty-six-year-old graduate student told a reporter at the University of Wisconsin. "There's no indication that this generation will be any less piggy than the rest."

The disillusionment and fragmentation of student attitudes had its parallels in cultural and sociological developments. Faded jeans with embroidered patches remained the uniform of the youth army. But its troops appeared, increasingly, to be marching to different drummers. The fervid racial unity of the late 1960s disintegrated; on many campuses, black racial pride led to reverse segregation of dormitories and dining tables. Even tastes in music diverged. The deafening volume of sound that has become a youth hallmark also became a social weapon. In campus "music wars," whites would turn up the gain on their stereos, playing hard rock, to try to drown out the soul music favored by blacks.

Many young people stayed with marijuana. Some sought satisfaction in progressively harder drugs. Others discovered a campy new high: alcohol. Still others, enlarging on previous trends, turned away from artificial stimulation altogether, seeking "to turn on to life" or mysticism or idealistic religiosity. This last reached a peak in June 1972 when some 75,000 young "Jesus freaks" from around the country assembled in Texas for Explo 72, a massive festival marked by exhortation from evangelist Billy Graham and football-like cheers: "Two bits, four bits, six bits, a dollar. Everyone for Jesus stand up and holler."

For all the signs of fragmentation, youth in general appeared to remain solidly monolithic in one fundamental respect: the desire to work for social welfare, justice, and reform. Impatience with the corruption or sluggishness of existing institutions led to the development of new ones. A notable example was a movement to "law communes," such as one in Carbondale, near Southern Illinois University. These "collectives" carried to the step of communal living an idea that has increasingly attracted the young: pressing test cases, with wide potential benefit to the disadvantaged. Often such cases challenge government itself, calling on the courts to order municipal, state, and federal agencies to obey dormant laws and reform restrictive regulations.

By far the most important impact of the youth pressure for social reform, however, was on existing institutions: even the most venerable adapted their behavior. In January 1972, for example, a two-year study by the National Council of Churches produced an indictment of ten major denominations for complicity, through their stockholdings, in the "irresponsible, immoral, and socially injurious acts of 29 corporations holding military contracts." On the same day, after a three-year study, the National Conference of Catholic Charities announced that henceforth it would not stop at traditional services but would become politically active in social reform. Four months later, a similar message came from Yale's gothic towers. The university announced it had decided to take an activist role "as a major corporate citizen" in connection with its $500 million securities portfolio. Its investments henceforth would be guided by the principles developed in a campus seminar and published under the title *The Ethical Investor*.

As the year went on, American youth gave a progressively more decisive showing of its ideals and its muscles in the most traditional way of all: politics. The primary elections of 1968 saw the emergence of a "children's crusade" on behalf of the anti-war candidacy of Senator Eugene McCarthy (D-Minn.). By 1972 young activists were able to add an asset even more important than their earlier energy and enthusiasm—numbers. For on July 1, 1971, when Ohio became the thirty-eighth assenting state, the

Twenty-sixth Amendment went into effect. It lowered the voting age to eighteen and, at a stroke, gave youth 20 percent of the potential vote. Experts estimated that 11,462,000 eighteen- to twenty-year-olds became eligible; another 14,213,000 had turned twenty-one since the 1968 election; the new youth voting total, then, was 25,675,000. The entry of this great bloc of new voters had some immediate effects on the political process. One was the advent of some public officials who were very young indeed— such as seventeen-year-old Lawrence Hamm who was appointed to the Newark Board of Education the day after the new amendment went into effect. A more divisive effect was the movement in some college communities, such as Amherst, Massachusetts, to prevent the new rush of student voters from overwhelming the views of year-round local residents by attempting to force students to vote in their home communities rather than their college districts. In the long run, many experts predicted, the most decisive effect of all may well be on national politics.

A final aspect of the power of youth was evident from the current state of population peristalsis. The youth bulge soon will no longer be a youth bulge at all, but a young adult and middle-age bulge. During the survey year, the leading edge of the baby boom generation passed its twenty-fifth birthday—an age when preoccupation with the needs of society is likely to yield to more inward concerns—marriage, first home, first child. "The next 15 years," Census Bureau Director George Hay Brown said in a personal interview in 1970, "is the era of the young married." Yet, even in their approach to domesticity, these young adults demonstrated some striking changes of character and style. It is in these differences that the whole youth movement intersects with —and strongly reinforces—the second major source of current social change: feminism.

ANOTHER KIND OF PIG

Women's liberation notwithstanding, sexism still abounded in American society. *Playboy*, which had long flaunted breasts and buttocks, now added public pubic hairs. Miami and other major cities saw the development of a new business, called, variously, "Rent-a-Girl," "Rent-a-Bird," and "Supergirl," whose purposes vary, allegedly, from legitimate escort service to call-girl camouflage.

But it was also a year of notable progress against the male chauvinist pig. There were historic legal advances. There were dramatic changes for working women. And, most striking, there were signs of deep change in attitudes toward sex, marriage, and children that portends a very different form of population peristalsis in the future.

The legal changes came with accelerating speed during the year. Over a period of months, federal courts across the country handed down a mass of decisions aimed at striking down all state laws restricting kind of work, hours, and promotion of women. The federal Equal Employment Opportunity Commission stiffened its regulations against female job discrimination. And on March 22, 1972 came the ultimate step, the culmination of a forty-nine-year feminist struggle. By a vote of 84 to 8, the Senate completed congressional action on the Twenty-seventh Amendment, forbidding discrimination based on sex by any law or governmental action. By the end of 1973, when a sufficient number of state legislatures will have been in session, women's rights should be firmly established in the Constitution.

Paralleling these legal changes came a wave of changes in access to work. Feminists assailed the president for failing to appoint a woman to the Supreme Court, but that was one of the few positions women failed to achieve. Representative Shirley Chisholm (D-N.Y.) ran for her party's presidential nomination and experienced little of the public ridicule heaped on such forerunners as Victoria Woodhull or Belva Lockwood after the Civil War. In other symbolic gains, the president appointed a woman to the Council of Economic Advisers. New York City named a woman as a police inspector. Women became telephone linemen, stock market officials, jockeys. Many of these were mere token gains; the mood of feminism remained angry. Still, the proportion of all adult women at work grew further. In 1920, only 23 percent worked; in 1972, the figure neared 50 percent. The rise was most striking among married women. The work rates were, clearly, highest among poorer women, who work because they have to. But they were high, also, among more affluent women, suggesting that they work because they want to.

The idea of women working for fulfillment appeared to be an inescapable consequence of the strong gains women have made in education. Compared with 1960, the proportion of white women with at least a high school diploma climbed from 65 percent to more than 80 percent. Women's college attendance shot up 60 percent faster than men's, although female totals were still lower.

All such gains notwithstanding, there was substantial doubt that women had gained much according to the bluntest index of progress: equal pay for equal work. A study by Herman P. Miller and Lawrence E. Suter, presented at the American Sociological Association in September 1971, reported that women in the same job status—even if they had worked constantly and had the same education—averaged only 62 percent of male earnings. Many women were disappointed, also, in the outcome of congressional efforts against yet another obstacle to work: lack of adequate day-care and child-development services. Although enacted by both chambers, a bill to promote such services was vetoed by President Nixon. He described it as a blow to the integrity of the family. Echoing criticism from the far right (which assailed the bill for proposing the "Sovietization" of American youth), the president denounced emphasis on "communal approaches to child-rearing." The politics of the day-care veto may well have been sound at the time, but it could be asked how long they would remain so. For there may be no aspects of American life that are in greater flux than those of sex, marriage, and children.

Repeatedly, the United States has learned that major social dislocations inevitably flow from the widespread adoption of new technology. During the 1960s, American women rushed to adopt one of the most revolutionary forms of technology of all time: easy, secure contraception. In 1971 and 1972, moreover, the wide use of the pill and the intrauterine device was facilitated. New York, Maryland, and other states, for example, greatly liberalized their abortion laws. From rigid restrictiveness that drove many women to quacks or coat hangers, the trend was to leave the abortion decision to a woman and her doctor. This was the most elemental form of women's liberation—the freedom to control her own body. The Catholic Church and right-to-life organizations persuaded the New York legislature to repeal the new state abortion law, but this was undone by Governor Nelson Rockefeller's veto. Whether further conservative efforts can succeed in the future is unclear. An opinion survey, released by the president's Commission on Population Growth and the American Future in October 1971, showed that public approval of liberalized abortion policies has climbed to the 50 percent level.

It might fairly be said that secure contraception and liberalized abortion have helped generate a whole new attitude of freedom about sexual intercourse. In spring 1972, for example, the *New York Times* published a front-page article on a subject that would have been unimaginable five years ago: whether parents should allow teenage children to engage in sex in their own homes. As the fear of pregnancy has subsided, so also have moral strictures appeared to lose their force. Indeed, if only for practical reasons, the mood of relaxation may have gone too far. In May, a population commission study by Melvin Zelnick and John F. Kantner reported that 46 percent of all young women have had sexual relations by the time they are nineteen. Most, the study found, have never used contraceptives at all, or used them only sporadically.

The combination of more education for women, more women working, freer attitudes toward sex, and the current dominance of the youth culture could be expected to affect marriage and child-bearing attitudes. A series of Census Bureau studies published in 1971 and 1972 confirmed that expectation. For one thing, young women are marrying later than ever before. For twenty years, their median age at first marriage remained stable at about age twenty, the Census Bureau reported in 1971. But the change in the 1960s alone was so strong that it brought the median age among all women almost up to age twenty-one. Among young women alone that means the typical age at marriage may be up to twenty-four or twenty-five.

In November 1971 the bureau issued some companion findings. It found a striking increase in the number of young women who stay single. As recently as 1960, about a third of those aged twenty-one were unmarried. Now the proportion is about half. There is no way to tell whether this means a permanent change. This finding may suggest only that women are waiting still longer, but will get married eventually. It is also possible, however, that —with enhanced freedom to engage in satisfying work and satisfying sexual relations outside marriage—the prospect of spinsterhood may have lost its sting for many women.

A different kind of marriage phenomenon was evident at the other end of the age spectrum. As longevity continued to rise, the male-female sex ratio among older adults also widened.

At birth, there are about 104 males for every 100 females. At age nineteen, the ratio is about even. But by age sixty-five, there now are only about 75 men for every 100 women, and by age seventy-five, less than 65. This imbalance is magnified increasingly by the growth of the over-sixty-five population. While the total population has doubled since 1920, the older population has *quadrupled.* Then, it was 5 percent of the total population; now, it is 10 percent. And in many areas, the impact of this senior population is still greater both because of in- and out-migration. The movement of older adults south has been so strong that 15 percent of Florida's population (and 50 percent of Miami Beach's population of 87,000) is over sixty-five. At the same time, migration of younger adults out of midwestern agricultural states left a disproportionately large share of older adults. States such as Iowa and Nebraska ranked next after Florida, with about 13 percent of over-sixty-five residents.

The sex imbalance appeared to be a strong reason for the movement of older adults to the Miami Beaches of the country. The sight of older women looking for the companionship of older men became a commonplace at lecture series and cha-cha classes. Some, even while condemning the easy morality of youth, took up "living in sin" themselves, in casual liaisons made economically beneficial by social security. While benefit levels shot up 20 percent, effective in September 1972, payments to two single individuals remained higher than if an older couple were to marry formally.

A BABY BUST?

It was the altered marriage patterns among young women, however, that bore the seeds of major change for the future. Young American women—rich and poor alike—are having fewer children than at any time in the nation's history. Birth rates dropped low in 1971. The total fertility rate in 1972, to judge by partial-year birth rates, now will graze and perhaps even reach what demographers call the magic number: 2.11 children per woman, the number needed to replace each set of parents, single people, and girls who die before they reach child-bearing age.

A Pollyanna could whoop at such news, delighted that the utopian goal of Zero Population Growth is at hand. At last, the cheer would go, America can hope to relieve the strain on the quality of life and the quantity of resources caused by too many people. Such a judgment would be frivolously premature. A fertility rate of 2.11 children or lower is an essential precondition to ZPG. But it would have to continue not for one year, but possibly seventy years before the population size finally stabilized. And even then—if the process began today—it would be a population of some 320 million, compared with the present 209 million. (To understand why, recall that there are twice as many twelve-year-olds as thirty-eight-year-olds. When the twelve-year-olds reach thirty-eight, presumably having an average of two children, they will have precisely replaced their own cohort. But it will still be twice as large a cohort.)

Demographers have learned to measure fertility trends in generations, not years. They know that what goes down rapidly can also go up rapidly, as the wide fluctuations in the American fertility rate attest—1937: 2.23 children; 1947: 3.27; 1957: 3.77; 1967: 2.57. Considering the size of the baby boom now reaching adulthood, there still is a population "bomb" latent in America, should attitudes change again. "The oldest war babies still have years of reproductive life left," Professor Philip M. Hauser, a noted demographer at the University of Chicago, said in a personal interview in November 1971. "The youngest ones have their entire reproductive life ahead of them. They haven't been heard from at all yet."

Still, the strong trends in work, education, and liberation give adequate reason to believe that low fertility will persist for at least a few years. That would not bring ZPG. But it would be enough to generate a whole new round of social dislocations. Indeed, it is already doing so. For example, society has now come full circle from the teacher shortages of the 1950s. The current drop in primary school enrollment has produced such a surplus of teachers that several education schools have severely restricted admissions. The National Education Association estimates that, at the current rate, there will be a surplus of 730,000 teachers in five years.

The larger effects of slower population growth chill the hearts of uninformed businessmen, boosters, and patriots. The president's population commission has now offered careful and complete reassurance. More working women and fewer babies means more income, to be disposed of in different ways. (The cost of bringing up a child, a commission study released in December 1971 calculated, now ranges from $80,000 to $150,000 depending on family income level.) The simple message is that if a family has fewer mouths to feed and more wage earners, it has more to spend on sailboats, stereo sets, and second homes.

Other changes, however, cannot be so clearly foreseen. A stabilizing population is an aging population (the median age has already hit bottom at 27.6 years and appears to be heading up again toward thirty). And often, an aging population is a more conservative population. What will happen to the social idealism of the present youth culture as it matures—to be followed in the nation's age structure by a diminishing number of young? Will what is now a youth bulge continue to dominate social attention as it passes progressively through the stages of man? Will its pluralist pressures shift, from demonstrating for social justice now to lobbying for increased social security forty years hence? The record of the past year gives no answers; only questions.

The People Speak

This new generation of kids will have to change their views about drugs—or else the country will go to pot.
     a New York City housewife

I'm happy that the youth have the right to vote now so we can all voice our opinions.
     a twenty-year-old linotype operator in New York State

I don't think the eighteen-year-olds are capable of voting. I don't know how to vote yet—and I'm seventy-two.
     a retired California woman

What I'm afraid of most is the hippies—they make too many waves.
     a waiter in the South

I don't worry about anything. I've just come back from Vietnam. I've gone through the worst part of my life.
     an unemployed twenty-year-old in Florida

I hope I can see all the boys with haircuts—and working instead of laying around.
     a hospital employee in Kentucky

I'd like to be able to do what I want to do, without any interference from anybody. To mow my own lawn and to play with my grand-children and see my children when I feel like it.
     a seventy-eight-year-old man in a New York suburb

With inflation, how's the elderly people going to live with only social security?
     a housewife in a small Illinois town

I think I would like to see women in more political jobs and in the job market in general.
     a male teacher in a Middle-Atlantic suburb

I like the child development program which helps mothers. It allows me to work while my kids are taken care of.
     a domestic servant in Atlanta

The young, the old, the women all have their own particular brand of problems. Especially associated with youth are the problems of education and, in these days of youthful Babylon, attitudes frequently at variance with their elders on sex and drug use. The old are at a psychological disadvantage in a society in flux that idealizes an image of youth and, with the breakdown of the multigenerational family, wants to sequester oldsters in quiet havens reserved for the elderly. But, above all, the problem of the old is poverty: an unusually large proportion of the elderly are in the lowest income bracket. The most deeply felt problem of the women is socio-psychological: discrimination that denies them not only equality but a full measure of human dignity.

We asked the public in June 1972 what they thought about the major problems associated with these three groups. We asked for an evaluation both of the current state of affairs and of the progress or lack of progress that had been made in each area in the past year. What the people had to say follows.

EDUCATION

Americans have long placed a high value on education, including college training for growing numbers of young people. In general, our educational efforts have been at least quantitatively successful. The great majority of young people today have attained a higher educational status than their fathers, let alone their historically less advantaged mothers. Educating the children of newly urbanized blacks and desegregating our school systems have created special problems, which will be taken up in Chapter V. Here, we are interested in the American people's evaluation of their schools and of public support (or lack of support) for more federal involvement in specific educational programs.

In the eyes of many competent experts, there exists a crisis in the field of education today, a combined crisis of inadequate resources and of what has come to be called "relevance." The majority of the public, however, does not share this view. Whether soundly or not, they believe that the public schools their children go to are good.

We asked: *Turning now to the matter of education, how would you rate the public schools in the neighborhood or area where you live?*

Excellent	15	percent
Good	42	
Only fair	24	
Poor	10	
Don't know	9	
	100	percent

The most noteworthy disparity on this question was between suburbanites, who tended to rate schools in their localities very favorably, and city dwellers, whose opinions were almost equally divided between favorable and unfavorable. Ratings assigned by black Americans were definitely on the negative side.

To our question of educational progress, the prevalent answer was that our educational system is getting better, not worse. Asked how we have done "in providing adequate education for young people as a whole, both white and nonwhite, throughout the country" during the past year, almost two-thirds sensed at least some upward movement. Their evaluations:

Made much progress	14 percent
Made some progress	50
Stood still	15
Lost some ground	12
Lost much ground	4
Don't know	5
	100 percent

The overall composite score * on the question of educational progress was an optimistic 65 on a scale of 100. Residents of the largest metropolitan areas exhibited on the whole a sense of progress that was slightly less than average. Interestingly, however, black Americans as a group were a hair more sanguine than whites. (See Table A-13.)

Despite a sense of progress, Americans put such a high priority on education that majorities of our respondents indicated their belief that the federal government should augment its educational efforts in at least two respects. Here are the figures on a question about whether federal spending on "programs to improve the education of children from low-income families" should be increased, kept at the present level, reduced, or ended altogether:

Increased	62 percent
Kept at present level	28
Reduced	3
Ended altogether	2
Don't know	5
	100 percent

Responses to a similar question about federal spending "to make a college education possible for young people who could not otherwise afford it" were almost equally generous:

Increased	54 percent
Kept at present level	32
Reduced	7
Ended altogether	4
Don't know	3
	100 percent

---

* The method by which composite scores are calculated appears in Appendix 5.

Far higher-than-average composite scores on both these questions were given by the young, who presumably have a special degree of self-interest and faith in the long-term benefits of education. Their views were shared by non-homeowners, liberals, and especially black Americans, who appear very conscious of the upward mobility that education offers their children. Among those who were more reluctant than average in supporting increased federal spending for educational purposes were respondents with only a grade school education and Republicans, who consistently in our survey appeared more reluctant than the public as a whole to increase public spending for almost any purpose. (See Table A-7.)

DRUGS

The problem of drug addicts and narcotic drugs ranked near the top of the list of current concerns of the American public. And a good deal of this concern is understandably directed toward youth.

A Gallup poll released in March 1972 pointed out that the percentage of American adults who have tried marijuana had nearly tripled over the preceding two and a half years: from 4 percent in October 1969 to 11 percent, the latter representing about 15 million people. Use of marijuana was highest by far among eighteen- to twenty-nine-year-olds; three in ten stated they had used the drug at least once, with a far higher incidence among young people with a college background. Another Gallup poll conducted in February 1972 on college campuses showed that nearly one student in five (18 percent) had tried LSD or other hallucinogens. And 51 percent had tried marijuana.

Whatever the merits of the case, the March 1972 Gallup poll found eight out of ten members of the public opposed to the legalization of marijuana. In related fashion, a Harris Survey released in August 1972 reported that a majority of likely voters —by a proportion of 54 to 40 percent—were opposed to easing drug-related criminal penalties, even for the use of marijuana. (Slightly more than 60 percent of the eighteen- to twenty-nine-year-olds and 57 percent of the college-educated disagreed with this majority view.) In the same vein, a Harris Survey released in July 1972 showed that almost eight out of ten members of the public favored "stiffer penalties on hard-drug users."

In short, a national consensus exists, at least for the time being, in favor of a hard-line approach to the problem of drugs and drug users.* This arises, in all likelihood, because the public is frightened by the insidious drug malady to which young people especially seem prey and (as we shall see in Chapter VI) pessimistic about the progress made in overcoming it. A public figure who exhibits a permissive attitude toward marijuana, let alone hard drugs, is apt to be judged by the people as up to no good.

TRUST AND CONFIDENCE IN YOUNG PEOPLE

Despite the enormous attention given to drug proclivities on the part of young people, despite relaxed and permissive sexual standards so disturbing to traditionalists, despite riots and demonstrations associated with the young in recent years, despite hippies, yippies, and zippies, the public, according to our findings, has kept its faith in young Americans.

Following a series of questions about trust and confidence in various institutions of our society, we asked: *Now let's consider young people as a whole today—that is, those in their teens and early twenties. How much trust and confidence do you have in the young in general when it comes to facing up to their own and the country's problems in a responsible way?*

A great deal	27	percent
A fair amount	49	
Not very much	17	
None at all	4	
Don't know	3	
	100	percent

Most population subgroups exhibited an equally high degree of trust and confidence in the young. (See Table A-8.) The overall composite score for this question was 67 (on our scale of 100). The most marked exceptions, showing less confidence in the young, were registered by two interrelated groups at the

* Along somewhat the same lines, a Harris Survey released in August 1972 reported that a majority of the public, by 53 to 38 percent, opposed another type of permissiveness toward the young: the granting of amnesty to those who fled the country to avoid military service.

very bottom of the socio-economic ladder—those with only a grade school education and those with family incomes under $5,000 per year.

There may, indeed, be a generation gap today, but it hardly appears that older people are in the midst of any real "crisis of confidence" in the young.

THE ELDERLY

We turn now to the other end of the age spectrum.

In the listing of public concerns in Table 1, it may or may not be significant that "problems of our elderly" ranked just below "disposing of garbage, trash, and other solid wastes." Whatever the meaning of that juxtaposition, the composite score on the question of concern about the elderly was an impressively high 78. The replies to the question about how worried or concerned respondents were about problems of our senior citizens were:

A great deal	47 percent
A fair amount	37
Not very much	11
Not at all	2
Don't know	3
	100 percent

This concern was particularly high among city dwellers, blacks, families at the bottom of the socio-economic pyramid, and, of course, those of our respondents over fifty years in age. (See Table A-4.)

Although clearly alert to problems of the elderly, a large proportion of the public at the same time tended to feel moderately optimistic about the degree of improvement in dealing with these problems. Asked about progress in handling problems of the elderly over the preceding year, the American people answered:

Made much progress	5 percent
Made some progress	44
Stood still	29
Lost some ground	9
Lost much ground	5
Don't know	8
	100 percent

Among the least sanguine elements of the population on this question were westerners, the college-educated, and the young. (See Table A-13.)

Three-quarters of our sample wanted to bring about further improvements by increasing spending on federal programs to help elderly people, "for example, by increasing the social security payments they receive." The increases in social security benefits enacted into law in July 1972 were evidently approved in large measure by all segments of the population—most of all by the poor, city dwellers, people living in the South and West, black Americans, and, of course, the group most directly affected, older people themselves. (See Table A-7.)

THE FEMALE OF THE SPECIES

Historically, women were slow to react to, let alone rebel against, the ingrained, systematic discrimination that affects their lives from cradle to grave. Nevertheless, what today we refer to as the "women's lib" movement is not altogether new: it is an extension, in fact, of the suffragist wave that led to the adoption of the Twentieth Amendment to the Constitution in 1920, giving women the right to vote. Much discrimination remains though, especially in such matters as equalization of wages. Nevertheless, there have been definite gains for women since the turn of the century. And the great majority of women seem to agree.*

Personal satisfaction and optimism are reflected in the ratings men and women give their personal lives on the imaginary ladder of life. In our mid-1972 survey, the average personal ladder rating for the present given by women was slightly higher (although the difference was not statistically significant) than that given by men. And women showed every bit as much sense of progress from past to present as men and were equally

---

* It is certain that sexually biased views will be with us for some time to come. If it is necessary to point up the problem in attitudes women still face, it should be enough to cite the statement made in the spring of 1972 by Representative Dave Smith, a member of the Florida House of Representatives: "I am a male chauvinist. I believe that women should be coddled, loved, kissed, and hugged. I believe they should be honored, that doors should be opened for them, chairs pulled back for them, and old-fashioned grace be accorded them. They should be well scrubbed and always smell sweet."

optimistic about their personal futures. The personal ladder ratings of men and women are given in Table 3.

TABLE 3   PERSONAL LADDER RATINGS OF WOMEN AND MEN *

	Women	Men
Past	5.6	5.4
Present	6.6	6.2
Future	7.7	7.4
Shift from Past to Present	+1.0	+0.8
Shift from Present to Future	+1.1	+1.2

* A shift of 0.6 of a step is considered statistically significant.

The clearly positive outlook implicit in these ladder ratings is borne out in responses to another question in our survey. We asked: *Turning to another topic, there is a lot of talk these days about discrimination against women and women's rights. Taking into account this question of discrimination and all other aspects of their lives, how would you, yourself, rate the situation of women in general in this country today: excellent, good, only fair, or poor?*

	Women	Men	Total Sample
	(in percentages)		
Excellent	17	25	21
Good	54	50	52
Only fair	22	18	20
Poor	5	4	4
Don't know	2	3	3
	100	100	100

Significantly more than one-half of female respondents thought their current situation was at least "good," and an additional 17 percent that it was actually "excellent," making a total of more than seven out of ten who gave upbeat answers. Males, to be sure, labeled the situation of women "excellent" more often than did women themselves, but the discrepancy was not so large as to suggest a markedly different overall perspective.

When it came to holding a job or staying at home with the children, the answers were fairly evenly divided. We asked:

Do you think that women with school age children should feel free to take full-time jobs if they want to, or, in your opinion, should they stay home and take care of their children?

	Women	Men	Total Sample
	(in percentages)		
Take jobs	51	53	52
Stay home	40	39	40
Don't know	9	8	8
	100	100	100

In this case, no less than 53 percent of the men joined 51 percent of the women in reacting affirmatively to women working full time. Moreover, the public was fully willing to facilitate this trend, our study showed, by providing facilities for the care of children of working mothers. We asked: *Would you favor or oppose the U.S. using tax money to set up day care centers for the care of children whose mothers are working away from home?*

	Women	Men	Total Sample
	(in percentages)		
Favor	63	58	61
Oppose	28	35	31
Don't know	9	7	8
	100	100	100

Support for federally financed day-care centers was considerably lower than average among the more traditionalist elements of our society: labor union households; people living in small towns, villages, and rural areas; conservatives; and especially Republicans, of whom only 44 percent were in favor. Exceedingly large majorities supporting government-financed day-care centers appeared among the top income and business and professional groups; the college-educated; people living in cities of more than 50,000 population; Democrats; liberals; and, most of all, young people and black Americans, among whom approval proportions reached 76 percent and 85 percent, respectively.

IV.
Urban Affairs

The cities are dehumanizing our people.
        a building superintendent in New York State

My greatest hope for the country is that there will be comfortable housing for all.
        the black wife of a mechanic on the West Coast

If they raise the subway fare any more, I won't be able to get to work.
        a retail clerk in New York City

The Record Speaks

By the beginning of 1972, the plight of the American cities was well known. With rare exceptions, the nation's urban centers were beset to varying degrees by systematic forces that no one within could do much about. Every year, even as the nation prospered in many ways, great cities such as New York, Philadelphia, Baltimore, Cleveland, St. Louis, and Chicago experienced an advance in urban decay, a loss of the middle class to the suburbs, an increase in social problems, and a decline in tax base.

But no one was quite prepared for the ominous development that was disclosed early in 1972—the abandonment of block after block of housing in a number of the central cities at the very time of a generally acute housing shortage. The puzzling phenomenon had various forms. Usually the federal government was left holding the property (much of it structurally sound), one indication among many of the federal government's inability to come to grips with the urban crisis.

In one sense, the nation was simply abandoning its central cities and moving on to newer urban settlements in the suburban ring, in much the same way that it abandons automobiles when they are worn out or mining towns when the mines shut down. But the shift was not without great pain and distortions of the society. Against all this was juxtaposed a range of other significant developments—from increasing financial failures of mass transit systems to the forming of biracial coalitions of central city residents in a desperate effort to do something about the forces that were tearing at their lives.

Trouble in the cities, building for several decades, had greatly accelerated during the 1960s. Long a repository for poor minorities both from rural areas of this country and from abroad, the cities earlier in the century could absorb and civilize the dispossessed and uneducated. But that was before technology displaced great numbers of unskilled jobs that served as a conduit for the under class into middle-class productivity. It was before the decline of the urban political machines which, however corrupt some may have been, served to meet the social needs of millions. And it was when the migrants came largely from cultural backgrounds that kept families together and permitted upward mobility in American society.

It was after World War II that the current trends began. Becoming more and more dependent on automobiles, Americans moved to new settlements outside the established city boundaries. In the old cities of the East and Midwest—where most of the urban problems are now concentrated—the new centers that offered cheap housing and low taxes refused to be incorporated by the central cities and, instead, set up their own governments, schools, and other services. At the same time, there was an enormous migration of blacks from depressed rural areas of the South to the slums and marginal neighborhoods in the central cities that the white minorities, now more prosperous, had begun to abandon.

The result was large concentrations of poverty, high unemployment, soaring welfare rolls, broken families, and high crime rates. There was little chance for upward mobility, either into the more prosperous white communities or into the job market that had been the salvation for white ethnics. Not surprisingly, there was considerable social unrest. At the same time, the cities were losing political power. The rural bloc that once thwarted the cities in the state legislatures, and to some extent in Congress, was joined by the even more powerful suburban bloc that had little sympathy for the peculiar problems of the cities, even though its constituents had a part in bringing about those problems.

Then came the riots of the 1960s, a national rebellion by blacks and Puerto Ricans impacted in central city slums. Although there was some positive reaction from the white majority in the form of more jobs for minorities and enactment of civil rights laws to attempt to open the suburbs, the uprisings in many ways worsened the situation. Much property was damaged or destroyed, the cities had to increase greatly their police forces, and the urban slums went right on festering, and in many cities spreading. The suburbs by and large remained exclusionary, through zoning or other practices. The white middle class, and some more affluent blacks as well, moved out of the central city at an even faster rate.

When the 1970s opened, some Americans were surprised to find they had created a new kind of city—a doughnut-shaped one surrounding the old core city, composed usually of a proliferation of municipalities and other jurisdictions, unwieldy and uncoordinated, but in fact the real city. Here was where most of life was—the homes, the schools, the industry, the jobs, the stores, the new high-rise apartments and the office buildings, all connected by countless miles of roads and expressways. A number of central cities, of course, remained at least in part places of bustling vitality—Manhattan and the Chicago Loop, for example, But in almost every major city the majority of the suburban dwellers did not work in the central city, but in some segment of the suburban ring.

Census Bureau figures and other studies from Detroit, compiled in a study entitled "Abandonment of the Cities," prepared by Stanley H. Ruttenberg and Associates for the National Urban Coalition, provide a case study of what had happened in one city. From 1960 to 1970, the white population of the central city declined almost 30 percent while the nonwhite population increased almost 38 percent, with an overall population loss of almost 10 percent. Between 1965 and 1970, the number of jobs in the central city dropped sharply while an even larger rise was recorded in the suburbs. For example, the number of manufacturing establishments in the central city declined by more than 10 percent while increasing by almost twice that figure in the suburbs. By 1971, there were almost five times as many people on welfare in the central city as in the suburbs, although the latter had almost 70 percent of the population. Polls showed that many suburban residents had quit going downtown altogether. The central city, once known as the center of activity, was now the place to shun.

Under the Nixon administration, which did not choose to stress the problems of the core cities or to emphasize innovations in urban matters, the central cities became more invisible. Federal programs enacted in the 1960s barely made a dent in the urban crisis. George Sternlieb, director of the Center for Urban Policy Research at Rutgers University, writing in *The Public Interest* in the fall of 1971, suggested that the function of many central cities is essentially like that of a child's sandbox:

A sandbox is a place where adults park their children in order to converse, play, or work with a minimum of interference. The adults, having found a distraction for the children, can get on with the serious things of life. There is some reward for the children in all this. The sandbox is given to them as their own turf. Occasionally, fresh sand or toys are put in the sandbox, along with an implicit admonition that these things are furnished to minimize the level of noise and nuisance. If the children do become noisy and distract their parents, fresh toys may be brought. If the occupants of the sandbox choose up sides and start bashing each other over the head, the adults will come running, smack the juniors more or less indiscriminately, calm things down, and then, perhaps in an act of semi-contrition, bring fresh sand and fresh toys, pat the occupants of the sandbox on the head, and disappear once again into their adult involvements and pursuits.

That is what the city has become—a sandbox. Government programs have increasingly taken on this cast.

Sternlieb maintained that policies could be drawn to restore a useful economic function for the central cities but that the country seemed to be "opting for the sandbox. What this will mean for our society in the future we do not fully know: but that the consequences are likely to be cruel and disagreeable has become only too clear."

His words were underscored at the beginning of 1972 when a series of revelations exposed the tragic extent of housing abandonment, previously viewed as only a minor problem. In old neighborhoods where real estate values have declined sharply it is not unusual for housing that can no longer be maintained without economic loss to the owner to be abandoned to the city in lieu of taxes. But in cities such as New York, Newark, Detroit, Cleveland, St. Louis, and Philadelphia, massive abandonment occurred without apparent reason and extended to property that could have been rehabilitated and made to serve housing needs for generations to come. In Detroit, where the government holds title to some 8,500 houses that no one wants, entire neighborhoods have been wrecked and vandalized. St. Louis never had a major riot, but block after block there looked as if the city had been bombed. Fires ravaged the Woodlawn section of Chicago prior to abandonment, reportedly the efforts of owners to collect insurance.

The cause was a combination of widespread corruption in the real estate and mortgage businesses operating in the central cities —the more reputable firms had moved to the suburbs with the middle class—and of the forces of social distress, massive poverty, crime, and neglect at work in the core city neighborhoods.

In a typical case a speculator would purchase an old house, make superficial repairs, and sell it to a low-income family at an inflated price under a mortgage guaranteed by the Federal Housing Administration (FHA). Shortly after moving in, the family would find the property in need of extensive repair. Not having the money for repairs and not having much equity in the property, the family would move out, with the property going to the FHA at a sizeable loss to the government.

Apartment buildings were also a problem. Even with government subsidies the owners frequently could not make the mortgage payments for a variety of reasons—corruption and theft in construction of the property, too high a concentration of poor families unable to pay rents, an unexpected rise in taxes due to the continuing decline of the city, or wage demands of municipal workers. George Romney, Secretary of Housing and Urban Development, estimated that the federal government would soon hold about $1 billion in properties, due largely to the erosive influences within the cities.

More than the housing itself was involved. The massive failures were a strong indicator that the central cities were in more trouble than many people had been willing to admit. The federal government under the Nixon administration had made only a limited investment in the central cities. It had invested rather heavily in subsidized housing—about 25 percent of the 2 million housing starts per year were in subsidized units—but this by itself could not stand against the tide of urban decay. As for meeting the housing needs of the general population, the government did succeed in reaching on a yearly basis the housing goals established under the 1968 Housing Act, but so many dwellings were being lost to abandonment and demolition to make way for highways and public buildings that President Nixon acknowledged in a report to Congress in mid-1971 that the housing shortage in many areas was likely to continue for a long time. Further, housing costs were going up so rapidly that about 40 percent of the population was eligible for limited housing subsidies. And most of the good housing that was going up was being built under the subsidy programs in the suburbs for moderate-income families with jobs, not for the poor in the central cities.

Secretary Romney publicly acknowledged the extent of the crisis and the shortcomings of his own department in dealing with it. "After long and careful study," he said in testimony to the Housing Subcommittee of the House Banking and Currency Committee on February 22, 1972, "it is my considered belief that the housing problem in our central cities results from all the social, economic, and physical problems now afflicting our urban areas. And it is abundantly clear that the rotting of central cities is beginning to rot the surrounding suburbs. Despite all our efforts, despite the billions of dollars that have been expended, the decay of core cities goes on. We continue to suffer continuing losses of human and economic resources."

But in fashioning a remedy, Secretary Romney did not appear to have the support of the White House. In his view, the problems of the central city would have to be attacked by the metropolitan area as a whole, a procedure that was very rare. The prevailing attitude in the predominant suburban ring was one of indifference, if not hostility, to the central city, even though, as the secretary pointed out, the decay was spreading. Romney went to the White House late in 1971 with a plan for making incentive grants to metropolitan areas that agreed through government and civic leadership to take on central city problems and solve them on an areawide basis. But the White House rejected the plan.

In a report to Congress on February 29, the White House staff, responding to a congressional mandate for an annual report from the executive branch on urban growth, said that the administration had no plan for an urban growth policy and, indeed, did not believe that it should. In effect, it said, the burden rests on local leadership.

Romney then went to some of the metropolitan areas—Detroit; St. Louis; Wilmington, Delaware; and others—in an effort to inspire a voluntary, metropolitan-wide approach. But this was not considered likely to have much effect, even within Romney's own department. Efforts were being made to open the suburbs to poor minorities, through administration of civil rights laws and pressing of lawsuits against exclusionary zoning. But this, too, was widely considered inadequate to deal with the massive distress of the central cities.

Another indication of the extent of the problem was the organization in March 1972 of a broad national coalition of central city dwellers, a new phenomenon in American history. Meeting in Chicago's west side—an area stunned by blight and abandonment—about 370 grassroots community organizations from cities across the country formed the National People's Action on Housing. What gave rise to the organization were deep feelings on the part of white ethnics, blacks, Spanish-speaking people, and others living in the central cities that they were being treated unfairly by the private and governmental institutions that control housing development, zoning, insurance rates, and real estate practices. Gale Cincotta of Chicago, chairman of the new coalition, told the House Government Operations Subcommittee on Legal and Monetary Affairs on May 4:

I am here to testify on a specific case of conspiracy, the outright murder of our neighborhoods in America, aided and abetted by the FHA, the mortgage industry, the insurance industry and the unscrupulous real estate industry. These four institutions are working together to systematically destroy what is left of America's cities. The blacks, the browns and the whites across the nation are sick and tired of the conditions which exist in our cities today, and our anger is mounting. Our inner-city neighborhoods are ringed by surburbia where indifference to the city dweller is an everyday word and "keep the minorities out" is a way of life. We are being manipulated by every fast-buck artist in the business.

Whatever the accuracy of Mrs. Cincotta's analysis of the motives, there was little doubt about the ultimate effect of the problems that stirred her complaints or the extent of the anger of central city residents.

The development of the new city outside the old, however disjointed in government and coordination of services and policy, could be viewed as a positive achievement. It was new and prosperous and many who lived there found little fault with it all. But it posed numerous problems nonetheless. One in particular was the matter of public transportation.

In the old concept of the city, public transportation was a fairly simple matter. The business section of the city was located at the center. Radial rail, bus, or subway lines could be established to take people to the center from the perimeter and back again, and a few circular routes would solve the cross-city problem, when needed. But in the new city the distances are magnified many times. If a majority lives in the suburban ring and works in another segment of the ring, the solution is no longer to get people back and forth from the center—nor for shopping, going to the dentist, or taking the children to music lessons. Yet some people still work in the central city and need to get back and forth, great distances, without driving automobiles. Others must travel from the central city to new job openings in the suburbs. Many more people have to be transported in many more different directions at much greater distances.

It was not surprising that the old public transit systems began to fail. Not only did they not get people where they wanted to be nor prevent the streets and expressways from becoming clogged with private automobiles; in addition, the transit companies, both public and private, were going broke. In 1965, according to a March 4 report in *National Journal,* only 12 urban transit systems across the country were receiving operating subsidies to cover their losses. By 1972 there were 130, and a number of others were on the verge of joining the list. The private Nashville Transit Company served notice on Nashville officials that it would go out of business in 1973 unless federal subsidies were forthcoming. In Cincinnati, attempts to sustain first a private franchise and then a publicly run transit system failed.

Part of the trouble in urban transit was in management and part in greatly increased labor costs. But much of it was due to the physical realities of the new city. In sprawling Los Angeles, for example, officials shudder at the cost of establishing an efficient mass transit system.

Yet, with more and more transit systems failing, Congress in 1970 had enacted a multi-billion-dollar program for assisting local governments in making new capital outlays for buses, subways, trains, and novel means of moving people. In 1972 a coalition of urban and business interests lobbied Congress extensively for subsidies to pay operating deficits. Pending legislation to this effect was considered sure to pass, if not in 1972, then in 1973. It was simply a matter, sponsors insisted, of the federal government spending money beyond current budget to keep the cities from collapsing altogether for want of adequate transportation. It was generally expected that operating subsidies would soon run $1 billion a year or more.

Some transportation plans did have the potential of making the real city—core and suburbs—more unified and livable. In Atlanta, for example, both the core city and the suburban ring voted to impose on themselves a sales tax that would provide cheaper transit rides and make it possible for residents to move about with some efficiency in the vast metropolitan area without going by automobile. San Francisco was building an extensive subway and rail system that would greatly cut down on automobile traffic and provide much greater mobility for a number of residents.

But critics of federal transit subsidies charged that no amount of federal subsidies would bring about really efficient transit systems for the new city built for the automobile culture. They charged that the subsidies sought are merely a stop-gap measure, not one that will come to grips with the basic problems, no matter how expensive the costs might ultimately be.

In 1971 the Nixon administration proposed extensive governmental reorganization that most experts believed would ultimately help the federal establishment cope with its urban problems. Federal agencies and departments concerned with the development of cities, towns, and counties are fragmented, and there is considerable duplication and overlapping of effort. Under the Nixon reorganization plan, the Department of Housing and Urban Development would be restructured as the Department of Community Development. Those agencies concerned primarily with the social and physical development of both the cities and small towns would be included in this new department. For example, the community action agencies funded by the Office of Economic Opportunity, the major anti-poverty agency, would be brought under the new department and meshed with similar programs already under HUD, such as Model Cities. From the Department of Agriculture would come the agencies that oversee small town and rural housing and community projects. Since each individual agency has its own constituency that can put pressure on Congress, and since the restructuring would challenge existing committee organization in Congress and therefore upset the seniority system, such a reorganization is difficult to bring about. In any event, Congress was very slow to move on the proposal. But at least partial reorganization along the lines suggested by the president was expected to come about in time. Although reorganization does not get to the crucial matter of solving programmatic problems, it at least would provide the framework for developing a rational means of dealing with growth and development of all kinds of communities.

Many other kinds of solutions have been proposed for dealing with the problems of the central cities and bringing about a rational urban growth policy. They include: an urban homestead plan under which the federal government would open central city lands to new development; extensive land reform and new zoning practices; and two-level government that would decentralize functions such as education and police while centralizing pollution control, housing, and planning. But no one has achieved a national consensus for any of these.

The prevailing view in mid-1972 was that what has happened to American cities is one of the great traumas of our time—one that is crying out for a rational solution that can only be reached through the consent of an informed and concerned majority.

The People Speak

Our neighborhood is falling apart but we can't move at our age.
Awful people move into these run-down houses. They're all on relief.
> the fifty-one-year-old wife of a disabled man in Harrisburg,
> Pennsylvania

I look around the inner city and it is like a tooth which has had no
dental attention after decay has started.
> a black business development specialist working for the federal
> government in Baltimore

I don't think it's fair for the government to subsidize housing for the
shiftless while the hard-working people can't get new homes.
> a Michigan housewife

I hope there won't be any more fighting in this part of town.
> an unemployed man living in Hartford, Connecticut, where
> rioting occurred the preceding year

I am afraid they will build too many freeways, especially through the
cities.
> a retired midwesterner

Condemned houses should be fixed up because the kids playing there
could get hurt. They should fix them because, when they tear them
down, they just leave the empty lots with sticks, glass, rocks, and
everything else right there.
> a diesel mechanic in New York City

My worst fear is that I will always have to live in a ghetto.
> a twenty-five-year-old black telephone operator in Brooklyn,
> New York

Rebuilding run-down sections of our cities, providing adequate housing for all the people, improving mass transportation systems, and handling urban troubles in general—these big-city problems fell lower on our scale of concerns than issues affecting Americans wherever they may live. (See Table 1.) That such problems are not personally experienced by people living outside the large cities inevitably brings down the degree of overall public interest. But another explanation for this lower level of concern was implicit in our findings: the American public as a whole does not seem to realize how seriously the cores of our cities have deteriorated in recent years. We asked three different questions about progress in handling urban problems over the past year. In all three cases, the answers we received did not reflect the state of affairs that experts and statistics tell us exists.

We asked: *How have we done in the field of mass transportation within and between metropolitan areas by bus, train, or, in some cities, subways; In providing adequate housing for the American people as a whole, both white and nonwhite;* and *Finally, how much progress, if any, do you feel we have made in handling the overall problems of our cities generally?*

The answers we received were:

	Mass Transportation	Housing (in percentages)	Urban Problems in General
Made much progress	4	8	2
Made some progress	27	52	42
Stood still	27	21	26
Lost some ground	16	9	14
Lost much ground	8	4	4
Don't know	18	6	12
	100	100	100

On the question about mass transportation, the overall composite score * was 51 (on a scale of 100), indicating a predominant evaluation that the country had "stood still" in this respect. Many experts would surely claim that the more valid assessment is that the country had lost ground. Even more unrealistic was the relatively high composite score of 64 on the question about providing adequate housing. The composite score on handling the

---

* The method by which composite scores are calculated is described in Appendix 5.

overall problems of the cities was a more restrained 57, but even this score indicated a feeling that at least a small degree of progress had been made over the past year on the urban front, an assessment clearly open to challenge.

GOVERNMENTAL SPENDING ON URBAN PROBLEMS

Reflecting lessened concern and awareness over the problems of America's cities, our sample was cautious when it came to supporting federal spending for city problems. Although the public favored maintaining at least the present levels of government expenditures on urban problems, the proportions of Americans supporting increases were much lower than was the case with problems of more widespread impact.

More than seven respondents out of ten, for example, wanted to augment federal spending in such fields as problems of the elderly, crime control, and drugs; and more than six out of ten in the cases of education, health care, and air and water pollution. In contrast, and despite the public's customarily liberal, even casual, tendency to approve governmental spending not directly related to tax increases, the proportion opting for increased expenditures to deal with problems peculiar to big cities dropped to about four in ten—significantly below the majority level. And sentiment for cutting spending, while still in minority proportions, was correspondingly higher than in other problem areas. (It may be that this reluctance to enlarge expenditures for dealing with urban ills is attributable in part to a sense of disillusionment with past spending programs and of frustration over their apparent inability to contribute to lasting solutions.)

This pattern of caution in recommending increased federal spending emerged with striking consistency when our sample was asked its views on spending for a whole range of activities: for "the federal program to help build low-rent public housing;" "programs to provide better and faster mass transportation systems in and between metropolitan areas, such as buses, trains, and, in some cities, subways;" "programs to rebuild run-down sections of our cities;" and, finally, spending designed to meet "the overall problems of our cities generally."

The public's answers to these five questions follow:

	Public Housing	Housing in General	Mass Transportation	Urban Renewal	Urban Problems in General
			(in percentages)		
Increased	40	37	41	51	41
Present level	40	48	39	29	44
Reduced	12	7	9	11	6
Ended	4	3	3	5	1
Don't know	4	5	8	4	8
	100	100	100	100	100

Although there was overwhelming support for maintaining at least the present level of governmental spending in all of these areas, in only one instance did the percentage advocating increased spending achieve a bare majority: 51 percent in the case of urban renewal. And here a comparatively high 16 percent called for either a reduction in spending or an end to the program altogether, a clear confirmation that urban renewal continues to be a controversial program.

It should come as no surprise that the highest composite scores in favor of increased spending were evident among those groups we found to be most concerned about these problems: the big-city dwellers, sometimes joined by suburbanites; the young; blacks; and those who characterized themselves as liberals. (See Table A-7.) Much lower composite scores appeared among those groups expressing least concern about big-city problems: people living in towns, villages, and rural areas, and Republicans. On the whole, the scores of these two groups were just above the "maintain present level" point on our scale.

One exception to this pattern appeared in the answers to the query about increased spending for mass transportation. Here, older people were far more in favor of increased spending than the young or middle-aged, obviously because the old are more dependent on public transportation.

FROM CITIES TO SUBURBS?

It is debatable, of course, whether increased governmental spending alone can reverse the painfully obvious process of urban blight. Americans, perhaps reflecting an awareness of this, presented no national consensus in favor of new, massive, and costly efforts.

How, then, did they feel about other possible solutions for our urban ills? How receptive were they, in particular, to the relocation in the suburbs of significant numbers of people now living in central cities?

To determine the acceptability of such an approach, we asked: *Considering the problems now faced by people living in our large central cities, please read the two propositions listed on this card and then tell me how you feel about each of them. Obviously, you can favor both; or favor one and not the other; or oppose both.*

A. *The government should undertake huge rebuilding programs in our central cities to provide adequate housing and facilities for the people who now live there.*

B. *The U.S. should force surrounding suburban areas to permit the building of more low- and medium-cost housing and facilities to take care of people in the central cities who would like to move there.*

First, would you be for or against proposition A?

For	60	percent
Against	32	
Don't know	8	
	100	percent

And would you support or oppose proposition B?

Support	47	percent
Oppose	44	
Don't know	9	
	100	percent

These two propositions were intentionally linked, for we wanted to see whether the public would prefer solving the problems of urban decay by action within the central cities or by dispersing poorer central city citizens in the suburbs. The answer is fairly clear. Even though the public had not indicated strong support in principle for massive new federal spending on the cities, it reacted differently when faced with the possibility of a federally directed population shift from the central cities to the suburbs. In short, considerably more Americans were in favor of huge rebuilding programs within the central cities (60 percent) than of opening the suburbs (47 percent).

Above the national average in favoring massive urban rebuilding were young people; non-homeowners; easterners; city dwellers in general and those living in our largest metropolitan areas in particular; and black Americans. Among those groups least in favor of rebuilding programs in central cities were middle-of-the-roaders on the liberal-conservative spectrum, Republicans, and Independents.

The pattern of responses on forcing the construction of low-cost housing in the suburbs was for the most part predictable. Predominantly in favor were young people; those with low incomes and little education; union households; non-homeowners; easterners; big-city dwellers; Catholics; Democrats; liberals; and, particularly, blacks. Predominantly opposed were the college-educated (a larger-than-average proportion of whom live in the suburbs); those with annual incomes in the $7,000 to $15,000 range; white collar workers; southerners; rural people; Republicans; Independents; middle-of-the-roaders; and conservatives.

Most interesting of all were the responses of those who called themselves suburbanites. At first glance, one would expect to encounter among them the strongest resistance of all to an enforced breach of their enclaves. Surprisingly, this was not the case: although 50 percent were opposed to our proposition B, almost as many, 46 percent, were in favor.

The overall conclusion, however, is clear: there is no consensus in favor of forcing the suburbs to permit construction of more low- and medium-cost housing and accompanying facilities. In fact, the public is virtually stalemated on the issue. At the present time, this particular approach for alleviating central city problems does not appear eminently practical, at least from the standpoint of public acceptance and political realities.

POTENTIAL POPULATION REDISTRIBUTION

The question remains of how many people now living in cities would actually like to move into the suburbs if they could. In a broader framework, the issue becomes one of potential population redistribution. Are the residents of cities, suburbs, towns, villages, and rural areas satisfied with their present environments? If obstacles—legal, social, and economic—were removed, would they prefer to relocate elsewhere?

The answers to one question about location were astounding: almost nine out of ten Americans indicated reasonable satisfaction with the neighborhood or locality in which they were living. Only one in ten expressed dissatisfaction. Our question: *How satisfied are you with living in the neighborhood or locality where you are now located: a great deal, a fair amount, not very much, or not at all?*

A great deal	56	percent
A fair amount	32	
Not very much	8	
Not at all	2	
Don't know	2	
	100	percent

Geographically, people living in small communities and rural areas expressed by far the highest degree of satisfaction with their present places of residence. So did those in upper-income groups. Understandably, non-homeowners were markedly less satisfied than homeowners. Also predictable was the lower-than-average satisfaction indicated by people now living in the cities; young people, most of whom have not yet established a fixed residence; and black Americans, especially.

Even among blacks, however, 33 percent indicated "a great deal" of satisfaction and 48 percent "a fair amount," making a total of more than eight out of ten who were reasonably pleased with their neighborhoods. Only 17 percent expressed dissatisfaction. Considering the conditions of many of the neighborhoods in which black Americans live, it seems likely that their reactions reflected a sense of resignation, fatalism, or the good spirit that exists in many inner-city neighborhoods. (As the resident of a black neighborhood scheduled for urban renewal in Washington, D.C., told a *Washington Post* reporter in the summer of 1972: "They might call this the ghetto, but the way we get along in the ghetto is A-OK with me.")

But if all bars were down—racial, economic, social—what kind of environment would people see as ideal? Where, in short, might they locate the residence of their dreams, no matter how satisfied they are with their present locale?

To get at this admittedly speculative issue, we asked respondents first to classify the type of place in which they now live and then to specify the kind of locale they would choose if they could live anywhere they wished. Their replies were:

	Present	Preferred
	(in percentages)	
City	36	18
Suburb	22	22
Town or village	15	19
Rural area	18	38
Don't know	9	3
	100	100

The results show some most interesting contrasts: while almost six respondents out of ten currently classified themselves as city dwellers or suburbanites, only four in ten would prefer to live in cities or suburbs. Conversely, while only one-third said they now live in towns, villages, or rural areas, almost six out of ten said that is what they would prefer.

Putting the matter another way, the figures suggest that if the American people could follow their inclinations, the population of our cities would be cut in half. The proportion of suburbanites would remain the same. The percentage of people living in towns and villages would increase significantly. And the proportion enjoying country life would more than double, from less than two in ten to almost four in ten.

This last finding may be discounted in part on the grounds that our sample may simply have reflected one of the most enduring of American myths: that true happiness is to be found in the country, close to nature. Intriguingly, however, analysis of our survey results seems to support that supposed myth. We cross-correlated present places of residence with preferred places of residence to see who was most happy where. The results are given in Table 4. They show that, while only four out of ten present city dwellers want to stay in the city, no less than nine out of ten of those now residing in the country say they are just where they want to be.

TABLE 4   PRESENT PLACE AND PREFERRED PLACE
          OF RESIDENCE
          percentages

Present Place of Residence	Preferred Place of Residence					
	City	*Suburb*	*Town or Village*	*Rural*	*Don't Know*	*Total*
City	*41*	18	14	27	—	100
Suburb	5	*57*	11	25	2	100
Town or village	5	6	*60*	27	2	100
Rural area	2	3	5	*90*	—	100

Because of the current debate over desegregating the suburbs
and over the direction future metropolitan development will take,
we looked at the present and preferred places of residence of two
special groups—black Americans and eighteen- to twenty-nine-
year-olds. The results are given below:

	Black Americans		Young People	
	Present	*Preferred*	*Present*	*Preferred*
		(*in percentages*)		
City	68	32	39	16
Suburb	9	26	21	19
Town or village	6	11	14	18
Rural area	10	30	16	44
Don't know	7	1	10	3
	100	100	100	100

While almost seven blacks out of ten in our sample are now
city dwellers, only about three in ten would like to remain such.
One-quarter would prefer to live in the suburbs, a shift that would
increase the proportion of blacks who are currently suburbanites
from 9 percent to 26 percent. One in ten blacks, almost double
the present proportion, would like to live in a town or village.
And no less than three in ten would prefer life in the country,
a change that would triple the proportion of blacks now living
in rural areas.

In view of the huge numbers of blacks who have attempted

to escape rural poverty by migrating to the cities, these findings take on special significance. Many blacks, it would appear, have found the complicated and frustrating life of the cities, combined so often with the vise of poverty and other deprivation, unsatisfying. The end of the rainbow, in short, is not to be found in the cities after all.

Also significant in terms of any future redistribution of the population are the views of the young. If left to their own devices, large numbers of young people would move out of the cities, not to the suburbs, but to towns, villages, and, especially, rural areas, where considerably more than four out of ten said they would most like to live.

While there may be room for conjecture, of course, as to the lasting significance of these various choices, an interesting alternative may be trying to make itself heard: the public appears to be suggesting that we alleviate the present crisis conditions in our cities by reversing the decades-long trend of migration from country to city, perhaps in part by making small town and country life more economically and culturally attractive.

Despite a notably high degree of satisfaction with the neighborhood or locality where they now live, the American people seem at least potentially receptive to shifting residences on a grand scale. And their readiness to do so might be substantially enhanced if appropriate incentives and encouragement were provided through private initiative and federal, state, and local governmental efforts.

V.
Minority Groups

It would be wonderful if there were no racial tensions, a complete elimination of American hypocrisy, especially in regard to blacks and us Puerto Ricans. Then there might be equal opportunities for all people.
   a female General Motors employee in New York City

My fear is that I will have to go on living in the same way I am now, with no way out: closed up in a ghetto, having a job I don't like, my children getting an inferior education.
   a twenty-two-year-old black machinist in Chicago

The Negroes now have as much a chance of getting jobs as the white people.
   a white IBM supervisor in an eastern city

The Record Speaks

The widespread discontent displayed in many areas of American life during the past year was evident in race relations, too. Blacks, Indians, and Mexican-Americans not only continued to voice dissatisfaction with their lot in society but also created new mechanisms to amplify their protest. White Americans, on the other hand, displayed heightened resistance to further reforms aimed at combating poverty and discrimination. This polarization was reflected in election-year politics, most notably by the symbolic weight attached to the issue of school busing to achieve desegregation. Underlying the public debate over this and other highly visible issues were basic trends affecting, both favorably and unfavorably, minority living patterns, economic opportunity, and political participation. How the American people ultimately choose among these alternative trends will determine the nation's future as a single or a divided society.

INDIANS AND SPANISH-SPEAKING AMERICANS

In general, the Spanish-speaking and American Indian minorities continued to experience disabilities similar to, but often more severe than, those of blacks—disproportionately high unemployment, low income, educational deficiencies, inadequate housing, and so on. Also like the blacks, these minorities exhibited heightened activism and pressure for greater self-determination. But there were also marked distinctions—in the case of the Spanish-speaking, who number about 9.6 million, special problems imposed by language and cultural differences; in the case of Indians, who number about 800,000, the uniqueness of tribal and reservation status, as well as a historically special relationship with the federal government.

The two major Spanish-speaking minorities, Puerto Ricans and Mexican-Americans (Chicanos), have had little in common, geographically and otherwise. An attempt to change this situation, at least on the political level, took place at a national meeting held in Washington, D.C., in the fall of 1971, where some 2,000 representatives of Puerto Rican and Mexican-American voters gathered. The significance of the meeting was primarily symbolic, but as a precedent it may turn out to have both political and cultural importance. Economically, Chicanos continued to press for better wages and working conditions through the organization of migrant workers in such states as California and Florida, primarily under the banner of Cesar Chavez's United Farm Workers union. Other organizing efforts concentrated on problems of schooling, housing, employment, and prison conditions.

Indians displayed a growing desire to participate in planning and policies affecting their status. Heretofore, the most visible and prominent spokesmen for these interests have been urbanized Indians. In the spring of 1971, reservation Indians founded the National Tribal Chairmen's Association to put their case to the Nixon administration in general and the Bureau of Indian Affairs in the Department of the Interior in particular. Their demands generally were twofold: reforms in the Bureau of Indian Affairs favorable to greater self-determination, and repudiation of policies seen as "terminating" the Indians' special status under treaties with the national government. Self-determination in practice was little evident, except for the creation of Indian boards of education overseeing the operation of local schools. The establishment of three Indian junior colleges was also a significant educational development.

The American Indian Movement (AIM), a recently organized protest group, played a major role in public expressions of the new Indian militancy. Under AIM's leadership, Indians occupied and laid claim to abandoned federal installations and also staged demonstrations in protest against alleged acts of brutality against Indians.

Urban Indians (variously estimated at 28 to 50 percent of the total Indian population) scored a modest gain in the form of four model urban Indian centers supported by $1 million in federal funding. The Native American Rights Fund was granted $1.2 million from the Ford Foundation to litigate on behalf of Indian rights. Its court action focused on the relationship of the tribal councils to ecology and the commercial exploitation of natural resources on Indian land. Broadly speaking, the thrust of litigation was that the tribal councils should be entitled to exercise full authority in this field, without usurpation by the Department of the Interior or private interest.

Because of their geographic concentration and their relatively small numbers, Chicanos and Indians were until recently America's "invisible" minorities. Events of the past year, however, made it increasingly evident that the nation would have to reckon with their demands as well as those of black Americans.

BLACK AMERICANS

Economics

Black Americans, numbering 23 million and constituting 11 percent of the population in 1971, achieved substantial economic progress during the 1960s. But special analyses of Census Bureau figures also revealed that in many respects black gains were outdistanced by white gains. Between 1960 and 1971, median nonwhite * income increased from $4,236 to $6,440 (about 52 percent), while white income rose from $7,664 to $10,672 (39 percent). As a result, black income as a percentage of white stood at 60 percent, up from 54 percent as recently as 1964, but down 1 percent from 1970. And the dollar gap actually widened by $804, so that by 1971 white median income exceeded nonwhite by $4,232.

Similarly, the pattern of unemployment among blacks showed some improvement during the 1960s, although the black-white differential shrank only slightly. The 12.4 percent nonwhite unemployment rate of 1961 had declined to 6.4 percent by 1969. But, with the recession of 1970–71, it rose again to 10.5 percent, averaging 9.9 percent for 1971. This was slightly less than double the white rate, although the actual increase in unemployment due to the recession was proportionately less for nonwhites than for whites. For certain categories of blacks the rates soared. For black teenagers, unemployment in 1971 stood at 31.7 percent, as contrasted with 15.1 percent for white teenagers. And in the heavily black central cities, unemployment in 1971 reached 10.6 percent, while the overall rate for whites was only 6 percent.

Although a disproportionately large number of blacks were still on the lowest rungs of the economic ladder in 1971, their position had improved noticeably over the preceding decade. The number of nonwhites employed as white collar workers, craftsmen, and operatives increased by 69 percent, from about 3 million in 1960 to about 5 million in 1971, while the white increase was about 23 percent. Still, this left almost 41 percent of nonwhites in lower-paying jobs, as against only 20 percent of whites. About one-third of the black population and 10 percent of the white were below the low-income or poverty level ($4,137 for a family of four in 1971), compared with more than 50 percent of blacks and 17 percent of whites eleven years earlier.

It followed that blacks were greatly over-represented among the more than 25 million Americans classified as low-income and the nearly 15 million receiving one or another form of public assistance. General discontent with mounting welfare rolls

---

* Since blacks constitute about 90 percent of nonwhites, Census Bureau figures for nonwhites are generally reflective of the status of the black population.

and the patchwork system of welfare administration had major racial overtones.

President Nixon's proposed program of welfare reform, first advanced in 1970, drew fire from left and right. Conservatives criticized it as an inordinately expensive move in the direction of "guaranteed income" that would swell rather than reduce welfare rolls. Spokesmen for welfare recipients, many of them black, criticized the low level of support proposed ($2,400 for a family of four) and the compulsory work requirements for all but mothers of children below school age.

The legislation embodying the Nixon welfare provisions was passed by the House of Representatives on June 22, 1971. The Senate, however, appeared to be moving toward passage of a bill even more stringent in its work requirements. In June 1972 the Senate Finance Committee gave preliminary approval to a measure that would require virtually all able-bodied welfare recipients to accept jobs. (The exceptions were mothers of children under six and mothers who are students.) In contrast to the House bill, the "workfare" obligation would not depend on the availability of jobs; if none were available, the federal government would be obliged to create them. Under this plan, the president's guaranteed income proposal would, in effect, be replaced by a guaranteed job paying no less than $2,400 a year.

Black criticism of the Senate committee's bill was even harsher than that which greeted the House bill. For this, among other reasons, the prospects in mid-1972 for early passage of a welfare bill were far from certain.

Politics

During the past year, blacks and other minorities showed a growing tendency to look to political activism as a chief—perhaps *the* chief—avenue of advancement. By March 1972, there were 2,264 black elected officials throughout the country, serving at all levels of government. While this figure represents a disproportionately small percentage of the national total, the rate of increase during the past few years has been impressive. In the South alone, blacks in elective public office increased from 72 in 1965 to 873 in 1972. This change reflected, in varying degrees from place to place, the trend toward predominantly black cities, a marked rise (particularly in the South) in black registration and voting, and an accompanying growth of political consciousness generally among blacks and other minorities.

The Congressional Black Caucus, comprised of the thirteen black members of the House of Representatives, was organized as an ongoing, staffed entity. After several unsuccessful attempts, the caucus members were given an appointment on March 25, 1971 with President Nixon to discuss their collective dissatisfaction with administration policies. Subsequently, at the president's request, the caucus submitted its demands in the form of 60 proposals for action by the executive branch, some of which were later implemented. Through negotiation with the White House, with the majority leadership in Congress, and, by means of public hearings, with other institutions, the caucus has signaled its intention to serve as an official watchdog of black interests.

A broader effort to unify black efforts in the political sphere was launched in Gary, Indiana, in March 1972. Conceived at an earlier meeting of two hundred black elected officials, the National Black Political Convention sought to bring together black representatives of every geographic area and every significant point of view in the United States to chart a common course for the presidential election year and beyond. Almost 3,000 official delegates, plus a somewhat larger number of observers, gathered under the joint chairmanship of Gary's Mayor Richard G. Hatcher, Congressman Charles C. Diggs (D-Mich.), and black nationalist playwright Imamu Baraka (the former LeRoi Jones). After several days of frenetic activity and debate, the convention adopted a Black Agenda, consisting of eighty-eight recommendations, and provided for the establishment of a continuing body of 427 members to be known as the National Black Political Assembly.

The ambitious aim of the convention and its offspring, the assembly, was to create a new force, independent of the established political parties, that would enlist all important expressions of black opinion under the banner of "unity without uniformity." At the end of the Gary proceedings, most black spokesmen agreed that the convention had been successful in those terms, despite heated discussion and sharp disagreements. Two controversial resolutions dominated the news of the convention. One denounced "forced integration" and "busing of black children" in favor of community-controlled schools financed by an equal share of all educational money; another condemned Israel for her "expansionist policy" and "forceful occupation" of Arab territory.

Proponents of the new black unity argued that these recommendations (particularly the one on busing, which was later modified) were magnified out of proportion. The real meaning of the convention, they maintained, was in the diversity it accommodated within a strong common commitment to black advancement. The national political impact of this development was not immediately apparent, nor was its influence on the outcome of the presidential election. Like the presidential primary campaigns of black Congresswoman Shirley Chisholm (D-N.Y.), the new assembly seemed likely, at least for the moment, to be one of several liberalizing pressures on the Democratic Party rather than the beginning of an autonomous political movement.

The Black Political Convention was not the only warning that minority votes might not be taken for granted. Leaders among Spanish-speaking Americans were also expressing dissatisfaction with the degree to which their support was assumed by the Democratic Party. The Republican administration demonstrated its awareness of the balance-of-power importance of Mexican-American and Puerto Rican voters by appointing an unprecedented number of Spanish-surnamed persons to important federal executive posts. A switch of as few as 6 percent of these voters to the Republican column could make a significant difference in electoral votes.

To charges that it was insensitive, even hostile, toward minority advancement, the Nixon administration in February 1972 responded with a seven-page catalog of "progress in civil rights and related social programs." Among the accomplishments claimed were the following:

- An increase in federal civilian minority employment from 389,251 in 1969 to 390,051 in 1971 (despite a 28,000 decline in overall federal civilian employment), bringing the minority percentage up from 19.2 percent in 1969 to 19.5 percent in 1971.
- Appointment of seven black ambassadors, promotion of five black military officers to general or flag rank, and an increase in the number of blacks in the top grades of federal employment from 63 to nearly 100.
- A nationwide decrease in the percentage of black children

in all-black schools from 40 percent in 1968 to about 12 percent in 1971; a doubling of aid to black colleges.

- An increase in the Justice Department's staff of civil rights attorneys from 93 in 1969 to 185 in early 1972. (The Office of Management and Budget also reported a rise in the federal civil rights enforcement budget from $190 million in 1971 to a projected $602 million in 1973.)
- More than a doubling of federal aid to minority businesses and an increase in public housing starts for low- and middle-income families from 156,000 units in 1969 to an estimated total of 566,000 in 1973.

Education

Black Americans greatly improved their educational status during the 1960s. As in the case of all other socio-economic indicators, however, blacks continued to lag far behind whites in years of education completed. For example, in 1971, among blacks twenty-five to twenty-nine years old, 54 percent of the men and 61 percent of the women had completed high school. The figures five years earlier were 49 percent and 47 percent, respectively. For whites, 80 percent of men and women twenty-five to twenty-nine years old had finished high school by 1971. Although black college enrollment almost doubled between 1965 and 1971, only 18 percent of blacks eighteen to twenty-four years old were enrolled in college in 1971, compared with 27 percent of whites of the same age.

By mid-1971, school segregation created by law—mainly a southern phenomenon—had been vastly diminished by court orders and federal civil rights requirements. By the most optimistic count, only 9.2 percent of black pupils in the South continued to attend all-black schools, a lower percentage than in the rest of the country. But the trend, north and south, was toward resegregation of schools as a result of increasing residential concentration by race. In an effort to curb the substitution of *de facto* for *de jure* segregation, federal judges have handed down a series of decisions ordering, among other things, busing of pupils as one of several means to achieve a measure of racial balance.

School busing is scarcely a new practice, or even one related primarily to racial considerations. It was estimated in 1971 that some 42 percent of the school population was bused, only 3 percent of it for purposes of racial desegregation. Nevertheless, the resistance to such busing fueled the presidential primary campaign of Governor George Wallace and influenced the public statements of other candidates, including President Nixon. Various anti-busing proposals were advanced, ranging from a constitutional amendment to the president's advocacy of a legislated moratorium on all new busing until mid-1973 and permanent restrictions on the busing of younger pupils. Others urged more and less stringent measures, or no legislative action at all.

In June 1972 Congress enacted a compromise provision in the form of an amendment to the Higher Education Act. Effective until January 1, 1974, it provides that no court-ordered busing plans shall go into effect until all appeals are exhausted. Some liberal and civil rights spokesmen denounced the measure as an infringement on the constitutional rights of black children; opponents of racial busing, including President Nixon, criticized it as being too weak. Reluctantly signing the bill, President Nixon said: "Congress has not given us the answer we requested. It has given us rhetoric. It has not provided a solution to the problem of court-ordered busing; it has provided a clever political evasion. The moratorium it offers is temporary; the relief it provides is illusory."

Although there seemed little or no likelihood of further action on busing in the current session of Congress, busing promised to be a major issue during this election year and beyond.

No conceivable resolution of the busing issue will eliminate the substantial amount of school segregation resulting from black concentration in the central cities. It can be argued, therefore, that the issue of reform in school finance is at least as important as desegregation to the education of black children. During the survey year, a landmark decision by the California Supreme Court, in *Serrano* v. *Priest,* held it unconstitutional for the amount spent on a child's education to be based on the taxable wealth of the district where he or she happens to reside. Subsequently, the U.S. Supreme Court agreed to hear an appeal from a similar ruling in a Texas case.

If the lower court is upheld, the new principle will have immense implications for the schooling of children in the less wealthy districts, where most nonwhites live. What those implications are will depend on the nature of the remedy devised in the name of greater equity. The problem is complicated because central city educational costs are higher than in most other areas—and the educational handicaps of the children more severe. Hence, a simple formula of dollar equality might well end up penalizing the very children whose needs are greatest. In the end, the people themselves, acting through their state legislatures and perhaps the Congress, must decide what constitutes a fair definition of equality in the complex field of school finance.

Living Patterns

The problems surrounding school desegregation were symptomatic of a more pervasive contradiction in American life. Most measures of public opinion indicated a continuing increase in the number of Americans professing allegiance to the principles of desegregation and equality. Yet, at the survey year's end, the nation's population was more segregated than at the beginning. This situation extended a trend best illustrated by the fact that between 1960 and 1971 blacks living in central cities grew by 3.3 million, while the white population there remained the same. As a result, by 1970, of the thirty cities across the nation with the largest black populations, sixteen were at least 50 percent black. Only three had been in 1960. This pattern reflected class, as well as racial, factors. Overt racial discrimination was less important than the suburbs' application of land-use controls to prevent the building of lower-income housing—the only type of housing the majority of nonwhites could afford.

Proposals that federal subsidies be used to force the lowering of such suburban bars as economically exclusionary zoning were firmly rejected by President Nixon in a 1971 message. Although court decisions and other pressures led the federal government to establish some criteria intended to promote greater dispersal of subsidized housing, the outlook for basic change in housing patterns was doubtful. Meanwhile, the housing conditions of low-income blacks in the central cities continued to deteriorate; older structures no longer considered economic by landlords were being abandoned at an alarming rate. The net result was a growing deficit in standard housing for most blacks and other low-income residents of the large cities.

Blacks and other nonwhites experienced a further liability as a consequence of racial concentration: blue collar jobs of the sort most minority group members must rely on for employment were steadily moving to outlying areas, far from central city ghettos. For example, in ten metropolitan areas analyzed in the 1971 *Manpower Report of the President,* almost 80 percent of the employment growth in manufacturing during the 1960s had taken place in suburbs, and commuting time and expense for low-income workers had become virtually prohibitive. Civil rights organizations, through lawsuits and demands for governmental regulation, sought to force both public agencies and private employers to relocate only when they could assure nearby housing for their lower-income workers, including minorities. But the obstacles to a breakthrough on this front remained forbiddingly high.

No set of public issues affecting the status of nonwhite minorities was more complex, controversial, and farther from solution in mid-1972 than those determining where low-income families could live and work. All indications were that most Americans were little disposed to confront the alternatives posed by this situation. To continue on the present course will inevitably mean ever poorer and blacker central cities of doubtful economic and social viability. To create the conditions for dispersion will require strong federal intervention in local land-use policies and private speculation. It will also require a much wider public acceptance of economically and racially mixed communities than presently exists.

The People Speak

I'd like to be able to send all my children to college.
        a black nurse in Cleveland

I want equality for myself and my people: clean, quiet surroundings; to live wherever I want to. To go anywhere I want to and be treated like what I am: a man.
        a black Vietnam veteran in the Midwest

All I want is equality for my children—equality in everything, in every phase of their lives. I think it was meant to be that way because people are people.
        a black domestic servant in a midwestern city

*If we don't curb them Mexican-Americans and colored, they'll be
getting jobs that rightfully should go to whites.*
        a retired woman in southern California

*I hope we can have complete desegregation. All children have to live
in this world together. Why can't they go to school together? It
would bring about an early understanding between people.*
        a black gardener in Illinois

The black man has more freedom now than he has ever had.
        a white oilfield worker in Indiana

*I see this country moving toward racial strife and tension. Will I be
able to buy a home where I wish and live in it in peace?*
        a black student in Detroit

I'm afraid the blacks will take over.
        a Memphis housewife

I hope the black people will take over.
        a black hostess in Washington, D.C.

Our survey included a good many questions about black Americans, but not about such other minority groups as Chicanos and American Indians. Since Spanish-speaking people and Indians tend to be heavily concentrated in a relatively few areas of the country, we concluded that the American people as a whole would not be familiar enough with the situation of these minorities to answer questions about them meaningfully. In this chapter, therefore, we concentrate our attention on black Americans.

The ratings blacks gave themselves on our "ladder of life" showed definite feelings of personal progress from past to present. And they were even more optimistic about their personal futures than were whites. (See Chapter I.) We must now, however, look at these ratings from a somewhat different point of view. The average personal ladder rating for the present among blacks was 5.5, significantly lower than the 6.5 of whites. This difference no doubt represents recognition on the part of black Americans of the unpleasant realities of discrimination. Blacks in general have moved upward in recent years in such matters as income, job status, and education, but their situation, whether on a relative or an absolute basis, remains markedly inferior to that of whites.

The problem of equality for black Americans continues. Yet, despite the persistence and magnitude of this issue, Americans as a whole do not appear to be deeply concerned. In our ranking of issues by degree of concern expressed by Americans, "the problem of black Americans" was almost at the bottom. (See Table 1.) The composite score on this question (derived by assigning values to the responses, ranging from 100 for "a great deal of concern" to zero for no concern at all, totaling these numbers, and then dividing by the number of respondents) was 65. Only one other domestic matter had a lower composite score —mass transportation, at 56.

Young people were more disturbed about the problems of blacks than their elders. So were those who are generally the better-informed elements of the population: the college-educated; families with incomes of $15,000 and more per year; and the professional and business group. (See Table A-4.) In much the same league were several groups whose inclinations are generally liberal: city dwellers; Democrats; and, of course, self-designated liberals. Naturally, however, none of these groups approached the high degree of concern registered among blacks themselves, a resounding 90.

PROGRESS IN RACIAL MATTERS

One of the main reasons for the low degree of concern about the situation of black Americans may be that the public has perceived signs of the indisputable progress that blacks as a group have made in recent times but are unaware of just how great the existing disparity between blacks and whites is. For discrimination against blacks—frequently veiled, habitual, and not always consciously intended—continues to affect important nerve centers of American life.

Reflecting what may be an overall myopia about the extent of discrimination that persists, the American people's evaluation of progress on racial matters was remarkably—many would say unrealistically—sanguine. We asked: *When it comes to handling the problem of black Americans in general, do you, yourself, feel that we as a nation have made much progress, some progress, stood still, lost some ground, or lost much ground over the last 12 months?*

Made much progress   12 percent
Made some progress   51
Stood still   17
Lost some ground   10
Lost much ground   5
Don't know   5
                           ___
                           100 percent

Almost two-thirds of the respondents gave a positive response, with the overall composite score a cheerful 64. (See Table A-13.) Indeed, this rating was higher by far than the progress scores on all but two of the other domestic problems covered—education, at 65, and housing, at 64.

Blacks, with a composite score of 66, were even more confident that progress had been made in their behalf than their white counterparts. Apparently the black community as a whole, with its optimism heightened by gains already made and by the increased visibility of blacks in our society, interpreted their current status in a more positive fashion than the official statistics themselves suggest.

GOVERNMENTAL SPENDING TO HELP BLACK AMERICANS

Mirroring the relative lack of concern about the problems of black Americans and the sense of progress in dealing with those problems, support for increased spending to help blacks was low. Asked whether the amount of tax money now being spent "to help improve the situation of black Americans" should be increased, kept at the present level, reduced, or ended altogether, Americans answered:

Increased   33 percent
Kept at present level   43
Reduced   11
Ended altogether   7
Don't know   6
                           ___
                           100 percent

The composite score on this question was 57, close to the "kept at present level" point. (See Table A-7.) This was the third lowest composite score of all questions about governmental spending on domestic problems. (The two lower were welfare programs, with a composite score of 53, and the space program, with a score of 25.) Looked at from another perspective, the composite score for spending on behalf of black Americans (57) was lower than that for financing more highways and thruways (63).

Apart from the blacks themselves, there were only two groups among whom a majority or near-majority favored increased financial assistance: young people (with 49 percent in favor) and those classifying themselves as very liberal (with 51 percent in favor). Along with the three groups just mentioned, the highest composite scores were given by the college-educated, families with incomes of less than $5,000 per year, manual workers (but not the labor union elite among them), city dwellers, Democrats, and those who considered themselves moderately liberal or very liberal. Generosity was most restrained among families in the $10,000–$14,000 income category, ruralites, southerners, Republicans, and those who called themselves moderately conservative or very conservative.

SCHOOLS AND BUSING

Even though the public was not enthusiastic in the abstract about increased governmental spending on urban problems, it reacted differently when confronted with two linked alternatives involving huge and costly rebuilding programs in our central cities on the one hand and forced integration of the suburbs on the other. (Here, the public was more approving of the former, regardless of cost. See Chapter IV.) Much the same pattern was evident in reactions to various approaches for educating black children.

Having already indicated that, in general, Americans did not favor increased governmental spending to improve the situation of black Americans, our respondents, when faced with the alternative of busing, overwhelmingly preferred spending more for higher-quality education in the schools where black children are now located. The question we asked and the people's responses follow:

Which one of the approaches listed on this card do you think would be the best way to give black children throughout the country a better education, while at the same time being fair to white children?

A. *By requiring all public schools to become thoroughly integrated, mixing black and white children, and using enforced busing where necessary.*   9 percent

B. *By allowing any child, with the consent of his or her parents, to pick the public school he or she wants to attend, providing busing for this purpose.*   18

C. *By forgetting about busing to achieve racial balance, and instead spending more money to provide the best possible education for children in whichever schools they now attend.*   62

D. *By maintaining the school setup as it now stands without increased spending.*   7

Don't know.   4

100 percent

Only blacks themselves supported enforced busing in significant proportions, and even those supporters were in the minority (24 percent). Sentiment in favor of the busing-by-choice alternative, on the other hand, was endorsed by about one-quarter of assorted groups: black Americans; those with only a grade school education; families in the top income bracket (many of whose children go to private schools); white collar workers; southerners (far more of whom [25 percent] endorsed busing-by-choice than in any other region of the country); people living in middle-sized cities (50,000 to 499,999) and in the suburbs; and Democrats, curiously associated in this case with the handful of respondents who said they were very conservative.

On the other hand, sentiment in favor of "quality education in place," the majority position and the solution endorsed by the Nixon administration, was especially pronounced among men (far more than women); the young; those in the middle-income bracket ($7,000 to $9,999); union households; westerners; people living in small communities and rural areas; Republicans; and especially Independents (71 percent of whom opted for this alternative and thus reflected much more than average aversion to busing, whether enforced or on the basis of choice.)

The reactions of black Americans to the dilemma they face in obtaining good educations for their children are juxtaposed against the views of whites below:

	Blacks	Whites
	(in percentages)	
Enforced busing	24	7
Busing by choice	23	17
Quality education "in place"	41	65
Present school setup and funding	4	7
Don't know	8	4
	100	100

Close to half of the blacks favored one or the other busing proposal in about equal measure; a plurality supported improving the quality of the schools their children now attend.

OPEN NEIGHBORHOODS

In the preceding chapter we saw that more than one-half of the blacks now living in urban surroundings would like to move elsewhere—to the suburbs, to small communities, or to rural areas. The problems of desegregation accompanying such a shift are apt to be most severe in the suburbs.

We also noted that the public was divided almost exactly down the middle on the issue of forcing suburban communities to allow construction of more low- and middle-class housing into which central city dwellers might move. The public was thus sharply split when the question was one of socio-economic class, though not specifically of race. What, then, would the public's attitudes be about receiving into their neighborhoods an increased number of blacks? And how linked are socio-economic and racial factors?

To determine the answers, we asked a series of questions. First, *Would you be happy or unhappy to see black families of a lower income and education level than yourself who are now living elsewhere move into the neighborhood or area where you live —or wouldn't this make much difference to you one way or the other?*

Happy	7 percent
Unhappy	40
Wouldn't make much difference	48
Don't know	5
	100 percent

The proportion of "happy" replies exceeded one out of ten only in the case of blacks themselves; but, even among them, only 29 percent said they would actually be happy to have less-fortunate members of their own race move into their midst. "Unhappy" answers, on the other hand, were given by about one-half of: older people (fifty and over); those in the lowest educational and highest income brackets; white collar workers; homeowners; Republicans; and, most of all, people living in the South. Showing far less unhappiness over the prospect of an influx of poor blacks were the college-educated; westerners and midwesterners; liberals; and, not altogether in keeping with their "hard hat" reputation, manual workers in general (a group that includes, to be sure, a large proportion of blacks) and labor union households in particular. Among these last two groups there apparently has not been as much backlash reaction as commonly supposed.

To find out whether the attitude of whites on admitting blacks of lower status into their neighborhoods was based primarily on socio-economic or racial factors, the whites in our sample were asked two additional questions:

And what about black families of about your own income and education level *who are now living elsewhere? Would you be happy or unhappy to see them move into the neighborhood or area where you live—or wouldn't this make much difference to you one way or the other?*

And how would you feel about white *families of a* lower *income and education level than yourself moving into the neighborhood or area where you live?*

The responses (and the views of whites on the earlier query about admitting lower-status blacks) were:

Attitude of Whites	Addition of Lower-Status Blacks	Addition of Lower-Status Whites	Addition of Similar-Status Blacks
		(in percentages)	
Happy	4	6	11
Unhappy	44	37	24
Not much difference	47	53	60
Don't know	5	4	5
	100	100	100

The configuration here is significant: although the "unhappy" responses were highest of all in the case of an influx of lower-status blacks, whites appeared to be less reluctant to admit higher-status blacks than lower-status whites. Race is clearly an influence, but the controlling consideration appears to be socio-economic. People just don't want others of lower economic and educational standing moving into their neighborhoods, especially if these new neighbors happen to be black.

This general mood of opposition was not much different among suburbanites, although they did seem more concerned about the addition of lower-status whites than did the public as a whole. Their responses are given below. (The first column contains the answers of black and white suburbanites; the other columns, of white suburbanites only.)

Attitude	Addition of Lower-Status Blacks	Addition of Lower-Status Whites	Addition of Similar-Status Blacks
		(in percentages)	
Happy	8	10	14
Unhappy	46	46	25
Not much difference	43	42	57
Don't know	3	2	4
	100	100	100

Taking into account where political power now tends to reside in our society, it seems unlikely that many lower-status blacks will be allowed to move unhindered into the suburbs of their choice in the very near future. The alternatives more open to those who do wish to leave large metropolitan centers would appear to lie in towns, villages, and small cities, and in rural areas (where, of course, economic opportunities are uncertain and could well be worse than in the large cities).

POLITICAL POWER

To find out how much resistance there might be to a continued increase in black political power, we asked: *Suppose more blacks were elected to public office to serve as mayors, congressmen, governors, or senators. Do you think this would be a good thing or a bad thing—or wouldn't it make much difference to you one way or the other?*

Good thing	31	percent
Bad thing	15	
Wouldn't make much difference	49	
Don't know	5	
	100	percent

As might have been anticipated, the "wouldn't make much difference" replies were the most numerous. More than three out of ten Americans and more than one-quarter of the whites (26 percent) said more blacks in office would be a "good thing." This feeling was especially widespread (although still in minority proportions compared to the "not much difference" replies) among: the young; the college-educated; upper-income groups; westerners; city dwellers in general and residents of medium-sized cities (50,000–499,999) in particular; Democrats; and, as would be expected, self-designated liberals. On the other hand, such affirmative responses were lowest among the following categories: those at the bottom of the socio-economic pyramid in terms both of education and income; older Americans; the nonlabor occupational group (made up mostly of retired people); homeowners; people living in rural areas; and Republicans.

Clearly, the predominant mood was affirmative—eight out of ten respondents either favored more blacks in public office or said that such an increase would not make much difference. This suggests that the way is open to blacks for significant accretions of political power, surely one of the most promising paths to a fundamental improvement of their position.

VI.
Justice, Crime, and Law

The crooks and robbers are so bold that many places of business are closing up because of the danger involved. I fear that this country is headed for destruction unless there is a big change. The laws are too lax. Too many people are getting away with commiting crimes.
    a black housewife in a large midwestern city

The worst thing is children taking dope, escaping from the nothingness that is all they have to look forward to—I mean the black children especially.
    a black steel-mill worker in Chicago

I would like to see someone do something about crime in the streets and robbing homes. I'm afraid to go anywhere.
    a practical nurse in a Virginia city

Less crime, better control over the kids, more power to the police, law and order—that is what would help us.
    a retired automobile worker in Detroit

The Record Speaks

In the 1971–72 survey year, the Supreme Court appeared to fulfill President Nixon's campaign promise of four years earlier to redress what he regarded as an imbalance in the tribunal's criminal law decisions. With Nixon's four appointees forming the core of a new court majority on many issues, the justices reversed the trend of the revolutionary rulings expanding defendants' constitutional rights made by the Court under former Chief Justice Earl Warren.

Some of the Court's new decisions went beyond drawing the line on continued expansion of suspects' safeguards. They chipped away at the earlier holdings, thereby undercutting their impact. It takes time for high court turnarounds to filter down to the lower courts and affect trials and appeals. By mid-1972, the full effects of the new decisions had yet to appear in the form of a sharply increased conviction rate or a pronounced reduction in reversed convictions. Such results appeared certain, however, especially as the president appointed men and women he described as "no nonsense" judges to district and appellate court benches.

The Supreme Court shift on criminal law was all the more dramatic because it came after President Nixon had been initially blocked in carrying out his campaign vow by Senate rejection of two of his nominees, Judges Clement F. Haynsworth, Jr. and G. Harrold Carswell. And the president made his third and fourth appointments, Lewis F. Powell, Jr. and William H. Rehnquist, only after an American Bar Association committee gave his widely rumored first choices for the vacancies embarrassingly low marks.

Nixon's eventual success in gaining Court seats for men who shared his misgivings about key Warren Court holdings was, however, unmistakable. On the matter of police lineups, for example, the four Nixon appointees—Powell, Rehnquist, Chief Justice Warren E. Burger, and Justice Harry A. Blackmun—were joined by Justice Potter Stewart in limiting sharply a 1967 decision that entitled suspects to a lawyer before they could be placed in a lineup. The new ruling: only defendants who have been indicted are entitled to legal representation at the lineup.

On searches and seizures by police, the Nixon appointees formed the core of a six-man majority that went well beyond the Warren Court's limited endorsement of police authority to "stop and frisk" suspicious persons. The Court ruled that an officer had such authority even if he had not personally observed suspicious conduct but was acting merely on information from a tipster who was never made known to the accused.

In a 5–2 ruling written by Powell, the Court held that granting a grand jury witness only limited immunity from prosecution to compel him to testify satisfied the Fifth Amendment protection against self-incrimination. Such limited immunity was provided for in the administration-backed Organized Crime Control Act of 1970. The hand of prosecutors was strengthened still further when the Court broke with six centuries of unwritten Anglo-American law and upheld verdicts in state criminal trials reached by less than unanimous juries. The vote was 5 to 4, with all Nixon-appointed justices in the majority.

Not all the rulings, to be sure, followed the administration's position. Without dissent, the court rejected the Justice Department's claim that it could use wiretaps without getting a judge's permission against persons and organizations the attorney general suspected of subversion. And the justices extended the landmark 1963 ruling guaranteeing every person a lawyer in felony cases. They held that a lawyer must be furnished to anyone charged with an offense that could land him in jail, even if for only a day. In a 5–4 decision, with the Nixon justices dissenting, the Court held that the death penalty violates the Eighth Amendment ban against "cruel and unusual" punishment when its imposition is left to the discretion of judge or jury. Since such discretionary provisions are found in most federal and state laws that carry the death penalty, the ruling sharply curtailed the number of cases in which capital punishment is likely to be inflicted. The decision did, however, leave the door open to laws making the death sentence mandatory for specific offenses, and it appeared likely that some legislatures would enact such laws to punish police and prison-guard killers.

These decisions, though, were more the exception than the rule as the emerging coalition, spearheaded by Nixon appointees, began to dominate Court rulings. The justices gave every sign of making the kind of decisions the president had said he wanted from the Court in the years ahead. And the possibility of additional appointments to fill future vacancies also remained. After the justices recessed for the summer, President Nixon commented on the Court's showing at a June 29, 1972 press conference. "I feel at the present time that the Court is as balanced as I have had an opportunity to make it."

BATTLING CRIME

The Supreme Court's harder stance on criminal law emerged just as the spiraling crime rate that characterized the mid-1960s and early 1970s was slowing down. For the first quarter of 1972, according to the Federal Bureau of Investigation (FBI), serious crime * in the nation increased only 1 percent over the same period of 1971. This was the smallest first-quarter increase in eleven years. A comparison of serious crime rates between 1970 and 1971 showed a 6 percent increase in the first quarter of 1971, itself an improvement over the 13 percent jump from 1969's first three months to 1970's.

Most heartening for the incumbent administration in a presidential election year, the FBI's measurement showed that serious crime had dropped 6 percent during the first quarter in the nation's six largest cities, those with populations exceeding 1 million. But while big-city crime dropped, suburban crime continued to climb—up 4 percent in the first quarter. Rural crime increased fastest of all in the first three months of 1972, up 8 percent over the 1971 level.

The slowdown in the national crime index continued a trend that already had appeared in the annual figures. FBI figures reported a 7 percent increase in serious crime in 1971, down from the increases of 11 percent in 1970, 12 percent in 1969, and 17 percent in 1968.

The validity of the FBI-collected data is open to some challenge. For one thing, the figures are supplied by local police forces and the temptation to report an improvement grows during an election year. In the District of Columbia, which reported a 30 percent reduction in the serious crime rate in the first quarter of 1972, the police department has been publicly accused of scaling down reported offenses so they fell below the level that would be reflected in the statistics.

Then, too, it has been demonstrated that only a fraction of actual crime is reported. Citing authoritative surveys, the President's Commission on Law Enforcement and the Administration

* Serious crime includes murder, forcible rape, robbery, aggravated assault, burglary, larceny ($50 and over), and auto theft.

of Justice (popularly known as the crime commission) concluded in 1967 that the actual crime rate is several times that
reported in the FBI's *Uniform Crime Reports.* Nothing has occurred in the intervening years to make that observation any less
appropriate in 1972.

Nevertheless, it is doubtful that the marked drop in crime rate
increases reflected only statistical gamesmanship or a sudden reluctance of victims to go to police. The question remained whether
the slowdown was a cyclical phenomenon, a mirror of the relative
quiet that enveloped the nation's campuses and other more traditional centers of dissatisfaction and unrest, a result of steps
taken by the managers of the criminal justice system, or some
combination of these and possibly other factors.

In the District of Columbia, the only city where the federal
government has sole responsibility for the criminal justice system,
the sharply reduced rate of lawlessness seemed directly related to
a crash anti-crime program the administration launched soon
after taking office in 1969. The factor cited most often was the
expansion of the city's police force to 5,100 men—more than
double the 2,400-man force Washington had employed four years
earlier. ("Wall-to-wall police" was a term some used to describe
the size of the federal city's department.)

There were other factors as well. The badly overburdened
court system was reorganized and expanded, prosecutors were
added, and narcotics enforcement and treatment programs were
stepped up.

Federal efforts elsewhere in the nation were far less effective.
The primary tool was the Law Enforcement Assistance Administration (LEAA), the agency created by the Omnibus Crime
Control and Safe Streets Act of 1968 to channel hundreds of
millions of dollars to upgrade state and local police, courts, and
prisons. By 1972, LEAA had one of the fastest growing rates of
budget increase in government as Congress approved $850 mil-
lion for fiscal 1973, some $151 million more than the 1972
budget.

Critics contended LEAA was spending the money poorly. In a
blistering report released May 18, 1972, the House Committee on
Government Operations charged the agency with "inefficiency,
waste, maladministration, and in some cases corruption." The
committee recommended cutting off anti-crime grants until LEAA

could set its own house in order. The outvoted Republican minority on the committee dismissed the criticism as partisan and said the agency's administrator had already moved to correct the shortcomings detailed by the report.

When Administrator Jerris Leonard took over the infant agency in May 1971 (at that point it had been headless for ten months), he went through an unusual exercise for Washington officialdom: he confessed the administration had made mistakes in implementing its anti-crime program. Leonard said LEAA had taken too long to hand out money, had moved too slowly on research goals that seemed confused, and had spoken with too many voices.

LEAA, regarded by the administration as a showcase for revenue sharing (much of the agency's money is disbursed in block grants to the states, with little control exercised by Washington), faced problems that went beyond simple mismanagement. A leading one was how to influence a system of criminal justice that had seldom viewed itself as a system, but rather as three separate institutions—the police, the courts, and the prisons. The task was complicated by the need to minimize pressure from Washington, leaving decisions up to state and, in some instances, local governments.

Eager for results that could send crime rates plummeting and reacting to criticism that the agency had not invested anti-crime funds where the problem was most acute—the cities—LEAA launched a high-impact program in January 1972. Eight major cities (Newark, Baltimore, Atlanta, Cleveland, Dallas, Denver, St. Louis, and Portland, Oregon) were designated to receive about $20 million apiece in LEAA funds through June 30, 1974 to combat street crimes and burglaries. The goal was to reduce these two categories of crime by 5 percent in the two years (and 20 percent in five years, assuming the program continued). Cities selected had populations between 250,000 and 1 million, big enough to be plagued by the two types of crime but small enough so that the money could have a measurable impact on the crime rate.

The agency took other steps aimed at increasing the likelihood that the $2.4 billion it will have invested by June 30, 1973 would finally produce concrete anti-crime results. With the effort scheduled for full-scale congressional review in 1973 before further funds are authorized, prospects were that the battle over more or less controls from Washington would be fought again, harder than ever.

THE DRUG CAMPAIGN

The campaign against illegal drugs fared better. After years of effort, the United States won what appeared to be an at least partially effective ban by Turkey on growing opium poppies, the estimated source of more than half of the heroin consumed in America. In return, the United States agreed to compensate the Turks by about $35 million to help peasants substitute new crops and to offset the loss of income incurred by discontinuing the legal exportation of opium. Earlier, agreement had been reached between the attorney general and his French counterpart for the detailed coordination of an all-out attack on illicit drug traffic between France and the U.S., with prime emphasis on destruction of heroin laboratories in southern France.

While the Turkish supply was being shut off, a glut of heroin built up in Southeast Asia, reflecting the withdrawal of a highly lucrative market there—American troops. Internal documents at the Bureau of Narcotics and Dangerous Drugs reportedly warned of the "Chinese connection," a reference to the expectation by narcotics agents that a network of Chinese drug smugglers would try to dump the glut into the U.S. domestic market. With cooperation from the Central Intelligence Agency and the State and Defense departments, U.S. narcotics agents worked with their foreign counterparts to disrupt international drug traffic at its points of origin. As seizures of dangerous drugs and arrests and convictions of traffickers increased, so did the domestic price of heroin. By summer 1972, the street price of heroin in the eastern United States was running 10 to 50 percent higher than a year earlier, and the quality was dropping.

With anti-drug programs under way in thirteen separate federal agencies, the administration moved to coordinate the effort by creating (within the White House, as an apparent signal of presidential interest) the Special Action Office for Drug Abuse Prevention. On the occasion of signing the legislation creating this new office, President Nixon warned that the heads of "petty bureaucrats" would roll if they tried to obstruct efforts at coordination. But divided authority for combating illicit drugs continued to cause problems.

In January 1972, the federal government, dissatisfied with state and local efforts to disrupt heroin traffic, organized a major campaign to drive pushers, particularly wholesalers, off the streets of the nation's cities. In mid-1972, five months after the program was begun, it was operating in thirty-three cities where the heroin problem was considered acute. The anti-heroin drive, directed by a new Justice Department office, included special federal grand juries and used tough provisions of a 1970 crime law. Domination of the effort by the federal government conflicted with the administration's philosophy of leaving essentially local crimes to local authorities. The conflict underscored the degree of national concern over the continually worsening heroin problem and the failure to control it.

On marijuana, President Nixon rejected the central finding of the National Commission on Marijuana and Drug Abuse, which urged the elimination of criminal penalties for personal possession and private use of the drug. The commission, nine of whose thirteen members were appointed by President Nixon, did recommend that states retain criminal penalties for trafficking in marijuana. It also called for outlawing public use of the drug, but subject only to a $100 fine and seizure as contraband.

In commenting on his rejection, President Nixon said: "I oppose the legalization of marijuana and that includes sale, possession, and use. I do not believe you can have effective criminal justice based on a philosophy that something is half legal and half illegal."

Because of the president's opposition to even partial legalization, and because the recommendation came in a volatile election year, there was scant chance it would be adopted. But the weight of the commission's conclusion that public fear of marijuana was based "much more on fantasy than on proven fact," as well as its call for de-emphasizing marijuana as an issue, may pave the way for the drug's ultimate legalization. Support from unexpected quarters lined up for a less punitive position on marijuana. In February 1972, a month after he retired as the No. 2 man at the Bureau of Narcotics and Dangerous Drugs, John Finlater came out for discontinuing jail sentences for marijuana use. Liquor and tobacco have far more harmful effects, he said. And the conservative American Medical Association (AMA) proposed an end to making possession of "insignificant amounts" of marijuana a felony.

The proposal represented a marked change from the AMA's 1969 position that marijuana was a dangerous drug and that, while penalties for its use were often "unrealistic," more research and evaluation was needed.

THE PRISON SYSTEM

The one element of the criminal justice system in daily touch with more lawbreakers than any other—the prisons—showed the least sign of undergoing change. Public concern over prisons mounts dramatically at a time of headline-making trouble, such as the 1971 Attica riot; it tends to subside equally dramatically once the prisoners are locked back in their cells and the high walls conceal any trouble within. Congressional hearings on the Attica revolt, for example, seemed to examine Attica as a one-of-a-kind aberration rather than as a symptom of the appalling conditions of U.S. prisons.

In June 1972 the prestigious Committee for Economic Development published a study, *Reducing Crime and Assuring Justice,* that echoed the president's crime commission report five years earlier on the sad state of the prison system. "Callous neglect has produced a debacle of major proportions in the nation's misguided and under-funded correctional efforts," the study by the organization of business leaders said. "There are 1,600,000 convicts under current correctional controls. The curative quality of these efforts is so ineffective that society continues to suffer from subsequent violations by these same individuals. . . . State governments bear primary responsibility for the abuses and inadequacies found in the corrections system today. They must now provide the moral leadership and financial support for substantial change."

Still, there were scattered signs of change in the field of corrections. The leading example was the increased willingness of courts, particularly federal courts, to have a new look at prison policies under the light of constitutional civil rights guarantees. Courts traditionally have kept out of prison matters, granting wardens and other officials wide discretion in disciplinary matters.

In Arkansas, the entire prison system has been declared unconstitutional, as have particular prison practices in such states as California, Florida, Illinois, Maryland, Virginia, and West Virginia. A federal court in the District of Columbia ordered the federal Bureau of Prisons to drop wherever possible its policy against press interviews of inmates, a ruling the Justice Department promptly appealed.

Civil suits by prisoners, claiming their rights had been violated, were mushrooming. In 1971, there were more than 12,000 prisoner suits filed, accounting for some 16 percent of all civil actions before federal district courts; in 1938, prisoner petitions numbered only 625, less than 2 percent of the civil suit docket.

Under pressure from the courts, the U.S. Board of Parole decided for the first time to reveal the reasons why inmates are denied parole. The parole process and administrative punishment within the prison often head the list of prisoner grievances. It was not clear how extensive the Parole Board's explanation would be, and lawyers for prisoners challenging parole practices said they would continue to press for making all the board's records public.

With prison litigation mounting, it appeared that the courts could play the same role in this area as they did earlier in school segregation and legislative malapportionment. They seemed reluctantly ready to take the lead in forcing change. Whether Congress would move with legislative changes remained to be seen.

AT THE FBI

The death of FBI Director J. Edgar Hoover on May 2, 1972 opened the door to changes within the leading federal law enforcement agency. Hoover's virtually autonomous stewardship of the FBI had come under increasing criticism in the last years before his death. President Nixon appointed an acting director, thereby avoiding Senate confirmation and a potential election-year review of the agency—a review that critics claimed was long overdue. Such an examination will certainly unfold when a permanent nominee faces senatorial approval.

The president's choice for the interim position, L. Patrick Gray III, was immediately challenged because he had served in 1960 on the personal staff of then Vice President Nixon. Gray, making no secret of the fact that he wanted the job permanently, quickly introduced changes inside the bureau. He declared the FBI open to women agents, took steps to increase minority hiring, relaxed rigid requirements of dress, discontinued punishing agents by transferring them to undesirable duty posts, and intensified the bureau's attack on organized crime. Although Gray maintained these were merely matters of style, close observers of the bureau thought the changes were much more substantial. Aside from its leading role in federal law enforcement, the FBI exercises considerable influence over state and local police through its training programs, and the changes could reverberate throughout the criminal justice system.

AT THE JUSTICE DEPARTMENT

The replacement of John N. Mitchell as attorney general by Richard G. Kleindienst seemed initially to indicate a possible easing of the hard-line stance the Justice Department had taken under Mitchell (who resigned effective March 1 to direct President Nixon's re-election effort and later relinquished that post to return to private law practice). But any voice Kleindienst might have raised in that direction was bound to be muffled by the protracted Senate battle over his nomination, a battle that proved embarrassing to the administration.

Discussion and disagreement over the department's positions was most intense in the areas of subversion and political dissidence. Critics charged that authorities were attempting to stifle political dissent by pressing actions against the dissenters for alleged crimes the department would not normally pursue. Examples cited on the federal level included the conspiracy case against the Reverend Philip Berrigan and six other defendants in Harrisburg, Pennsylvania. On the state level, the most frequently cited example was the murder and conspiracy charge against Angela Davis, the acknowledged communist and former faculty member of the University of California at Los Angeles. The fact that the Berrigan case ended in a hung jury (with only two of the jurors believing that a conspiracy existed) and that Miss Davis was acquitted only added to the pervading sense of controversy that surrounded the entire field of justice and law in our survey year.

The People Speak

My fears are many: crime, dope, muggings, breaking-ins, and shootings.
     a retired Detroit man

Our country is still bringing our boys home from Vietnam hooked on dope and we aren't doing much about it.
     a manual worker in Illinois

I wish I could feel safe going to and from work.
     a female lab technician in an eastern city

I can't use my air conditioner for fear I won't hear someone breaking into the house.
     the wife of a disabled man in a Middle Atlantic city

The main thing I would like is a little more law and order, instead of people tearing up and destroying things. There's no discipline. People don't discipline their children.
     a woman living on social security in Wilmington, Delaware

They go on protecting the heroin and drug pushers, forcing our children to pay the price.
     the wife of a sales manager in a small New York city

I'd like to move out of this neighborhood. Maybe I'll go back south, where you can walk the streets in the dark without carrying a pistol in your pocket all the time.
     a black janitor in Chicago

I hope my boys can make it through their teens without killing somebody or getting themselves killed.
     a ghetto dweller in a large midwestern city

Our law enforcement officers are not allowed to enforce the laws. Criminals are too protected.
     the assistant manager of a California restaurant

Crime and drugs were almost at the top of the list of the problems worrying the American people,* outranked only slightly by infla-

---

* Public attitudes toward the federal judiciary are examined in Chapter XII rather than here.

tion and violence in American life. (See Table 1.) And no wonder. Robberies, muggings, deaths from drug overdoses, crime in the streets, thefts by narcotic addicts, organized crime, rape—these are the daily litany of most of our national press.

The degree of concern about these problems is almost completely uniform among population subgroups. (See Table A-4.) Suburbanites are every bit as worried, and those living in rural areas only a shade less so, than residents of our largest metropolises, where the incidence of both crime and drug use is unquestionably much higher. The main reason, no doubt, is provided by FBI statistics: although serious crimes show signs of decreasing in our largest cities, suburban crime has continued to climb, and rural crime, although still at a low rate, has increased fastest of all. In short, the introduction of even a very small but growing apple can disturb the tranquility of any Garden of Eden; it is the frightening novelty of the thing that gives it impact.

PESSIMISM OVER CRIME AND DRUGS

To determine the public's evaluation of efforts to deal with crime and drug abuse, we asked the American people to rate the progress they believed the country had made in the past year in "combating crime" and in "coping with the problem of narcotic drugs and drug addicts." Their answers were:

	Combating Crime	Preventing Drug Abuse
	(in percentages)	
Made much progress	1	3
Made some progress	19	31
Stood still	26	21
Lost some ground	32	23
Lost much ground	19	18
Don't know	3	4
	100	100

One half of the public—51 percent—thought that the country had lost ground in its crime-control efforts. Only two in ten sensed progress. And the people's judgment of the nation's effectiveness in coping with the drug problem was almost equally pessimistic.

The composite scores * on both of these questions were below the "stood still" point of 50: 44 in the case of drugs, signaling a predominant feeling that the country had lost some ground in handling this problem, and a very low 37 in the case of crime, indicating the loss of a good deal of ground. In fact, on only one other topic were respondents more pessimistic about national progress: they felt the country had lost even more ground in the fight against inflation (with a composite score of 36).

Evaluations of progress (or nonprogress) by various sub-groups of the population were remarkably uniform (just as were the ratings on degrees of concern). (See Table A-13.) The most pessimistic groups on both drugs and crime were respondents with only a grade school education and those who characterized themselves as very conservative; the least pessimistic were young people twenty-one to twenty-nine. In the case of drugs, those in top income, professional, and business categories and suburbanites joined with the young in evaluations slightly less unfavorable than the public as a whole.

GOVERNMENTAL SPENDING TO COMBAT CRIME AND DRUG ABUSE

This combination of high concern and low estimates of progress inevitably produced widespread approval for throwing more resources into the fight against crime and drug abuse. Approximately three-quarters of the public opted for increased spending by the federal government. The answer to our queries about the level of governmental spending to combat crime and drug abuse were:

	Combating Crime	Preventing Drug Abuse
	(in percentages)	
Increased	77	74
Kept at present level	18	20
Reduced	1	2
Ended altogether	1	1
Don't know	3	3
	100	100

* The method by which composite scores are calculated is explained in Appendix 5.

The composite score on the question of federal spending to combat crime was a resounding 88 (on a scale of 100), which put that item at the very top of the public's list of spending priorities. The score on drugs was an almost equally high 86. Once again, the composite scores showed very little demographic variation. (See Table A-7.) The only noteworthy deviation, oddly enough, was among those who classified themselves as ruralites, who were even more in favor of increased spending in both fields than was any other group—another demonstration of how all-pervasive the fear of crime and drugs has become in our society.

CRACKING DOWN ON CRIME

We have seen in Chapter III that the public favored cracking down on drugs and drug users in hard-line fashion. Frankly, we had expected to find a similarly hard-nosed stance when it came to combating crime. In framing the following question, we anticipated that preponderant numbers of respondents would lean toward the harsher "law and order" alternatives listed below. We were in for a surprise. Our question:

Now I'd like to get your views about the best way to deal with some of our domestic problems here at home. First, which two or three of the approaches listed on this card do you think would be the best way to reduce crime?

A. *Cleaning up social and economic conditions in our slums and ghettos that tend to breed drug addicts and criminals.*	61 percent
B. *Getting parents to exert stricter discipline over their children.*	48
C. *Putting more policemen on the job to prevent crimes and arrest more criminals.*	22
D. *Reforming our courts so that persons charged with crimes can get fairer and speedier justice.*	37
E. *Improving conditions in our jails and prisons so that more people convicted of crimes will be rehabilitated and not go back to a life of crime.*	40

F. Really cracking down on criminals by giving them longer prison terms to be served under the toughest possible conditions.   35
Don't know   3

In short, when given a broad choice of alternatives, a majority of Americans exhibited an exceedingly sophisticated grasp of the probable roots of criminal behavior. The smallest proportions of our respondents believed that the best ways to reduce crime are by putting more policemen on the job or by cracking down hard on criminals. The majority view—that the best approach lies, rather, in cleaning up our slums and ghettos—was especially pronounced among young people; those in the top income bracket; professional and business workers; and westerners. (Since we have already determined that, at the abstract level, the American people are not keen about spending more money on big-city problems, the results on this question suggest that one of the most effective appeals for urban renewal programs may be to link them with an attack on crime.)

Certain other groups, perhaps sensing the financial implications of their answers, put less-than-average stress on costly measures to clean up slums and ghettos and more stress on the inexpensive alternative of getting parents to exert greater discipline over their offspring. These groups included Republicans; those with low incomes and little education; those few who called themselves very conservative; the nonlabor force; and older people. Almost six in ten of the older generation (58 percent) stressed this need for stricter control of children, an implicit confession perhaps that they, as parents, had been guilty of too much permissiveness in raising their own offspring—or that they believed their children had not been strict enough in raising the grandchildren.

The generally liberal tone of our findings was confirmed by answers to questions on prison uprisings reported in two Harris Surveys in February 1972. Asked about the main reason for prison takeovers by inmates, almost six out of ten respondents (58 percent) laid the blame on prison authorities' "not understanding the needs of the inmates." Harris also asked: "In general, what do you feel prisoners are trying to do when they take over a prison and hold guards and authorities as hostages?" Instead of blaming troublemakers, 29 percent said the prisoners were "crying out for attention to their problems" and 26 percent that the inmates "want better treatment, human respect"—far more than picked any other reasons. These surveys also showed that, in the event of a prison uprising, two-thirds of the public favored "sitting down with the prisoners and listening to their complaints" instead of resorting to force.

Louis Harris summed up the matter this way: "The simplistic, hard-nosed approach to law enforcement, talk of putting prisoners 'in their place' or ending the 'mollycoddling of proven criminals,' neither carries the day with public opinion nor is it very typical of even a significant minority of individual Americans."

Despite the intense concern about crime, it appears that the hard-line law-and-order pitch has little current appeal among the American people. Perhaps this mood helps explain why the law-and-order theme in the Republican congressional election campaigns of 1970 never took hold.

VII.
Health Care

*My greatest hope is to have more perfect health for myself and my
family, especially the children.*
        a twenty-year-old black mother of two in the Midwest

*I would like to see improvements in medicine, such as cancer cures
and research on heart disease.*
        a woman living on social security in Wilmington, Delaware

*What am I worried about? There could be an accident; I could be
hurt; or there could be sickness. I don't have any other fears.*
        a housewife in a New York suburb

The Record Speaks

The state of the nation's health care system was under intense
scrutiny again in this survey year, with special attention focused
on health care costs, which outstripped inflationary trends in the
overall cost of living for the preceding decade—and still continued
to rise. National expenditures for health in 1971 reached $75
billion, 7.4 percent of the gross national product (GNP); in
1960, they had totaled $26 billion, or 5.3 percent of GNP.

This high cost of health care was one reason President Nixon
gave for reasserting his 1969 statement that the nation's health
care system was in "crisis." In fact, the word crisis after health
care seemed to be in the air all year. Even Senate hearings on
proposed national health insurance measures were titled Health
Care Crises in America, 1971.

There was concern, on the part of both health professionals and public officials, about the uneven quality and availability of health care as well as the costs. The House of Delegates of the American Medical Association, in December 1969, adopted a resolution declaring health care as a right of all citizens, evidence that doctors' attitudes over the past decade had changed considerably. And for the first time in Congress a sizeable majority of its members sponsored bills to establish some form of national health insurance, a concept considered radical by most Americans twenty years ago.

FEDERAL ACTION ON HEALTH CARE

Historically reluctant to take any policy steps that would directly or indirectly affect the traditional practice of American medicine, Congress nevertheless moved toward passage of a bill in 1972 specifically designed to encourage a new kind of health care service. The pending legislation would provide federal funds to support the establishment of more Health Maintenance Organizations, known as HMOs, which are based upon group practice of medicine, a predetermined fee for which medical services are provided as needed, and the encouragement of preventive care. (At the time the legislation was introduced, there were about thirty similar arrangements in operation serving 6.5 million Americans.)

The AMA has objected to the government's helping foster a particular kind of medical practice, and many Americans themselves have indicated reluctance to switch from reliance on a single family physician to a group plan, where care may be provided by any one of a number of doctors. But the proposal for federal financing of HMOs, first suggested by President Nixon and subsequently endorsed by congressional leaders of both parties, may soon be part of a broad new federal effort to spur improvements in health care.

Similarly, in spite of the government's long reluctance to become directly involved in supporting medical education, Congress in late 1971 enacted legislation that not only accepted a major federal responsibility for helping to insure an adequate supply of physicians for the country but also, for the first time, declared the elimination of the present doctor shortage—estimated by the

Department of Health, Education, and Welfare and the Association of American Medical Schools at 50,000 physicians—to be a national goal.

The federal government made its debut in this activist role in 1965 with the enactment of medicare, which provides health insurance for the elderly, and medicaid, designed to help the poor get the care they need. The operation of the medicaid program has come under particular criticism, for both operational abuses and its unexpectedly large expenditures, and both programs have been charged with contributing to the continuing rise in health care costs. If they have aggravated that problem, they have apparently also begun to approach one of the intended goals; a recent study of health services utilization by Joseph P. Newhouse and Vincent Taylor of the Rand Corporation, *Medical Costs, Health Insurance, and Public Policy,* concluded that the poor and the aged are now receiving a little more of the physician's time, while others are seeing him a little less.

The medicare and medicaid programs may have opened the door to federal action, for public attitudes favoring the extension of government-subsidized health insurance beyond the old and the poor seem to be on the rise. Many doctors, threatened at first by the spectre of governmental intrusion, now accept the benefits of the programs as including guarantees of payment to them for services they might have provided anyway, even if they chafe under the additional paperwork that is required. Naturally, those whom the programs have directly benefited are its chief supporters.

The government opened up other fronts during the survey year as well as intensifying its action on some old ones. In December 1971 President Nixon signed a bill launching a new crusade against cancer with an annual appropriation of $500 million and what was claimed to be a strengthened and streamlined managerial organization to oversee the effort. In May 1972 the Department of Health, Education, and Welfare launched the National Health Service Corps (initiated by Congress) within the U.S. Public Health Service, which in its first year will send 152 newly graduated physicians—plus nurses, dentists, and other health personnel—into 122 U.S. communities that are now critically short of, or totally lacking, such manpower. The Veterans Administration (VA) received congressional approval to make its health care facilities available to the widows and children of veterans and began planning for wider sharing of its medical resources in communities where those resources are the only, or the best, ones available. And the government issued new regulations requiring hospitals built with federal funds under the Hill-Burton Act to increase their free care for the poor.

NATIONAL HEALTH INSURANCE

Where the new federal thrust was stopped, however, was on what is conceded to be the most important front—that of national health insurance. And this, despite a majority opinion among policymakers, health professionals, and the citizenry at large that the government should lead the way in developing a national health insurance plan.* The problem is that, upon close examination, the consensus turns out to be limited.

The Nixon administration is proposing that the government's involvement be confined to requiring employers to provide coverage for their employees and to subsidizing private insurance coverage for those not covered at work and not able to afford coverage on their own.

Senator Edward M. Kennedy (D-Mass.) and Congresswoman Martha W. Griffiths (D-Mich.), joined by a coalition including leaders of organized labor, senior citizens associations, and the American Public Health Association, took a different approach. The provisions in their Health Security bill would provide universal and relatively comprehensive coverage for all Americans, financed out of payroll taxes and general treasury funds and administered by the government through regional and local offices.

Prominent among a variety of other approaches were plans

---

* In answers to a public opinion survey conducted in late 1971, 57 percent of the American people thought that the federal government should remove high cost as an obstacle to good health care; 46 percent, that the federal government should have the main responsibility for a national health insurance plan; and 11 percent, that the government should be centrally involved, along with private insurance companies, in such a plan. Among doctors polled at the same time by mail, 51 percent favored congressional passage of "some form of national health insurance." The results of these special surveys, commissioned by Potomac Associates, are analyzed and interpreted in Stephen P. Strickland's *U.S. Health Care: What's Wrong and What's Right* (N.Y.: Universe Books, 1972).

calling for federal subsidies for what has been labeled catastrophic illness insurance. The appeal of this concept lies in its promise to remove a potential threat with which most Americans have some familiarity: a family's life savings being drastically reduced or even wiped out by prolonged bouts with cancer, spinal cord injury, or other intractable medical conditions. The appeal is a broad one, reaching even into high income brackets, for "catastrophic" illness strikes the rich as well as the poor.

The cost of these alternative proposals for national health insurance became as much, if not more, a part of the debate as their comprehensiveness, fairness, and efficacy. The Kennedy-Griffiths proposal had the highest price tag, estimated by its sponsors at $57 billion in fiscal 1974 and by administration opponents at $77 billion for that year. Whatever the cost to the federal government, the bill's supporters argued that their Health Security Program would not increase total national health care expenditures and would actually reduce personal health care expenditures for most Americans because it would eliminate the profits of the commercial insurance companies, which, they claim, have caused health costs to rise even more rapidly than inflation.

The administration estimated that the federal contribution to its Family Health Insurance Program would be $3 billion in 1974 (including a savings of $1.9 billion from medicaid, which would be more restricted in scope than at present). Additionally, under the employer-employee insurance plans that the administration bill would require, private contributions to such plans would increase by $7 billion annually over current contributions.

The American Medical Association estimated that the Medicredit plan it drafted, under which the federal government would pay insurance premiums for the poor and all others would be given tax credits for the insurance they purchased, would amount to an overall federal cost of $14.5 billion annually.

If the government adopted a plan providing federal protection against catastrophic illness only, along the lines suggested by Senator Russell Long (D-La.), the estimate of federal costs fell to $2.5 billion per year.

Some plans focused as much on the coordination of existing resources as they did on the provision of health care insurance. One proposal that assumed increasing importance, initiated by Congressman Al Ullman (D-Ore.), was based on a network of federally funded but locally controlled health care corporations. Such organizations would not only make sure that all persons within the community served had health insurance coverage, subsidized if necessary with federal funds, but would encourage coordination of all local health care resources in an attempt to insure that they were utilized to maximum advantage in serving the local population. One attraction of the plan was the greater decisionmaking it specified for local citizens in the organization's governance—a role that citizens seem ready and interested to perform.*

Each major proposal for national health insurance has important competing interest groups backing it. Indeed, the splintering of old alliances of professional organizations, such as the American Medical Association, the American Hospital Association, and the commercial insurance industry, was one reason why the consensus on the need for *some* federally sponsored health insurance plan had not produced legislation by the 1972 summer adjournment of Congress.

That 1972 is an election year was another key factor. The Democratic majority in Congress was not anxious to accommodate the Republican president by accepting the health proposals he advanced. In addition, congressional committee chairmen whose jurisdictions include health legislation either were avowed presidential candidates (Congressman Wilbur Mills (D-Ark.) of the House Ways and Means Committee) or perceived by others to be possible presidential candidates (Senator Kennedy of the Senate Health Subcommittee), a situation that did not facilitate agreement among them nor encourage them to embrace plans first advanced by others. The delay in developing a health insurance program thus resulted in part from a clash of interests, in part from political rivalries, and in part from the politicians' professed uncertainty as to what the people really wanted.

But there were other, perhaps more important, reasons for this legislative delay. There was a fundamental and genuine

---

* To a question about which groups should be primarily responsible for determining how local areas spend federal money allocated for the establishment of new health care services and the reorganization of old ones, the public placed local citizens in second place, right behind local doctors. The special survey of which this question was part is described in Stephen P. Strickland's *U.S. Health Care*.

concern on the part of policymakers that the next steps taken by the federal government provide real remedies to present weaknesses in the health care system, without locking that system into new organizational patterns and cost structures that might turn out to be no better than what we now have. Even among the most experienced and most concerned policymakers, and among many of their most knowledgeable and sophisticated advisers, there was a lack of the usual zealous certainty that a given national health insurance plan would indisputably bring better health care to the American people.

THE DRUG EFFORT

The growing phenomenon of drug use and addiction, particularly among younger Americans, prompted new federal action against drug abuse. Essentially endorsing the president's earlier creation by executive order of the Special Action Office for Drug Abuse Prevention, Congress passed legislation in March 1972 providing $1.1 billion to fund the office for four years. Under the law, the new office is charged with providing "overall planning and policy and establishing objectives and priorities for all federal drug abuse prevention functions."

Moreover, the administration proposed a budget of some $365 million for all federal drug abuse programs for fiscal 1973, an increase of $55 million over 1972. The Veterans Administration continued to intensify and extend its care of veterans with drug problems. In fiscal 1969 the VA treated 118 addict veterans; in fiscal 1971, when a special drug treatment program began, the VA treated 1,344 veterans with drug problems; and in fiscal 1972, the number jumped to 9,500. The National Institute of Mental Health estimated that its proposed 1973 budget of $39 million for narcotics programs would enable it to help provide treatment and rehabilitation for some 73,000 narcotics addicts—a goodly number of addicts, but a small proportion of the addict population of 559,000, estimated (conservatively, most would say) by the Bureau of Narcotics and Dangerous Drugs.

THE PRIVATE SECTOR

It was not only federal government actions that suggested a changing face, and changing structure, for American health care.

The health industry has always had commercial and industrial aspects as well as purely professional ones, with drug manufacturers and private insurance companies representing and receiving more dollars than medical practitioners or the installations in which they practice. But there were new indications that health is truly a business as well as a professional field and, in part, a governmental responsibility. Hospital and nursing home chains have proliferated rapidly in the last several years and in some instances have been acquired by conglomerates. Business firms providing health services were easy to identify on the stock exchange in 1972, and shares of many moved upward in price like all other aspects of health care.

New trends in professional practice were also producing changes in structure. While federal legislation to encourage such changes was pending, group medical practices operating on the basis of prepayment plans continued to increase in number, attracting younger physicians in particular. Medical foundations, also based upon group practice and in some cases providing fee incentives as well as salaries, were a new variation on traditional fee-for-service practice.

With changes in the structure of health care delivery, the practice of medicine has been changing, too. National investment in biomedical research over the last twenty-five years has altered, sometimes dramatically, the treatment for particular illnesses. Maladies as varied as rubella and hypertension are now easily controllable, and kidney failure no longer means immediate death for the victim—if he or she can get access to a dialysis machine.

As their expertise has been broadened by advances in medical science, though, doctors have felt increasingly constrained by another situation—the significant increase in malpractice suits against physicians and the notable number of court verdicts upholding the claimants. One effect of malpractice suits is simply an acceleration of the cost spiral, since doctors pass on at least some of the costs of their malpractice insurance to patients. A more important potential result is that the growth of such suits may affect the manner in which physicians approach medical treatment—sometimes to the advantage of a patient, sometimes to the disadvantage, especially when boldness may offer the only chance to save a life.

On balance, the evidence available in mid-1972 indicated that the health care system of the United States is at the brink of fundamental change. Alterations in the system appeared inevitable. But there was still widespread debate over exactly what form those changes should take—and to what degree those alterations would bring improvements in the health of the American people.

The People Speak

If you've got good health, you can be happy.
   a housewife in Illinois

My worst fear is sickness in the family that we can't pay for.
   an x-ray technician in an eastern suburb

I'd like to see less money spent on exploration of the moon and more money spent on diseases—cancer, sickle cell anemia, and heart disease.
   a housewife in Massachusetts

Health is the most important thing. With health you can do anything.
   a secretary in an eastern suburb

My life would be very bad if any one of my family were ill. If my son contracted a disease like cancer or leukemia, that would be awful.
   the wife of an executive in New York State

I hope that our income continues to provide for our wants and that my family continues to be healthy.
   the wife of an executive in an eastern state

More than eight out of ten Americans have at least a fair degree of confidence that they and their families can get good medical care when they need it, according to the special survey commissioned by Potomac Associates at the end of 1971 and described in Stephen Strickland's *U.S. Health Care.* Most surprisingly, this confidence was shared even by three-quarters of those whose income and educational levels placed them at the very bottom of the socio-economic pyramid.

Yet Americans continue to be highly concerned about health, illness, and medical care. In our mid-1972 survey, large proportions of respondents mentioned good health for themselves as a personal hope and illness as a personal fear (27 and 21 percent, respectively). This, of course, was to be expected; no matter how adequate available medical care may be, no one wants to become ill or have a family member laid low by disease.

But the concern of Americans is more than personal; it is also a social concern extending to the question of medical care for the population as a whole. In our ranking of public concerns about various problems, "insuring that Americans in general, including the poor and the elderly, get adequate medical and health care" was high on the list, above unemployment, poverty, and improving the educational system. (See Table 1.)

In fact, worry about adequate health care for all members of our society was uniformly high among nearly all population subgroups. (See Table A-4.) On this question, the most notable deviation from the overall composite score * of 83 was found among Republicans, who registered a relatively low 78.

GOVERNMENTAL SPENDING ON HEALTH CARE

This broad sense of public concern was paralleled by a feeling that the amount of governmental tax money being devoted to health care should be augmented. Asked if federal spending "to improve medical and health care for Americans generally" should be increased, kept at the present level, reduced, or ended altogether, more than six out of ten respondents came out on the "increased" side:

Increased	62	percent
Kept at present level	32	
Reduced	2	
Ended altogether	2	
Don't know	2	
	100	percent

The composite score on spending for this purpose (100 for "increased," 50 for "present level," zero for "reduced" or "ended altogether") was 80. This put medical and health care (along with education for low-income children and reducing air

---

* The method by which composite scores are calculated is explained in Appendix 5.

pollution) fifth in rank order of spending priorities among the twenty areas covered in our survey. (See Table A-7.) Most strongly in favor of increased spending were city dwellers in general, easterners, those in the lowest income bracket, and, most of all, black Americans. Lukewarm about increased spending were families with incomes over $15,000 per year and Republicans.

More than one-half of the public also favored increased federal spending specifically for "the medicaid program to help low-income families pay their medical bills," strongly suggesting that anxiety about this particular subject was not only personally but also socially motivated. The responses to our question were:

Increased	52	percent
Kept at present level	35	
Reduced	6	
Ended altogether	2	
Don't know	5	
	100	percent

The overall composite score in this case was 74, a good deal lower than the 80 registered on spending for health care for all the population. (See Table A-7.) But still high enough to put medicaid just a rung below medical care in general on the public's spending priorities list. City dwellers, the poor, and blacks again registered very high scores, joined by older people, who are particularly vulnerable to illnesses and whose need for governmental help in paying their medical bills is as great as, or greater than, that of any other group.

PROGRESS IN HEALTH CARE

The record suggests that there was more talk than action in the field of health care during the survey year. Nevertheless, the American people were convinced that at least some progress had in fact been made: almost six out of ten believed that advances had taken place in "providing adequate medical and health care for all our citizens, including the poor and the elderly." The composite score for progress in health care was 61, just below the midway point between "made some progress" and "stood still."

Despite the public's confidence in its ability to get medical care when needed and its general estimate that some progress had been made in the health field during the preceding year, the survey described in *U.S. Health Care* indicated that more than six out of ten members of the public nonetheless believed that "there is a general 'health care' crisis in the U.S. that will require some basic changes in how medical services are made available to the public." Most significantly, however, this sense of crisis was far more restrained than average among two of the very groups in which one might expect it to be most acute: nonwhites and people sixty years of age and over.

In other words, even where the shoe was most apt to pinch, it would seem it actually wasn't hurting very much. It is probably fair to conclude that sentiment in favor of change in the health care system was motivated more by social than personal reasons: a feeling that whereas I, myself, can get adequate medical care when I need it, there are many more disadvantaged persons who cannot. Yet, testimony of the disadvantaged groups themselves appeared to call that point of view into question.

NATIONAL HEALTH CARE PLANS

The principal changes that the public seemed to want in their health care systems were twofold: assured service, and adequate insurance coverage, especially in case of so-called catastrophic illnesses which, in the face of soaring medical costs, can ruin the fortunes of almost any family.

To determine the kind of institutional arrangements people thought would prove most beneficial, particularly in achieving the latter objective, we asked:

Which one of the health care systems listed on this card do you think would be the best way to provide medical and health care for all the people?

A. *A universal system of health insurance covering everybody and paid for by the federal government out of money raised by taxes.*   22 percent

B. *A system of compulsory health insurance covering everyone who has a job and his or her family, with employers and employees sharing*

*the costs, and the federal government providing
health insurance only for people who do not
have jobs.*   40

C. *The present system of voluntary health and
medical care.*   30

   Don't know   8
                                                                    ————
                                                            100 percent

The figures make clear that there is no consensus among Americans on this subject of health care systems. Three out of ten respondents favored retention of the present voluntary system (corresponding very closely to the 34 percent reported in *U.S. Health Care* who said there is no health care crisis and "things are going along pretty well as is at the present time"). Only slightly more than two in ten endorsed the basic principles of the Kennedy-Griffiths proposal now before Congress. The largest single bloc, but still less than a majority—four out of ten— favored a plan along the basic guidelines laid down by the Nixon administration.

Amplifying these findings are some other results from the surveys reported in *U.S. Health Care* which show that if a national health insurance plan paid for at least partially out of taxes were to be adopted, 40 percent of Americans thought it should be run by the federal government, 15 percent by state governments, 13 percent by insurance companies, 13 percent by local organizations run by citizens and doctors, and 7 percent by local governments, with the rest having no opinion. Once again there was no majority agreement as to a preferred administrator, although the federal government was certainly far ahead. The same survey also showed that Americans feel strongly that the chief contribution the federal government can make in the health field is to prevent high costs from denying needed medical care to citizens.

Americans appreciate and respect the basic values of our current health care system, but at the same time they perceive serious problems that will require some fundamental changes. There is not yet a clear consensus, however, about what an improved system should look like. Preponderant, but not majority, opinion would seem to favor the Nixon administration's plan requiring employers to provide coverage for their employees and having subsidized insurance coverage for the poor paid for out of tax money. While sentiment for such an approach is not overwhelming at the present time, at the very least our survey results suggest that it might gain easier public acceptance than any of the more sweeping plans now under discussion.

VIII.
The Environment

*One of the best things that has happened is the fight against
pollution. If we don't start fighting, we aren't going to have
any country left.*
     a lawyer in New York City

*My fear is that the population will continue to grow and get too big
for our resources. What you see in India and China could
happen here.*
     a fork-lift operator in a small eastern city

*I hope we can clean up this air pollution; eliminate the use of
pesticides in growing food; eliminate preservatives in food; eliminate
the hormones and other foreign substances used in raising
poultry and livestock.*
     the manager of a medical instrument plant in an eastern city

The Record Speaks

The nation's many environmental problems continued to cause
considerable anxiety over the survey year. In contrast to the
earlier, blustery sounds of alarm, scientists, government officials,
businessmen—and citizens without portfolio—appeared to have
braced themselves for the long, hard search for solutions, sorting
out the complex social, economic, and environmental tradeoffs
in the tough crucible of politics and law.

For the most part, the process of protecting and improving

135

the natural habitat remains gradual and laborious. Environmentalists scored some dramatic successes. But a vigorous reaction against their efforts also emerged—the so-called environmental backlash. Some representatives of government, industry, and the scientific community set up a crossfire of counterclaims. Regulations are too strict, they said. Costs are too high. Plants are being forced to shut down, jobs lost. Growth and progress are threatened. The public will not stand for it. Unfortunately, it is often difficult, if not impossible, for the public to distinguish between valid opposition and self-serving propaganda.

Some of the governmental reorganization necessary to deal with environmental problems has already taken place. The Environmental Protection Agency (EPA), established in 1970 to police the environment, assumed from other agencies several functions that had been linked with special interests—such as pesticides regulation in the Department of Agriculture. EPA was also charged with controlling air pollution, water pollution, solid wastes, noise pollution, radiation, and water hygiene.

The National Oceanic and Atmospheric Administration (NOAA), created at the same time in the Department of Commerce, also brought several environmental programs under a single umbrella. Still pending in mid-1972, after many years of discussion, was a controversial Nixon administration proposal for further consolidation of a far broader range of environmental activities in a new Department of Natural Resources.

The Council on Environmental Quality, a White House-level body charged with analyzing environmental problems, reviewing federal programs, and making recommendations to the president, was also established in 1970. Many states and local governments, reflecting a similar increase in environmental concerns, set up comparable agencies of their own.

GROWTH AND PLANNING

There was an unmistakable trend during our survey year toward more critical evaluations of actions that affect the environment —pollutant discharges, applications of technology, construction projects, mining and timbering operations, and many kinds of land use. These and other manifestations of "growth," especially those which resist quantification, are undergoing increasingly sophisticated analyses of costs and benefits. Congress moved forward on legislation to create an Office of Technology Assessment, which would provide regular and thorough evaluation of the costs and effects of proposed new spending programs. And the National Environmental Policy Act (NEPA), now almost three years old, has induced more and more comprehensive and rational planning.

NEPA requires that a detailed "environmental impact statement" be prepared for all federally funded projects with a significant effect on the environment. The statement must discuss "alternatives to the proposed action." (And it is *supposed* to be considered fully in the planning process.) Failure to adhere to NEPA led courts to halt construction of major highways, power plants, airports, and water resource projects (such as Tocks Island Dam on the Delaware River, Gillham Dam on Arkansas' Cossatot River, and the Tennessee-Tombigbee Waterway, a 253-mile canal from the Tennessee River to the Gulf of Mexico). The remarkable effectiveness of NEPA, in fact, inspired various efforts to amend and weaken its provisions. For the next few years at least, a major tug-of-war undoubtedly will be waged over NEPA.

The quality of planning is also likely to improve with passage of a national land-use law. Pending in Congress at midyear, the legislation, sponsored by Representative Wayne Aspinall (D-Col.) in the House and Senator Henry Jackson (D-Wash.) in the Senate would provide federal grants to states to develop comprehensive land-use plans for areas of special environmental concern, for key facilities such as highways and airports, and for large developments and regional programs such as mass transit. Federal funds would be available to help the states undertake the program. But these funds, as well as grants under other programs, would be frozen if a state failed to comply with federal criteria.

Environmentalists and others continued to mount a growing challenge to the orthodoxies of economic and technological growth—to the faith that "progress" can and must continue indefinitely. More and more communities questioned the value of growth, on both environmental and economic grounds. Quite a few inhibited growth through tighter limitations on building permits, zoning restrictions, denial of sewer hookups, and other techniques. A growing number of people have become convinced that current life styles will have to change, and on a national scale. Dr. Barry Commoner, in his book *The Closing Circle,** warned that the nation cannot long endure an endless stream of products like many that have come upon the scene since World War II. Quite a few of these products, he noted, are far more difficult to dispose of than their earlier counterparts; and their manufacturing causes considerably more pollution and requires a gluttonous consumption of electric power.

Another dimension of growth—population—remained the subject of intense debate. Environmentalists were cheered by the news that the nation's birth rate had fallen to its lowest level in history in the first quarter of 1972 and was, in fact, very close to the replacement (or zero growth) level needed to bring an eventual halt to the rise in population.

"Our population growth has developed its own momentum which makes it very difficult to stop, no matter how hard the brakes are applied," said the Commission on Population Growth and the American Future in its report in March 1972. The commission also concluded that "no substantial benefits would result from continued growth of the nation's population."

And finally, on an international scale, the problems of unchecked growth were explored in a widely discussed book *The Limits to Growth,*** which appeared in March 1972. Based on an eighteen-month computer model study at the Massachusetts Institute of Technology, the book warned: "If the present growth trends in world population, industrialization, pollution, food production, and resource depletion continue unchanged, the limits to growth on this planet will be reached sometime within the next 100 years. The most probable result will be a rather sudden and uncontrollable decline in both population and industrial capacity."

In an effort to begin sorting out these converging problems, feverish international environmental activity was undertaken during the past year, much of it in preparation for the United Nations Conference on the Human Environment. The 114-nation conference, held in Stockholm in June 1972, highlighted basic differences in outlook between richer nations seeking to control

* Barry Commoner, *The Closing Circle* (N.Y.: Alfred A. Knopf, 1971).
** Donella H. Meadows et al, *The Limits to Growth* (New York: Universe Books, 1972).

pollution and poorer nations concerned more with economic development. Yet the conference agreed on a declaration of twenty-six principles to protect and improve the human environment. And it voted, backed by limited funding, to set up a permanent U.N. organization to coordinate environmental activities. U.S. involvement in these and other developments at the Stockholm conference were certain to influence at least some U.S. policies and actions in the future.

AIR POLLUTION

The nation has made general, albeit slow, progress in controlling its air pollution. But improvement was uneven, and monitoring admittedly still spotty and unreliable. A rather crude measurement—estimated nationwide emissions of five pollutants by tons per year—showed an aggregate drop from 1969 to 1970 of about 6 percent. A general downward trend for three major pollutants (sulfur dioxide, suspended particulates, and nitrogen dioxide) was reflected in an index developed for the Council on Environmental Quality, based on measurements at eighty-two urban sites through 1970.

Further progress in abating air pollution must buck increasing growth in population, industrialization, and affluence. But considerably cleaner air can be anticipated to the extent that there is effective implementation of the stringent Clean Air Act Amendments of 1970, although they will not begin having a real impact until mid-decade at the earliest.

Under this federal law, states must receive Environmental Protection Agency approval of—and then carry out—their "implementation plans." The law requires that these plans lead to observance by mid-1975 of the air pollution levels for major pollutants set by EPA to protect health. The plans place restrictions both on stationary industrial and municipal sources of pollution and on mobile sources. If EPA disapproves any segment of a state plan, and the state fails to correct the deficiency, EPA itself can promulgate necessary regulations and enforce them. EPA did, in fact, disapprove many portions of state plans and on June 5, 1972 began proposing adjustments.

The stage was thus set for a long succession of battles over pollution-control restrictions on specific sources. One preview of what may lie ahead occurred in Delaware, when the state ordered the Delmarva Power & Light Company to reduce sulfur dioxide emissions at one of its plants by using cleaner fuel. Delmarva's fuel supplier, Getty Oil Company, balked, but EPA stepped in with a notice to Delmarva that it was violating the state's implementation plan, the first such court action under the 1970 act. EPA then issued an order to comply, violation of which carries a maximum penalty of $25,000 a day and a year's imprisonment. The case awaits a judge's decision.

EPA also made clear that it expected states to curb automobile traffic in urban regions where necessary to achieve the national air standards. But states have been hesitant to move forward with such controversial strategies as mandatory vehicle maintenance and inspection, parking fee increases, parking bans, road tolls, car pool incentives, smoother traffic flow, designation of traffic-free zones, and land-use controls. Recognizing the difficulties in assessing and imposing transportation controls, EPA agreed on May 31, 1972 to grant eighteen states a two-year extension—to 1977—to meet certain automotive pollutant standards in thirty-four urban areas.

Achievement of standards was also to be facilitated by Clean Air Act provisions imposing strict emission levels for new cars and trucks. After lengthy hearings, EPA on May 12, 1972 denied auto industry requests to postpone the original 1975 deadline by one year; but the manufacturers have taken the matter to the courts.

Industry continued to profess great difficulty developing effective, reliable, and durable emission-control devices for its cars. One result was intensified interest in finding an alternative to the internal combustion engine itself, and as soon as possible. Major possibilities undergoing research included cars driven by gas turbine, electricity, steam, natural gas, liquefied natural gas, and hybrids that can use two types of fuel.

During the survey year there were still occasional but severe air pollution episodes, most notably the one in Birmingham, Alabama, in November 1971, when a federal judge—under emergency federal law provisions—ordered a two-day shutdown of twenty-three industrial plants.

Concern grew over the effects of lead pollution, particularly on inner-city children. In El Paso, Texas, for example, several children were hospitalized in March 1972 for severe lead poisoning. Soon afterward, the city filed a $1 million damage suit against American Smelting & Refining Company, charging earlier large emissions of lead, cadmium, zinc, and arsenic. Prior to formal court action, the company settled for a fraction of the claim.

Pressure increased, and is likely to increase further, for a shift from regulatory techniques of limiting pollution emissions to the application of economic leverage such as taxes, emission charges, and economic incentives. Proponents of the latter insisted that such controls would more effectively induce polluters to cut down emissions and would be easier to impose. Prime candidates include a tax on lead in gasoline and a charge on sulfur oxide emissions. Specific legislative proposals were submitted both from within Congress and by the administration, but no final action had been taken by mid-1972.

The costs of air pollution control will be enormous though perhaps less than the fearful figures disseminated by some in industry and elsewhere. EPA, in a February 1972 report entitled *The Economics of Clean Air,* estimated that meeting air quality standards for both stationary and mobile sources would entail an aggregate increase in consumer prices from 1971 to 1977 of less than 1 percent. Well over half the increase would be due to 10 percent higher prices for new cars; much of the remainder would stem from a projected increase in the cost of electricity.

Such estimates did not seem to justify much hand-wringing about the costs of pollution control, though some plants—usually those operating marginally or losing money anyway—undoubtedly would be forced to close. Frequently overlooked are the benefits of cleaning up the air—in terms of better health, lower medical expenses, increased employment in and growth of firms making control devices, lower cleaning costs, reduced plant damage, and the like. Projections of benefits are even cruder than those of costs, but the EPA study estimated that in the year 1977, for example, control costs of $12.3 billion would be exceeded by benefits of $14.2 billion. The latter figure was considered extremely conservative since health benefits from reductions in carbon monoxide, oxidants, and nitrogen oxides had not been included due to lack of knowledge and data.

WATER POLLUTION

Measuring the extent of water pollution is a task even more elusive than quantifying air pollution. Nonetheless, various indicators showed that by and large the nation at best has been just "holding the line" in the face of increasing population, construction, and industrial activity. At the same time, noticeable improvements during the last year or more have been reported for various bodies of water such as Lake Washington, the Willamette River, the Hudson River, New York Harbor, and San Francisco Bay.

EPA reported in a May 1972 study, *The Economics of Clean Water,* that, of the total 260,324 miles of streams and shorelines in the U.S., an estimated 76,299 were polluted (by standards set according to use of the area) at some time during 1971. The figure represented 29 percent of total miles, up a bit from 27 percent in 1970. EPA, noting that these figures may be understated, continued its efforts to develop an index for better measurements of water pollution prevalence, duration, and intensity.

Projections in the same EPA document indicated that by the end of 1972 some 156 million Americans would be served by sewers (up from 152 million in 1971), and that 70 percent of their wastes (compared to 68 percent in 1971) would be undergoing secondary treatment—as opposed to rudimentary primary treatment or no treatment at all.

Almost everyone conceded that the basic federal water-pollution-control law has been a failure, and for nearly two years Congress worked on a revised law, versions of which were finally passed by both the Senate and the House. This legislation, awaiting House-Senate conference committee agreement in mid-1972, would scrap the current system under which a state decides how a stream is to be used and adopt instead the control measures it deems necessary to keep pollutants at low levels. The new law would rely chiefly on a combined state-federal permit program limiting effluents from particular industrial and municipal plants, in line with existing technology.

The legislation was expected to set goals—not necessarily requirements—that all waters be clean enough for swimming by 1981 and all polluting discharges eliminated by 1985. Observers predicted a great many economic qualifications and loopholes in the final wording; concern was also expressed over costs, which escalate rapidly as pollutant removal approaches 100 percent.

Meanwhile, in more flagrant cases, federal officials continued to make selective use of the 1899 Refuse Act, a long overlooked but bluntly effective tool for prohibiting discharges into navigable waters. For example, on December 10, 1971, Anaconda Wire and Cable Company paid a $200,000 fine under this act for discharges into the Hudson River. And in May 1972, under state law, New York sought to levy fines totaling $1.6 million against Consolidated Edison Company for the alleged "massive" killing of fish impaled on water intake screens at the Indian Point nuclear power plant on the Hudson. (The decision was still pending in early fall, 1972.)

Substantial funding continued for construction of municipal waste-treatment plants, but there was some shift in emphasis to expanded industrial control efforts, particularly changes in manufacturing processes and use of total recycling systems. Dow Chemical Company reported that in some new treatment programs it turned a substantial profit, mostly through recovery of usable materials; but this was still a distinctly minority view.

EPA reported that a relatively few, inefficient factories accounted for a very large portion of the water pollution burden. As with air pollution there was increasing interest in imposing taxes or other charges on effluents—according to weight, chemical composition, etc.—to get at major sources of pollution more effectively. Vermont initiated such a law two years ago.

What are the costs of controlling water pollution? So far one can only guess. Total capital investment, replacement, interest and operating costs, for both industries and municipalities, are measured in many billions of dollars. Much depends on terms of the new law, its enforcement, and other factors. EPA estimated that, under the law as of mid-1972, if the costs of industrial pollution control were passed on to consumers, with normal markups and profit margins fully maintained, the overall price of manufactured goods might increase 0.1 percent each year up to 1976.

The benefits of water pollution control are even harder to assess than those of air pollution reduction. Reliable analyses are rare. One study, which might provide some insights into this elusive issue, was made of Illinois waters by Bruce Barker of the Illinois Department of Transportation and reported in the May 1972 issue of *Environmental Science and Technology*. In a complex calculation, he added dollar benefits of clean water (by quantifying the increased value of recreation and commercial fisheries, plus savings in municipal and industrial treatment costs) to dollar losses associated with polluted water (current lost recreation and commercial fisheries values and increased costs of municipal and industrial treatment) to arrive at the tentative conclusion that the benefits of pollution control in the state are significantly greater than costs.

SOLID WASTES

The trend in solid wastes continued inexorably upward. In 1967 the nation generated an estimated total of 364 million tons, and this is expected to climb by 1977 to 554 million tons. Solid wastes in the past year probably equaled about 12 pounds per person per day, about half of it collected by municipal systems. Chief disposal techniques include open burning dumps (many of which are being closed down), incinerators (also air polluters), and sanitary landfills (though more than half of the nation's fifty largest cities were said to have sufficient space left for only ten more years of filling or less). Some wastes are also disposed of by ocean dumping, composting, and other recycling.

Although the public showed great enthusiasm for recycling centers, quite a few closed down in the past year. At the end of 1971, industry reported that the public was redeeming glass bottles and jars at the rate of nearly a billion a year—against yearly production of about 36 billion. Similarly, 35 million pounds of aluminum cans were being collected for recycling, in contrast to an estimated 929 million pounds shipped for container production.

Although interest in recycling continued to grow, each type of material also continued to present its own problems. Usually they were economic rather than technological—costs of transportation, difficulty of finding a market, costs of reprocessing, and so forth. Officials, environmentalists, and concerned citizens all awaited with interest the results of various demonstration projects that might give clues to future solutions.

PESTICIDES

On June 14, 1972 EPA prohibited most uses of the controversial pesticide DDT. The action followed a long administrative and legal dispute. EPA's order, which takes effect December 31, 1972, permits certain public health and minor agricultural uses of the pesticide. But EPA Administrator William D. Ruckelshaus ruled that the dangers of continued widespread use of DDT outweigh any agricultural and economic benefits. (More than 85 percent of the DDT in this country is used to protect cotton crops.)

Ruckelshaus said that DDT poses an "unacceptable risk" to the environment. (Diffuse and persistent, it accumulates in the food chain and is credited with great damage to fish and birds.) Ruckelshaus also noted the possible risk to man's health, since experiments have shown that DDT causes tumors in laboratory animals.

On the day of the ruling, DDT manufacturers filed an appeal to the courts to overturn it. But the domestic use of DDT is already on a long downward trend—due to warnings by scientists, public pressure, governmental restrictions, development of substitutes, and the increasing resistance of insects. About 12 million pounds a year are now used, far below the 79 million pounds at the time of peak consumption in 1959.

The recent decline in domestic use of all chlorinated hydrocarbons (of which DDT is one) has been sharp: from 103 million pounds in 1969 to 31 million in 1970. Total domestic consumption of *all* pesticides (insecticides, herbicides, and fungicides) has leveled off since 1966 and totaled 658 million pounds in 1970.

Pesticide users can be expected to rely much more on substitute chemicals which, while less long-lived, are more toxic. A major example is the organic phosphate parathion, domestic production of which has already been growing sharply (56.6 million pounds in 1970 compared to 50.6 million in 1969). Misused, parathion can be quickly fatal to humans, and there is concern that the number of accidental poisonings will climb.

Meanwhile, there was increasing, if belated, recognition of the long-term need to rely more on biological, rather than chemical, techniques for pest control. These include use of natural insect predators, pest diseases, sterilization, sex attractants, and different planting practices.

ENERGY AND FUELS

A combination of factors—not the least among them being problems of supply and environmental damage—have forced govern-

ment officials in the past year to confront more directly the web
of complex problems that make up the "energy crisis." Raw
resources of some fuels are plentiful. But there were snags in
meeting the nation's demand for energy (which has been rising by
4–5 percent a year, with electricity consumption increasing at up
to 9 percent a year, or more than doubling every ten years).
Among the problems were developing technologies to utilize fuels
and produce energy economically, doing it in time to forestall
blackouts and brownouts in many cities, and avoiding unacceptable environmental harm.

The only thing that seems certain is that consumer prices will
go up all around, and well into the future. For example, a Federal Power Commission survey, released in April 1972, predicted
a reversal of the long-term decline in the cost of electricity. Assuming 3 percent inflation, it estimated that the average price per
kilowatt-hour will more than double in the next twenty years—
jumping from 1.54 cents in 1969 to 3.51 cents in 1990. Major
anticipated causes included costs of environmental protection and
rising competition for available fuels, especially clean ones.

There are problems associated with all alternative solutions.
Natural gas, in great demand for its environmental purity, has
been in such short supply that distributors in some areas have
been forced to turn away customers. Known gas reserves are estimated to have declined to less than 250 trillion cubic feet, which
would probably not last eight years at current rates. Under the
more pessimistic estimates, an additional 1,200 trillion cubic feet
is susceptible to economical discovery and production, but even
this could be consumed before the turn of the century.

Similarly, recoverable oil reserves, if they had to meet domestic
demand without the help of imports or new sources of energy,
would, according to a report for the Senate Interior Committee
released in May 1972, be depleted by the year 2011 at the latest.
Oil imports, however, have come to account for about 22 percent
of domestic supply and are expected to increase rapidly. This has
raised widespread concern over the balance-of-payments, national
security, and environmental implications of our increasing de-
pendence on foreign oil, as well as costly liquefied natural gas.
The threats posed by tanker collisions and other spills are considerable.

Meanwhile, the Interior Department again went ahead with

plans for substantial Gulf of Mexico offshore oil and gas leasing. (It was postponed in December 1971, when a federal court agreed with environmentalists that a full discussion of alternatives was required by NEPA.) In the wings is a major dispute over whether to allow drilling off the Atlantic Coast.

Interior also gave its blessing in May 1972 to construction of the trans-Alaskan oil pipeline, but environmentalists continued to press for a court injunction. And even if the Alaskan North Slope oil potential were fully developed today, it would provide only an estimated 13 percent of domestic demand.

There are vast supplies of coal in the ground. But much of it has a high sulfur content, and the damage caused by strip mining is severe. Research continued (and undoubtedly will continue) on methods to utilize more coal by desulfurizing it and by transforming it into gas and liquid.

Nuclear power is expected to supply an ever increasing share of the nation's electric power—perhaps 50 percent or more by the year 2000, compared to about 2 percent now. But there are substantial problems of safety, radioactivity, and thermal pollution of water or air. Environmental lawsuits have at least temporarily held up construction and operation of a number of nuclear power plants, such as Calvert Cliffs in Maryland and Quad Cities in Illinois.

In addition, supplies of uranium for current reactors are by no means unlimited. Nearly 70 percent of federal energy research funds are going into the fast breeder reactor. If successful, this reactor will generate its own supply of uranium, but many consider the safety and environmental risks extreme.

Other long-range hopes are pinned on controlled thermonuclear fusion fueled by the virtually unlimited source of deuterium in sea water, solar energy, geothermal energy, fuel cells, and others.

The People Speak

Pollution is our worst enemy.
    a weaver in a small Maine town

I hope we can clean up the air and the water so people can live in peace and see trees and grass and breathe fresh air.
    a Long Island caterer

*I'm afraid pollution will hinder our health and the health of
future generations.*
        a baker's helper in Jacksonville, Florida

*I hope overpopulation can be prevented. This brings on the loss
of importance of each individual life. It makes it hard on all of us.*
        a housewife in New York State

*I'm afraid they'll try to control the black population with birth
control pills and operations so they can't have children.*
        an eighteen-year-old black college student in the South

Now every time you breathe, you breathe soot.
        a hospital worker in the New York metropolitan area

*I hope we can achieve a cleaner environment. Man must realize
that he is one with nature.*
        a retired college professor in Baltimore

*I'd like to live in a neighborhood where it is quiet and there
are grass and trees.*
        a black janitor in Chicago

I'm afraid pollution will finally kill us all.
        the wife of a teacher in a western state

Public concern about environmental problems has clearly burgeoned in recent years. When the Institute for International Social
Research asked a cross section of the public how concerned they
were about air and water pollution in 1968, the composite score *
(on a range from 100 for "a great deal" to zero for "not at all")
was 68. Now, just four years later, in answers to our questions, the score on water pollution came out at 84 and on air
pollution, at 83, representing an increase of 16 and 15 points,
respectively. This upward shift put these items near the top of the
public's concerns. (See Table 1.) And concern about "collecting
and disposing of garbage, trash, and other solid wastes" was only
slightly lower.

As mentioned earlier, there was considerable uniformity among
all elements of the population in the high ratings assigned these

---

* The method by which composite scores are calculated is explained in
Appendix 5.

subjects, with only relatively minor demographic variations. (See Table A-4.) Those groups generally exhibiting more concern than the norm included the young; the well-educated; the professional and business group; suburbanites; westerners; Catholics; political Independents; and those who classified themselves as at least moderately liberal. On the other hand, lower-than-average composite scores tended to be the rule among those with little education and little income (presumably less well informed and therefore less aware of pollution problems), and people living in rural areas (where pollution is generally less acute than elsewhere).

Nevertheless, whether based on fact or fad, well-nigh universal concern about problems of the environment was evident among Americans in mid-1972.

PROGRESS IN COMBATING POLLUTION

The preponderant feeling among Americans was that some progress had been made during the preceding year in lessening air pollution (an assessment in accord with the record) and in reducing water pollution (a conclusion not warranted by the record). When asked about progress in "cleaning up our waterways and reducing water pollution throughout the country" and in "reducing air pollution," the people replied:

	Water Pollution	Air Pollution
	(in percentages)	
Made much progress	4	3
Made some progress	45	46
Stood still	23	25
Lost some ground	12	11
Lost much ground	8	7
Don't know	8	8
	100	100

The composite scores yielded by these results were 57 in the case of water pollution and 58 for air pollution, not much above the "stood still" point of 50. (See Table A-13.) Young people appeared to be the most realistic in assessing the pollution situation. In contrast, those more optimistic than the record supports were the older generation (fifty and over), those with little education, ruralites, and midwesterners.

GOVERNMENTAL SPENDING TO COMBAT POLLUTION

Reflecting their deep concern about pollution problems, almost two-thirds of our respondents were in favor of increasing spending on water pollution and more than six out of ten, on air pollution. Asked whether the amount of tax money now being spent in these areas should be increased, kept at the present level, reduced, or ended altogether, Americans reacted as follows:

	Water Pollution	Air Pollution
	(in percentages)
Increased	64	61
Present level	26	28
Reduced	4	4
Ended altogether	1	1
Don't know	5	6
	100	100

The overall composite scores yielded by these results were 81 in the case of water pollution and 80 in regard to air pollution, which placed these two items toward the very top of the public's priority list for governmental spending.

Predictably, the demographic patterns on this question were basically similar to those on degrees of concern about air and water pollution. (See Table A-7.) Most eager to spend more on both problems were the young, families with incomes in excess of $10,000 per year, white collar workers, residents of our largest metropolitan areas, suburbanites, and westerners. Less-than-average (but still substantial) support for increased spending was evident among older people, the most disadvantaged groups in terms of education and income, those living in very small towns and rural areas, and blacks (who may look upon the abatement of pollution as something of a luxury compared to such immediate concerns as improved housing, urban renewal, better schools, and medicaid).

COOPERATION IN LESSENING POLLUTION

Unfortunately, the length of our interviews did not allow us to explore in depth the extent to which the public is willing to make personal sacrifices to help reduce pollution. We did ask several

questions along this line about air pollution, water pollution, and
solid wastes, however. First, we asked: *Do you use an automobile
regularly at the present time?*

Yes	82 percent
No	17
Don't know	1
	100 percent

To those who answered yes, we then asked: *As you probably
know, a great deal of air pollution comes from automobiles. How
much more would you be willing to pay for a car to cover the
cost of installing antipollution equipment?*

$0	22 percent	$50	17 percent
$5	5	$100	17
$10	3	$200	10
$20	9	$500	6
	Don't know	11 percent	

One-half of the 82 percent of our respondents who use an
automobile regularly were willing to pay $50 or more out of their
own pockets to reduce polluted emissions from the cars they
drive; almost one-fourth, on the other hand, said they did not want
to pay anything extra.

We also asked a related question about water pollution: *Turning now to water pollution, please tell me how much more in
taxes or water rates you would be willing to pay each year to help
clean up our waterways?*

$0	24 percent	$50	13 percent
$5	11	$100	9
$10	11	$200	5
$20	11	$500	4
	Don't know	12 percent	

In contrast to the one-half of the automobile users who were
willing to pay $50 or more for anti-pollution equipment on their
cars, only three out of ten members of the public as a whole were
prepared to make an equivalent contribution toward cleaning up
our waterways. The one-out-of-four proportion that wanted no
additional financial burden was essentially unchanged.

Finally, we asked about solid wastes: *As you probably know, many of our localities are having a great deal of trouble disposing of trash and other solid wastes. To help out, it has been suggested that drinks should not be sold in throw-away bottles or cans, but only in returnable bottles, on which a good-sized deposit would be charged. Would you favor or oppose a national law along these lines?*

Favor	81	percent
Oppose	15	
Don't know	4	
	100	percent

That eight out of ten members of the public would actually be willing to give up the convenience of throw-away bottles and cans and start lugging returnable bottles back to the stores is highly debatable. Nevertheless, on this issue the public's heart was obviously on the side of recycling.

Supporting our findings are results reported by The Roper Organization in October 1971. In response to a series of questions asking people whether they would pay more for certain items, if that turned out to be the only way to eliminate pollution, almost seven respondents out of ten said they would be willing to pay 10 percent more for detergents, gasoline, and automobiles; and around six out of ten said they would pay 10 percent more for electricity, magazines, newspapers, and airline tickets.

LIMITING ECONOMIC AND TECHNICAL GROWTH

That's all very well, some experts and concerned citizens may say, but limiting our view to such relatively small-scale approaches as increased governmental spending and personal contributions toward pollution abatement will never turn the tables on pollution. The problems involved, they might add, are so huge and so entrenched by now that only a truly fundamental approach, such as limiting the level of industrial activity, can possibly be successful. To test reactions to this concept, we asked: *Some people say the U.S. should put more emphasis on curbing pollution and improving the quality of life in this country by deliberately holding back on economic and technical growth, for example by prohibiting an increase in certain kinds of industrial activities. Others*

*say this would result in fewer jobs and a lower standard of living
in America. If you had to choose, would you favor or oppose the
U.S. deliberately limiting economic and technical growth in this
country?*

Favor	27	percent
Oppose	60	
Don't know	13	
	100	percent

   Only among a few groups did the proportion in favor of limiting
economic and technical growth exceed one-third. The percentage
among those in the eighteen- to twenty-nine age group was 37
percent, and among westerners, 36 percent. The only element of
the population that produced an actual majority (56 percent) was
the handful of respondents who classified themselves as very liberal. It is thus clear—and not at all surprising, given our national
devotion to economic expansion—that if those who believe in the
necessity of limits to growth are proved correct, the American
people will require considerable education before they will be
prepared to go along.

POPULATION CONTROL

Another fundamental proposal often advanced these days calls for
control of the size of our population. To test reactions to this line
of thinking, we asked: *Some people say that, in order to keep
pollution down and prevent overcrowding, the U.S. should deliberately try to cut down on the growth of our population by
such means as encouraging birth control and reducing tax exemptions and welfare payments for large families. Others say such
matters as family size should be left to the individuals involved
and their consciences. If you had to choose between these two
points of view, would you favor or oppose the U.S. deliberately
taking steps to limit population growth?*

Favor	47	percent
Oppose	44	
Don't know	9	
	100	percent

Obviously, these results amount to a virtual stand-off. Opposition to a policy of population control reached plurality, and in some cases majority, proportions among the following groups: people fifty years old and older; those with only a high school education; manual workers in general (but not higher-status labor union members); people living in the Midwest and the South and in small communities and rural areas; blacks (many of whom equate a policy of population control with a form of genocide against their race); and, especially, political Independents and Catholics.

In contrast, greater-than-average majorities favoring a policy of population control appeared among families with incomes over $10,000 per year; the college-educated; easterners and westerners; people living in large cities and in the suburbs throughout the country; Protestants; Republicans; and, most of all, the young.

The divergence of these views undoubtedly reflected clashing, emotion-ladened beliefs about such very personal matters as birth control and abortion. (A Harris Survey released in August 1972 reported, for example, that 48 percent of likely voters favored a national law legalizing abortions up to the fourth month of pregnancy; but almost as many, 43 percent, were opposed.) This conflict in outlook was undoubtedly heightened by the reference in our question to governmental action to control population growth, with its implications of official compulsion. Clearly, there is no national consensus yet in support of a government-sponsored policy of population control along the lines proposed, to President Nixon's evident displeasure, by the Commission on Population Growth and the American Future.

Looking, then, at the entire range of environmental issues, it would appear that the public at this stage would not only condone, but indeed welcome, a considerable new investment in solving the problems of air and water pollution and solid waste disposal. The people remain leery, however, about more sweeping and revolutionary attacks on environmental problems, if these approaches assume overtones of governmental control through such devices as officially limiting economic and technical growth or inhibiting an increase in population.

IX.
Economic Affairs

You wonder how you're going to live. You go to the store to buy food and think you'll have two dollars left, but you come out with nothing.
> a black woman, the wife of a parking-lot supervisor in Cleveland

The nation as a whole is very prosperous and, even with domestic troubles, our standard of living is still good.
> a twenty-one-year-old purchasing agent in the Midwest

There have been numerous factories in the U.S. that have closed. It's obvious we can't all have jobs if we all buy foreign products.
> a midwestern office manager

My husband has been out of work for two and a half years. His department closed down after he had been with the company for ten years.
> wife of a data processor in New England

The freeze on wages and prices ended up with prices going up but wages standing still.
> a construction worker in the South

The Record Speaks

On August 15, 1971 President Nixon stunned the nation and the world with his announcement of an integrated economic program designed to stimulate domestic economic recovery, dampen inflation, and protect the dollar from speculative attacks in international money markets. These actions were taken against a background of sluggish economic growth and high unemployment, inflationary wage settlements and rapidly rising prices, a sharp decline in the stock market, severe buffeting of the dollar in foreign exchange markets, and intense political pressures. Recognizing the interdependence of these complex problems, the president attacked on all fronts simultaneously. With this New Economic Policy (NEP), the U.S. launched a dramatic new era in its economic history.

THE DOMESTIC ECONOMY AND THE NEP

The domestic component of the president's surprise package was precipitated by a disappointingly slow recovery from the 1969–70 recession and attendant unemployment rate of approximately 6 percent, coupled with the persistence of rapid inflation. Although some strengthening of the economy was evident in the summer of 1971, the pace was frustratingly slow relative to the aspirations of the American public. Hence, to spur economic growth and expand employment, the president requested Congress to restore the investment tax credit on domestically produced machinery and equipment, repeal the excise tax on automobiles, and have scheduled increases in personal income tax exemptions and deductions take effect earlier than originally planned. To provide a framework within which expansionary monetary and fiscal policies * could be employed without further aggravating inflation, emergency powers were invoked under the Economic Stabilization Act of 1970, freezing prices, wages, salaries, and rents for ninety days.

YEAR OF RECOVERY

The pace of economic growth accelerated as the survey year progressed, and by summer 1972 a strong recovery clearly was under way, with the prospect of further impressive gains immediately

---

* Monetary policy seeks to promote economic growth and stable prices by manipulating the economy's supply of money and credit. Fiscal policy, on the other hand, attempts to achieve a growing full-employment economy free from either excessive inflation or deflation through the shaping of taxation and public expenditures.

ahead. The gross national product advanced $85.2 billion (8.4 percent) over fiscal 1971. All major sectors of the economy except inventories and net exports shared in the expansion. Much of the total gain in GNP, however, reflected increased prices. "Real" GNP grew 4.5 percent, roughly the nation's expected long-run average annual growth rate.

A strong expansion in consumer spending, necessary for a balanced and sustained recovery, took hold as the fiscal year progressed. The investment picture was mixed. Throughout the year, the boom in residential housing construction provided a solid foundation for the expansion, with housing starts setting an annual record of 2.3 million. Unusually small investment in inventories, on the other hand, exerted a substantial drag on the economy. Business-fixed investment showed marked improvement only after the turn of the year, as businessmen were held back earlier by the low rate of capacity utilization (about 75 percent), the lackluster performance of industrial production, and uncertainty about the future course of the economy.

For the first time in the nation's history, in 1971 more than half of the families in the U.S. moved into the five-figure income bracket, with annual incomes of $10,000 or more. Median family income—$10,290—was 4.2 percent higher than the 1970 level, but because of rising consumer prices it was about the same in constant dollars.

The U.S. net export position deteriorated drastically throughout the fiscal year to a deficit of nearly $3 billion. This reversal from the nation's historic trade surplus resulted from the worsening over a number of years of the U.S. price-cost performance relative to that of its competitors. In addition, special factors during the year had a negative impact on the trade balance, among them, more rapid economic growth in the U.S. than in Europe, dock strikes, and an unsettled international financial picture.

Governmental purchases of goods and services provided a substantial boost to the economy: defense expenditures, which had been declining, rose sharply; civilian and military pay was raised; and state and local governmental spending continued upward.

Monetary and fiscal policies were geared to assist economic recovery. Banks by and large held comfortable reserves; interest rates, particularly short-term, were low; and the Federal Reserve

Board generally carried out an expansionist policy that accommodated the recovery.

The fiscal 1972 federal budget deficit of $23 billion (one of the largest since World War II) also promoted the recovery— even though this deficit was considerably smaller than the administration had planned. (The smaller deficit was the result of both unexpectedly high revenues from overwithholding of federal personal income taxes and high tax receipts as a result of unexpected strength in the economy and smaller outlays because government departments and agencies were unable to spend as rapidly as anticipated and because the administration's revenue-sharing proposal was not enacted during the fiscal year.) Except for an immediate spurt in automobile sales, the initial impact of the fiscal policies proposed by the president on August 15, 1971 was primarily psychological. The investment tax credit and the speedup in personal income tax reductions were not passed by Congress until December 10; their importance lay primarily in adding stimulus to an already expanding economy.

The large 1972 deficit, the latest in a succession of red ink budgets, and apparently the forerunner of even larger ones, focused attention on the urgent and unresolved issues of what services the government should provide and how they should be financed. There was little disagreement with the conclusions of the highly respected Brookings Institution study *Setting National Priorities* * that a choice must be made among slashing federal expenditures, severely raising taxes, or condoning rapid inflation. (Another suggested alternative was continued deficit spending, balanced by rigidly enforced controls on price increases.) In addition, discontent with the burdens of the property tax and widespread resentment over alleged inequities in the tax system made tax reform one of the most popular—and political—issues of the year.

Faced with the dilemma of how to match spending requirements with inadequate revenues, the administration expressed a preference for cutting spending rather than attempting thoroughgoing tax reform. In seeking possible new sources of funds, the administration also began to take a serious look at a value-added

* Charles L. Schultze et al, *Setting National Priorities: The 1973 Budget* (Washington, D.C.: The Brookings Institution, 1972).

tax.* Under one variation being considered, proceeds from the tax would be distributed to states for support of public education, thereby helping to reduce the burden of property taxes now being used for this purpose.

Opposition spokesmen, on the other hand, stressed fundamental reform of the present tax system as the best means of eliminating inequities and providing revenue for proposed social welfare programs. Numerous studies suggested, however, that only a limited amount of new revenue could be raised by tax reform alone (or at least by reforms that had a realistic chance of passage). But, with Congress, the administration, and the public all expressing concern, some changes in the tax structure appeared likely in the near future.

The expanding economy absorbed an unusually large number of workers entering the labor force. Nonfarm employment grew by an impressive 2.6 million persons from May 1971 to May 1972. Nonetheless, in the face of such rapid labor-force growth, the pace of recovery failed to reduce the rate of unemployment from a yearly average of 5.9 percent.

With a large pool of unemployed, and the number of people classified as poor actually increasing during the recession years of 1970 and 1971 after a decade of decline in the 1960s, the problem of providing a minimum income for all Americans remained urgent. (Some income assistance was forthcoming when Congress on June 30, 1972 passed legislation to raise social security benefits by 20 percent, effective September 1, 1972.) The modest employment programs in effect during the year (primarily manpower training programs, public and private efforts to employ veterans, and a public service jobs program authorizing federal expenditures to underwrite the cost of hiring new employees for state and local governmental jobs) were inadequate to reduce the unmployment rolls substantially. Although there was at least some backing for the concept of attacking poverty by providing direct income support—with national benefit and eligibility standards and financing provided at the federal level—Congress was

---

* A value-added tax is similar to a national sales tax, levied on the value added to goods and services at each stage of their production or performance. The tax paid is added to the price at each stage so that each producer is reimbursed for the taxes he pays. The final consumer pays the entire tax, which is subsumed in the retail price.

unable to reach agreement on the long-stalled welfare reform bill. Given the wide disparity of views among members of the House and Senate committees involved, it increasingly appeared that final legislation (if, indeed, any would emerge at all) would not embody many of the reforms that had been introduced, to both praise and criticism, in the president's original proposal.

A NATIONAL INCOMES POLICY

Although success in promoting economic recovery was clearly evident during the survey year, the results of the wage- and price-control program were still ambiguous at the close of fiscal 1972. The ninety-day freeze on prices, wages, salaries, and rents expired on November 14 and was replaced by the more flexible Phase II program of wage and price restraint. To meet the Phase II objective of reducing the annual rate of inflation to 2 or 3 percent by the end of calendar 1972, responsibility for controlling wages, salaries, and fringe benefits was vested in a fifteen-member tripartite Pay Board composed of five members each from labor, business, and the public. A Price Commission, consisting of seven public members, was responsible for prices and rents. While these two bodies were expected to develop standards and make specific decisions in individual cases, the cabinet-level Cost of Living Council created by the president on August 15 retained the responsibility of establishing overall goals and determining the scope of the program.

The Price Commission aimed to limit the average annual advance in the general price level to 2.5 percent; the Pay Board announced a general standard for annual increases in employee compensation of 5.5 percent (with provision for specific exceptions by the board).

The Phase II inflation-control program began with a sweeping effort to control even the smallest economic units. By the summer of 1972 the program had been streamlined so that enforcement was focused on the largest firms and groups of employees thought to be "engines of inflation." But while overall coverage of the program was being narrowed to certain key groups, enforcement was being progressively tightened.

Both the Pay Board and the Price Commission were the objects of considerable criticism. Early policy decisions of the Pay Board were often difficult to interpret, regulations were slow to appear, and they were frequently revised and reconsidered after they had been announced. Moreover, early in its operation, the board approved raises for coal and railroad workers that were considerably in excess of its own 5.5 percent guideline. Although many decisions were favorable to labor, representatives dramatically expressed their dissatisfaction with the control program in March 1972 when AFL-CIO President George Meany and three other labor representatives—but not Teamsters Union President Frank E. Fitzsimmons—walked off the board following its decision to cut back the pay increases negotiated by the west coast longshoremen. President Nixon thereupon reconstituted the board as a semipublic rather than tripartite body, and it continued to function with its policies essentially unchanged.

The Price Commission was freer from criticism in its first weeks of operation, but it too came under fire as food prices soared, overall wholesale and consumer price indexes continued to rise rapidly, and corporate profits surged. As food prices, and meat prices in particular, continued to spiral upward, consumers (the American housewife most of all) became increasingly distressed. In response to this concern, the president on June 26 removed quotas on meat imports for the remainder of 1972 in an attempt

TABLE 5   PRICE AND WAGE CHANGES, Feb. 1971–May 1972
percentage change, seasonally adjusted annual rate

Price or Wage Measure	Six months prior to Phase I: Feb–Aug 1971	Phase I: Aug–Nov 1971	First six months of Phase II: Nov 1971– May 1972	Phase I and Phase II: Aug 1971– May 1972
Consumer Price Indexes:				
All items	4.0	1.9	3.5	2.9
Food	5.4	1.7	4.4	3.5
Commodities less food	3.5	.0	2.9	1.9
Wholesale Price Index	4.7	−0.8	5.2	3.4
Earnings of Private Nonfarm Production Workers *	6.8	1.9	8.1	6.0

* Hourly earnings in current dollars adjusted to exclude the effects of interindustry shifts and overtime pay.

to increase supplies and hold down prices. Several days later he extended price controls to previously exempt unprocessed foods (primarily fresh fruits, vegetables, eggs, and seafood), but only after they have been sold by the farmer.

Final judgment on the success of the control program could not be rendered after little more than a year of operation. As shown in Table 5, during the freeze, consumer commodity prices excluding food did not rise at all, wholesale prices actually declined, and increases in hourly earnings were cut sharply.

The months immediately following the freeze were a transition period to the more flexible Phase II program. As anticipated, prices and wages bulged as many of the previously forbidden increases were permitted to take effect. Although prices then rose slowly in some months, in others they continued to rise rapidly. Prices of agricultural products were particularly volatile. And the post-freeze bulge in hourly earnings was so large that the rate of increase for the post-freeze period was considerably larger than in the pre-freeze period.

In summary, in the six months after the freeze ended, prices and hourly earnings both rose at rates considerably higher than were consistent with the program's goals. Much of the increase clearly was attributable to the post-freeze bulge, but not enough time had elapsed to judge the effectiveness of the controls once the immediate post-freeze conditions had passed. In the absence of clearcut progress in the war against inflation, it appeared probable by mid-1972 that the economy would continue to live with formal controls for some time.

THE UNITED STATES AND THE INTERNATIONAL ECONOMY

In moves as dramatic and far-reaching on the international front as were his domestic economic actions, the president on August 15, 1972 suspended the convertibility of the dollar into gold or other reserve assets and imposed a temporary 10 percent surcharge on all dutiable imports.* The administration hoped through these

---

* In addition, the president requested Congress to: (1) exclude foreign-made capital equipment from the benefits of the proposed investment tax credit while the surcharge was in effect; (2) provide for the creation of Domestic International Sales Corporations in order to defer payment of taxes on profits earned from export sales; and (3) reduce foreign aid appropriations by 10 percent.

actions to force a realignment of exchange rates of the currencies of other countries in order to devalue the dollar, trigger international trade negotiations aimed at giving U.S. producers improved entry to foreign markets, and initiate an overhaul of the entire international monetary system.

In the years since the postwar international monetary system was devised at Bretton Woods in 1944, the economic strength of the U.S. vis-à-vis its trading partners had declined materially. A decade of continuous U.S. balance-of-payments deficits had resulted in a massive accumulation of dollars by foreign official institutions far in excess of demand, thereby reducing the dollar's value as the primary reserve currency. As foreigners exchanged their excess dollars for gold and U.S. gold reserves accordingly declined, it became more and more difficult for the U.S. to honor its commitment to sell gold for officially held dollars at $35 an ounce—a commitment that had provided the underpinning for a fixed exchange rate system.

These long-run problems were compounded in 1971 by a massive outflow of U.S. capital seeking to take quick advantage of the relatively high interest rates in Europe, and a turnaround from the traditional U.S. merchandise trade surplus to a trade deficit. As the balance-of-payments picture darkened, speculative pressures against the dollar grew. In the first two weeks of August 1971 alone, the U.S. paid out $1.1 billion in reserve assets, leaving the claims of foreign official institutions against U.S. dollar reserves more than three times greater than the reserves themselves. Under these circumstances, the U.S. commitment to maintain the dollar's convertibility was no longer tenable, and bold new action was clearly required to protect the dollar and strengthen our balance-of-payments position.

The president's action meant the end, in effect, of the previous fixed exchange rate system. In the weeks following August 15, many foreign currencies were set free, to let their value be determined by supply and demand. In the prevailing circumstances, the value of the currencies rose relative to the dollar, although most countries attempted to hold this shift to a minimum. Restrictions mushroomed on financial transactions and even on trade; other nations resented the import surcharge and denounced the U.S. for refusing to raise the price of gold as part of a total realignment package. Businessmen found themselves in a climate of such uncertainty that fears of a worldwide recession were pervasive. In a crisis atmosphere, feverish international negotiations got under way and culminated in the Smithsonian Accord of December 18, 1971 (named for the site at which the talks took place—the Smithsonian Institution's "Castle" in Washington, D.C.).

At the Smithsonian discussions the administration agreed to propose to Congress a devaluation of the dollar in terms of gold from $35 to $38 an ounce * and to lift the import surcharge. Foreign negotiators agreed to revalue their exchange rates and to open discussions on U.S. trade problems. The participants also agreed to widen the range within which exchange rates would be allowed to fluctuate. Trade agreements were shortly completed with both Japan and the European Economic Community (EEC), although by mid-1972 Canada and the U.S. still had not reached agreement.

With the signing of the Smithsonian Accord (hailed perhaps prematurely by President Nixon as "the most significant monetary agreement in the history of the world"), the extreme uncertainties of the preceding months were partially eased, frictions between the U.S. and its major financial and trading partners were reduced (although certainly not eliminated), and a major objective of the NEP—devaluation of the dollar through a realignment of exchange rates—was accomplished. The longer-range issues of trade liberalization and international monetary reform, however, remained to be resolved.

The new pattern of exchange rates negotiated in the Smithsonian Accord was expected over time to improve substantially the U.S. balance-of-payments position by slowing the growth in imports, strengthening exports, and boosting investment and tourism in the U.S. In the short run, however, the trade balance continued to deteriorate; merchandise imports exceeded exports by a record $3.3 billion in the first six months of 1972, compared with $1.6 billion in the previous six months. This widening trade deficit strengthened protectionist sentiment in the domestic arena. For example, the Burke-Hartke bill, a highly protectionist measure that would place a ceiling on almost all imports, received wide support

---

* The required Par Value Modification Act was signed into law on April 3, 1972.

from a number of quarters. This was particularly true in the case of organized labor, until recent years a strong proponent of free trade.

The fragile nature of the Smithsonian Accord was made clear on June 23, 1972 when the British reacted to intense speculation against the pound by discontinuing support of the pound at the rate agreed upon in December, and allowing it instead to find its own level on the open market.

Although the other Smithsonian rates and the recently achieved EEC monetary accord survived the British crisis, it did produce a new round of currency restrictions and fueled fears of an additional dollar devaluation. It also emphasized the urgency of resolving the details of the appropriate forum for further international monetary negotiations (which had been under discussion in the first half of 1972) and the critical need to get on with the myriad substantive issues for negotiation. This will undoubtedly take a number of years, but developments in the survey year 1971–72 were crucial in forcing a worldwide recognition of the necessity of building a workable international monetary system that will contribute to world economic growth, promote stability in exchange markets, and provide greater freedom from controls on trade and payments.

The People Speak

Prices are impossible. If things keep getting worse, we won't be able to eat at all ten years from now.
    an oil-field worker in Indiana

The wage freeze is a big fix: good for people who have money but bad for people who don't.
    a black electrician in rural Mississippi

I hope the dollar will get its muscle back; its value is still dropping.
    a black construction worker in Virginia

There ought to be some way to limit welfare. People should earn their own way. As long as we pay them to have children they will go right on having them. I believe after one child they should be fixed so they can't have any more until they can support them.
    a Baltimore housewife

*One good thing that has happened is food stamps. People who
need help until they can get on their feet are being helped.*
        a black housewife in Florida

The devaluation of the dollar hurt us economically.
        a manufacturer of pharmaceuticals in a Michigan city

*Levying duties on imports is a very good thing. It gives American
manufacturers more security and calls for better quality in
American and imported products.*
        a university student in the South

*They're talking about cutting down on relief. This is my biggest
worry. I don't see how poor people can manage if they cut
down the relief.*
        an unemployed white woman in a large western city

*I think anybody who wants to make a living for himself has
that chance. Our problem is those who don't want to.*
        the wife of a fireman in a small Maine town

A Harris Survey released at the end of January 1972 reported
that "after a sustained and extended period of deep pessimism,
there are now signs the American people feel the country may
be on the road to economic recovery." Two-thirds of the public
had felt in the spring of 1971 that "the country is in a recession
today," but by the beginning of the new year less than a majority
(49 percent) believed the recession was continuing. The release
went on to say that "for the first time in over a year, the number
of persons who say they feel that prices are rising more rapidly
than 12 months before has also dropped below the 50 percent
mark." Correspondingly, the proportion believing that unemployment in their immediate vicinity was still increasing diminished
even more—from a high of 70 percent in July 1971 to 43 percent
at the beginning of the new year.

    In late August 1972 another Harris Survey reported that those
who felt the recession was still under way (41 percent) were
slightly overshadowed by those who felt it was not (43 percent).
And the number who believed unemployment in their area was
still on the upswing had dropped to 35 percent. But the attitude
on price increases had turned around and was on the move again

—60 percent believed prices were rising more rapidly than a year earlier.

In our June survey, we wanted to go beyond the American people's assessments of the current situation to determine what the people thought of the dramatic economic moves that had been made over the past year and how they would deal with some of the economic problems still facing the nation. To do so, we asked a battery of questions, ranging over such topics as inflation, wage and price controls, welfare, and international trade.

INFLATION

In the ranking of public concern about various problems, "rising prices and the cost of living" appeared at the very top of the list. (See Table 1.) Inflation not only affects every American in one way or another, but, unlike some of the more abstruse aspects of economics, rising prices are visible to all as people do their daily shopping.

Statistics released by the Nixon administration in mid-1972 showed that, at least for the time being, significant progress had been made in slowing down the rate of inflation. In terms of direct impact on the public, however, statistics are one thing and price tags in the supermarket another. In our survey the public, judging the matter personally, we believe, clearly expressed discouragement about inflationary trends. Replies to a question about progress over the past year in handling "rising prices and the cost of living" came out like this:

Made much progress	3 percent
Made some progress	20
Stood still	17
Lost some ground	36
Lost much ground	22
Don't know	2
	100 percent

Almost six out of ten respondents thought the country had lost either "some" or "much" ground in controlling inflation during the preceding year. As a result, the overall composite score * on

* The method by which composite scores are calculated is explained in Appendix 5.

this question came out at a low 36 (with "made much progress" at 100 and "lost much ground" at zero).

The ratings among population subgroups were quite uniform. (See Table A-13.) Women, with more daily exposure to price tags, were more negative than men. On the other hand, suburbanites, those with annual incomes of $7,000 to $9,999, and Republicans took a slightly more favorable view than did the public as a whole. But the general mood was definitely pessimistic—a judgment perhaps not fully in accord with official statistics, but nevertheless widely held.

WAGE AND PRICE CONTROLS

In February 1972 another Harris Survey reported that a majority of the public believed that the basic policies of both the Pay Board and the Price Commission were fair and reasonable. By June, however, the Harris Survey reported that almost one-half of the public (including 44 percent of the labor union members) were of the opinion that there had been "too many pay increases," and almost six out of ten said there had been "too many price increases."

In our own survey, conducted at about the same time, one-half of the respondents (51 percent) thought that "the way the Pay Board has been controlling wages in recent months" had not been "fair and just." And, in the case of the Price Commission, this unfavorable judgment was shared by only a shade less than six out of ten (59 percent). There were, however, differences of view as to whether wage controls and price controls should be made more strict, less strict, or kept about as they are. The answers we received were:

	Wage Controls	Price Controls
	(in percentages)	
Kept as they are	36	24
More strict	30	55
Less strict	21	14
Don't know	13	7
	100	100

The results show an interesting ambivalence in the public mood: although a majority was in favor of cracking down on price increases, opinions on the subject of wage controls scattered on each side of the preponderant "keep them as they are" view.

UNEMPLOYMENT

The public's evaluation of progress in "handling the problem of unemployment" was somewhat less pessimistic than on inflation: the composite score was 45, as compared to the controlling-inflation score of 36. This was still below the "stood still" point of 50, however, indicating a prevailing opinion that ground had been lost in dealing with unemployment during the survey year. The answers to our question on unemployment were:

Made much progress	1	percent
Made some progress	27	
Stood still	30	
Lost some ground	24	
Lost much ground	12	
Don't know	6	
	100	percent

More sanguine views than average prevailed among southerners; people living in small cities, towns, and rural areas; and Republicans. (See Table A-13.) Not unexpectedly, some of the most critical evaluations came from groups that are among the first to be affected by any worsening of the unemployment problem: labor union households, residents of our largest metropolitan areas, and black Americans.

In assessing the impact of this issue, however, it must be borne in mind that unemployment is not a matter of top concern to the public as a whole. In the ranking of concerns in Table 1, it is evident that people generally were very much less worried about unemployment rates than price levels. In fact, unemployment was well down toward the middle of the list, below such current preoccupations as air and water pollution and consumer protection. The reason for this probably lies in an easily overlooked fact: if less than 6 percent of the working force is not employed, more than 94 percent is. In numerical terms, those with jobs in June 1972 numbered 82.6 million; those without, only 5.4 million. Furthermore, to most Americans, a large proportion of the unemployed are out of sight and therefore out of mind

—blacks and other disadvantaged minorities hidden away in the ghettos of inner cities, on prairie reservations, and the like. It may be unfortunate, but for both of these reasons unemployment for the great mass of Americans is more a matter of numbers than a deeply felt personal concern.

Such impersonal realities notwithstanding, almost half the public favored augmenting programs "to provide government-paid jobs for the unemployed." Asked whether the amount of tax money now being spent for these purposes should be increased, kept at the present level, reduced, or ended altogether, Americans answered:

Increased	48 percent
Kept at present level	31
Reduced	10
Ended altogether	5
Don't know	6
	100 percent

Although overall concern about unemployment was not great, the American people seemed to acknowledge a social obligation to those who are out of luck because they are out of work.

The composite scores on this question reveal a decided class alignment, with lower socio-economic groups strongly in favor of increased spending; the upper groups, only mildly so. (See Table A-7.) Apart from black Americans, who probably know better as a group than any other what it means to be unemployed, the scores farthest above the norm of 67 were to be found among young people and those few who classified themselves as very liberal. The lowest score of all was among Republicans—a 54, indicating predominant sentiment in favor of holding the line on spending to help the unemployed.

POVERTY AND WELFARE PROGRAMS

What constitutes poverty is, to be sure, a relative matter. In a good many economically underdeveloped countries in Latin America, Africa, and Asia, the average per capita income hovers around $100 per year. In the United States, any nonfarm family of four without an annual income in current spending power of at least $4,137 a year is officially poor. The Census Bureau reported in mid-1972 that 25.6 million Americans, some 12 percent of our population, were poor. One-third of the nation's 23 million blacks were in this category, representing just less than three out of ten of the total number below the poverty line. More than seven out of ten of the poor were white.

As America has grown more affluent, its citizens have accepted a steadily enlarged sense of obligation to the poor. But poverty is hard to overcome for those in its grip economically, socially, and psychologically. In a country such as India, the degradation of poverty may seem relatively less severe, simply because it is so widespread. In the United States, poverty is especially degrading because the vast majority of the compatriots of the poor are not poor, and poverty closes off the social mobility that is an imperative of the American dream. If you are poor in our society, you are at the very bottom; and, under today's conditions, with good jobs requiring education and skills for advancement, you are apt to stay there, often generation after generation. Unlike the situation in most countries of the Third World, there is enough to go around in America: but when it comes to dividing the pie, the poor are put at the end of a very long table.

The public is not altogether sympathetic in this matter. In accordance with a deep-seated and long-enduring American myth, many Americans equate poverty with shiftlessness or downright laziness and show a combination of disdain and lack of understanding for the root causes of need in a land of plenty. Underlying this pervasive prejudice is a cherished Puritan ethic: if one believes that virtue is rewarded in material ways, poverty becomes evidence of waywardness.

In keeping with this cultural vestige, studies conducted by the Institute for International Social Research in 1964 revealed that when a national cross section of Americans was asked "Which is generally more often to blame if a person is poor—lack of effort on his part, or circumstances beyond his control?" only one-quarter chose the "circumstances beyond his control" alternative. Three-quarters pointed either to lack of effort, or a combination of lack of effort and circumstances—both of which, of course, placed the stigma of blame on the poor for their own condition. In the same study, three-quarters of the public expressed the conviction that in general "any able-bodied person who really wants to work in this country can find a job and earn a living," (overlooking the fact that most of the physically able unemployed want to work but are unable to find jobs, either because of general economic conditions or lack of education, training, and skills). Holding this view, then, it was not surprising that two-thirds of the public in this Institute study accepted the old bromide that "the relief rolls are loaded with chiselers and people who just don't want to work." *

This background may help to explain some of the results of our present survey. To start with, our respondents showed a decent but still restrained concern about "reducing poverty in this country." The composite score of 77 on this item put it in twelfth place in our listing of public concurs, halfway down the list and, appropriately, at the same level as unemployment. (See Table 1.)

When asked about progress in handling poverty and welfare programs during the preceding year, the public responded:

Made much progress	3	percent
Made some progress	31	
Stood still	26	
Lost some ground	22	
Lost much ground	11	
Don't know	7	
	100	percent

The composite score on this question was 48, just below the "stood still" point of 50. (See Table A-13 for demographic breakdowns.) Even this response may have been more optimistic than the facts warranted: almost 15 million Americans were on one or another relief roll at the time of our survey.

When it came to further assistance from the government treasury to the poor, the general attitude was to hold the line. Asked whether federal spending on "welfare programs to help low-income families" should be increased, kept at the present level, reduced, or ended altogether, our respondents replied:

Increased	30	percent
Kept at present level	41	
Reduced	18	
Ended altogether	6	
Don't know	5	
	100	percent

* This study is described in Lloyd A. Free and Hadley Cantril's *The Political Beliefs of Americans.*

To be sure, slightly more than seven out of ten members of the public were at least in favor of maintaining the present level of spending on welfare, not a signal to the poor that their more fortunate countrymen want to put an end to this particular demand on the public purse. But, in larger perspective, the composite score on this question was only 53, the lowest spending score on any of the twenty domestic items covered, with the exception of the space program (if that can be considered a domestic program).

The demographic lineup on this issue followed the liberal-conservative orientations evident in the replies to so many other questions. (See Table A-7.) More generous attitudes toward the poor were evident among young people, those with low income and little education, city dwellers, Democrats, liberals, and especially black Americans. The more hard-nosed groups included families with annual incomes over $10,000, professional and business people, those thirty to forty-nine years old, respondents who classified themselves either as suburbanites or ruralites, and especially the self-designated moderately conservative and Republicans, who registered the lowest composite scores of all groups (42 and 43, respectively).

Welfare spending, then, can hardly be said to have evoked wide public enthusiasm. Yet there was general agreement that some governmental system for aiding the poor had to be continued. But what kind? To find out, we asked:

Let's turn now to the problem of poverty. Suppose you had a chance to choose between the alternatives on this card, which one do you think would be the best way to handle the problem of families with little or no income?

A. For state and local governments to continue their present system of welfare payments, with the federal government chipping in a good part of the tax money required.   37 percent

B. For the federal government in Washington to guarantee every family a certain minimum income even if one or more of its members are working for very low wages, with the government making up any shortage in family income out of federal tax money.   42

C. *For welfare payments to needy families to be
stopped, leaving the problem of poverty to
be taken care of by private charities.*   9
Don't know   12
                                                    ─────────────
                                                    100 percent

Less than one respondent in ten felt that welfare payments should be stopped entirely. The rest were fairly evenly divided between the present welfare system and the concept of a guaranteed minimum income. Support for the present system was stronger than average among such generally traditionalist groups as older people, the nonlabor force (made up mostly of retired people), white collar workers, those who called themselves moderately conservative, and Republicans. Joining them were Catholics and people living in the Midwest and, especially, the Far West. Support for the alternative of a guaranteed minimum income plan was above the norm among such liberally oriented groups as the college-educated; families with incomes above $15,000 per year; the professional and business group; easterners; residents of our largest metropolitan areas; Democrats; the handful of respondents who classified themselves as very liberal; black Americans; and particularly young people, of whom six out of ten opted for a guaranteed minimum income solution to the poverty problem.

In a special survey commissioned by Potomac Associates, two questions that go beyond our findings were put to a cross section of almost 1,600 individuals by The Gallup Organization in mid-June 1972. One question was:

What is the minimum income, if any, you think the government should assure a family of four to live on—either through cash payments or jobs?

No income should be assured by the government	15 percent
$30 a week or $1,600 a year	2
$50 a week or $2,600 a year	5
$60 a week or $3,200 a year	13
$100 a week or $5,200 a year	25
$125 a week or $6,700 a year	14
Over $125 a week or $6,700 a year	12
Don't know	14
	100 percent

A most amazing finding emerged: if a guaranteed income plan were to be adopted, slightly more than one-half (51 percent) of the public thought that the amount the government should assure a family of four should be at least $100 a week or $5,200 per year—a surprisingly liberal figure, and more than twice the annual level of $2,400 advocated by the Nixon administration.

But this mood of generosity was at the same time tempered by strong support for requiring able-bodied welfare recipients to go to work. Another question in Potomac Associates' special survey was: *Suppose it were to cost the government less money to give poor people a cash payment than it would to have the government train them, and find them a job, and, where necessary, provide care for their children while they are at work, would you prefer the less expensive system of giving them money and not requiring them to work or the more expensive system of getting them to work?*

Less expensive system	9	percent
More expensive system	81	
Don't know	10	
	100	percent

The chief reasons given for preferring the more expensive system were that "working is better for the recipient," along with the flat statement of principle that "able-bodied people should work." But whatever the underlying motivation, the public definitely wanted to put welfare recipients to work, even if it definitely cost more money to do so.

At the present time, by far the largest proportion of able-bodied welfare recipients who are not working are mothers of families receiving welfare. In our survey, a majority of respondents thought that even such mothers should be required to take jobs on penalty of losing their relief benefits. We asked: *Should mothers with school-aged children in families receiving welfare be required to take any job offered them, or should they be allowed to turn down a job and still keep their welfare payments?*

Be required to take jobs	53	percent
Turn down job, keep welfare	36	
Don't know	11	
	100	percent

Almost six out of ten Protestants thought that welfare mothers should be required to take jobs (influenced, one might conjecture, by the Protestant work ethic). Most surprisingly, they were joined by almost six out of ten of those in the very lowest educational and income categories. The chief deviations from the majority view were among professional and business people and Catholics, who by slight margins thought that welfare mothers should be allowed to turn down jobs without losing welfare benefits, and among blacks, who were of this opinion by a much larger margin.

INTERNATIONAL ECONOMIC AFFAIRS

Growing competition from international markets, balance-of-payments deficits, concern about loss of jobs here at home—these and other factors have led to considerable pressures in Congress and elsewhere for some kind of protectionist legislation. In an effort to plumb the depth of this mood, we asked: *Turning now to the question of foreign trade, do you think the U.S. should cut down on certain kinds of imports from foreign countries, or do you feel we should follow the principles of free trade?*

Cut down on imports	43 percent
Support free trade	50
Don't know	7
	100 percent

Protectionist sentiment reached or exceeded the one-half mark among the following groups: the $10,000–$14,999 income category; labor union households (who tend to be very conscious of the "save our jobs" theme); middle-of-the-roaders; and people living in small cities, towns, and rural areas. Far-below-average support for a cut in imports, on the other hand, was found among: white collar workers, those living in the largest metropolitan areas, westerners, black Americans, and especially those few respondents who considered themselves very liberal. Most significant of all were the view of the professional and business group: 39 percent favored cutting imports on a selective basis, but a substantial majority (56 percent) opted for the principles of free trade.

Free trade opinion thus prevailed, but by a narrow margin. More importantly, however, the public's reserved, but still basically positive, assessment of the domestic economic situation did not extend beyond our shores. Asked how the U.S. had fared during the preceding year in "handling economic matters in the international field, such as balance-of-payments and foreign trade problems," Americans answered:

Made much progress	1	percent
Made some progress	21	
Stood still	24	
Lost some ground	24	
Lost much ground	6	
Don't know	24	
	100	percent

The composite score was 46 on this question—below the "stood still" point of 50, and indicating a predominant opinion that the country had actually lost a little ground. This pessimistic view was particularly strong among big-city dwellers, the college-educated, and the well-to-do. (See Table A-11.) The latter two groups tend to be conversant with international economics and, therefore, particularly prone to drawing a negative conclusion from the record of the past year.

ECONOMIC AND BUSINESS CONDITIONS GENERALLY

While views about progress were predominantly unfavorable on the subjects of poverty, unemployment, and particularly inflation, the public nevertheless felt that the general domestic economic picture was not at all bad. When asked about progress over the past year at home in "economic and business conditions generally —that is, the overall prosperity of the country," respondents lined up as follows:

Made much progress	4	percent
Made some progress	42	
Stood still	24	
Lost some ground	17	
Lost much ground	5	
Don't know	8	
	100	percent

The composite score was a modest 56, showing not real enthusiasm but rather a restrained optimism that at least some slight progress had been made.

The least sanguine elements of the population were the very poor, people living in the East and in our largest cities, black Americans, labor union households, and the "very liberal." (See Table A-13.) Unusually ebullient, on the other hand, was a clustering of generally conservative groups: southerners, residents of small communities, self-designated conservatives, and Republicans.

In sum, then, the public appeared to have reached a mixed conclusion. At least some ground had been lost in coping with unemployment, poverty, and especially inflation. On balance, however, Americans thought that the general prosperity of the country had improved over the preceding year. Despite severe problems for some (and inflation for all), the great majority of Americans were just not hurting that much: economically speaking, they judged the twelve months from mid-1971 to mid-1972 as not a bad year.

X.
International Affairs

Our talks with China and Russia have eased the cold war. I feel the
Vietnam crunch is going to break for the good. The Middle
East is calmer.
     an accountant in the Midwest

I don't like the way things have been going: the naval blockade
and bombing of North Vietnam; American support of dictatorship
in West Pakistan; continued American investment in South Africa.
     a black student at Wayne State University in Detroit

I approved of the president's visit to China and the summit meeting
in Russia. It's like people shaking hands and becoming friends.
     a black auditor in Philadelphia

We're involved too much with the rest of the world and not thinking
of our own people. We've got our nose in everybody else's
business and don't take care of our own.
     a salesman in the South

The Record Speaks

In his third annual report to Congress on United States foreign
policy, *U.S. Foreign Policy for the 1970s,* President Nixon
described 1971 as "the watershed year" in the efforts of this
administration to reshape American diplomacy to the realities
of a new era. The description appears equally, if not more,
appropriate when applied to the twelve-month period reviewed
in these pages. Beginning just before the dramatic announcement

of the president's impending visit to Peking and ending just after the Moscow summit conference, the year extending from July 1971 through June 1972 was marked by a series of diplomatic initiatives and exercises in summitry that have no parallel in the years since the late 1940s. Only time will disclose the full scope of the change in America's world role reflected by the events of the preceding year. That the nation's role has changed, both in relation to its adversaries and to its allies, seems beyond dispute.

THE SOVIET UNION

Given the paramount importance attached by the president to developing a "new relationship" with the Soviet Union, the Moscow summit conference of late May stands out as the principal event of the year. The announcement of the meeting on October 12, 1971 followed a period of almost three years during which Soviet-American relations had oscillated from modest, though promising, beginnings in 1969 to a period of rising tensions in the fall of 1970, occasioned by the Middle East crisis, continuation of the Vietnam War, the ups and downs of the negotiations on strategic arms limitations and Berlin, and the apparent Soviet attempt to develop a submarine base in Cuba. But 1971 found some progress in the relations of the two superpowers. In May, the stalemate that had developed in the talks on limiting strategic arms was broken by the direct intercession of the White House. In September, agreement was reached on measures for reducing the prospect that Berlin would once again become the focus of a dangerous confrontation. In November, the U.S. Secretary of Commerce undertook conversations in Moscow with the goal of normalizing economic relations between the two countries.

These and other signs pointing to improved Soviet-American relations had to be balanced against developments that indicated a continuing competition and rivalry. The ambivalence with which the Nixon administration viewed Soviet foreign policy in early 1972 found striking expression, not without domestic political overtones to be sure, in the president's annual report to Congress. Noting the improvement in relations with the Soviet Union in 1971, the president declared that it nevertheless remained "unclear whether we are now witnessing a permanent change in Soviet policy or only a passing phase concerned more with tactics than with a fundamental commitment to a stable international system. Soviet weapons development and deployment activity, Soviet arms policy in the Middle East, Soviet behavior during the India-Pakistan crisis and the expansionist implications of Soviet naval activities, all raise serious questions."

Ironically, in retrospect, the president neglected to note the one Soviet activity that more than any other was subsequently to endanger the gradual improvement in relations preceding the Moscow summit—the greatly stepped-up supply of heavy weapons to North Vietnam. In equipping Hanoi with the means to launch a large conventional offensive against South Vietnam in April 1972, the Soviet Union set in motion a course of events that led—however unwittingly—to an American response that for a brief period threatened to escalate to a major confrontation between the superpowers on the eve of the summit meeting. That the mining of North Vietnam's coasts and ports, together with the intensified bombing of the North, did not (despite evidence of heated internal debate) lead the Russians to react sharply by calling off the conference was indicative of the very considerable interests at stake for the Soviet leadership in promoting a growing détente with America and Western Europe generally. And the Kremlin apparently concluded that a Soviet-American confrontation over the blockade held little promise of a Soviet victory.

The very fact that the Moscow summit was held at all, then, may prove at least as significant as the more tangible results of the meeting. The agreements on limiting strategic arms apart, the importance of the other agreements reached at the conference —on measures to prevent incidents at sea, cooperation in science and technology, peaceful exploration of outer space, health, and protection and enhancement of man's environment—may lie in their symbolism and potential (without in any sense denying their immediate intrinsic value).

If the prospects for a more constructive relationship were to be judged by the declaration of principles with which the Soviet and American leaders concluded their talks, as well as by the atmosphere in which the talks were conducted, the Moscow summit could logically be regarded as an historic turning point. Although the conference marked little if any progress in resolving conflicts of interest in the Middle East and Vietnam, there was evidence of a determination not to permit these divisive issues to forestall efforts toward achieving a generally more stable and constructive relationship. For the Soviet Union, immediate incentives were contained in the joint communiqué ending the summit—particularly in the promise of a European security conference and negotiations leading to a trade agreement.

A broadening détente between the United States and the Soviet Union, if it were to follow, would probably result as much from the constraints operating on the two parties as from positive incentives. For both sides, these constraints are partly domestic and partly international in character (and the domestic factors should not be underrated in either instance). The most important of the external considerations for the Soviet leaders, American power apart, is the conflict with China. That conflict, together with the initial steps toward American-Chinese rapprochement, clearly provided one compelling reason for the Russians to proceed with the summit conference despite the American challenge in the waters of North Vietnam. (Another, almost certainly, was the Soviet desire not to disturb the delicate progress in Bonn at that very moment toward ratification of the Soviet-German treaty.) The same conflict, and a continuing American-Chinese rapprochement, may be expected to moderate future Soviet relations with the United States.

CHINA

It was the emergence of the triangular relationship involving America, the Soviet Union, and China that, in retrospect, may well appear as the most significant development of the year. Slow to acknowledge the fact of Soviet-Chinese rivalry in the early 1960s, American policy was reluctant in the later 1960s to exploit any advantages that might have accrued from this rivalry. A seemingly implacable hostility resulting from the years of the Korean War, a persistent exaggeration of Chinese power and aggressiveness, and the coincidence of the Vietnam War with the cultural revolution in China together prompted an American policy during the 1960s that diminished the constraint China might have represented to the Soviet Union. It also delayed the emergence of a new power constellation in Asia that, in time, would pose the alternative of the United States playing a substantially reduced role in that region.

Although not generally recognized at the time, the announcement of the Nixon Doctrine in 1969 made easier the dramatic shift confirmed two years later in American policy toward China. For the logic of the Nixon Doctrine as applied to East and Southeast Asia required, if not a cooperative, then at least a competitive-cooperative relationship with China. Without this relationship, U.S. retrenchment in Asia would run the risks of tempting the Russians to expand their influence at Chinese and American expense, possibly forcing military confrontation with either the U.S. or China, and of impelling Japan to embark on an independent, and possibly militant, policy of her own.

The announcement of the president's prospective trip to Peking, made July 15, 1971, had an impact, domestic and international, almost without parallel in the past generation. Observers immediately discerned the advantages China derived from the dramatic move. Quite apart from enhancing Chairman Mao Tsetung's prestige and virtually guaranteeing China's entrance into the United Nations, the visit to Peking of an American president was bound to introduce an element of uncertainty and restraint in Soviet policy toward China. On the American side, the principal results hoped for were, as already noted, to induce China to accept a more cooperative relationship, particularly in Southeast Asia, to push the Russians faster and further along the road to détente, and to throw Hanoi (apparently with considerable success) into disarray.

Almost inevitably, the February 1972 trip to Peking was followed by widespread skepticism over what it had accomplished. Critics were ready to acknowledge that the "China Show" strengthened the domestic position of Chou En-lai and, in an election year in this country, scarcely hurt the image of President Nixon as a daring "peace" statesman. Although the final communiqué made clear that the parties were unable to reach agreement on any of the specific issues dividing them in the past, it also indicated that they were intent upon establishing a new relationship despite persisting conflicts of interest. And this, in turn, might eventually permit the two governments to view their long-standing conflicts in a new and more promising light.

The importance of the interests leading to an improved relationship with the United States was reflected in Peking's (as in Moscow's) surprisingly mild response to the closing of North Vietnam's ports and to the intensified American bombing of North Vietnam beginning officially in May 1972. There remained, to be sure, considerable room for doubt that either China or the Soviet Union was prepared to abandon North Vietnam, even if continued support for Hanoi threatened to impair the relationship each of the two great communist powers was developing with the United States.

INDOCHINA

The continuing American involvement in the Vietnam conflict remained, therefore, a critical factor in the evolution of the new triangular relationship involving the United States, the Soviet Union, and China. Indeed, the strong measures against North Vietnam initiated by President Nixon on May 8 may have been undertaken in part, in the administration's eyes, as the necessary precondition to serious negotiations leading to a genuine compromise settlement. For both Washington and Hanoi there were strong incentives to strive for such a settlement. Despite the apparent effectiveness of both the American blockade and the bombing of North Vietnam, the course of the fighting in the South had shown that truly successful "Vietnamization" remained a distant and elusive objective. Moreover, although the nearly complete disengagement of American ground forces from South Vietnam (27,000 support troops were scheduled to remain by December 1, 1972) had gone far toward muting the sharper edges of domestic opposition to the war, the depth of public antipathy was beyond dispute. The prospect in an election year of an indefinite American involvement, if only in the form of air and naval support, could scarcely appear an attractive one to the administration, particularly to the degree such continued involvement impeded progress on the grand design that promised, in President Nixon's words, "a generation of peace."

The incentives for Hanoi to compromise its objectives were no less apparent. The successes of the spring offensive in the South—the capture of the northern provincial capital of Quangtri and much of the surrounding territory south of the demilitarized zone, accompanied by an initial rout of South Vietnamese forces—had been obtained only at very considerable cost. And they were not immediately followed by the taking of what most observers assumed was a second round of objectives—An Loc, Kontum, Hue, and other sites. Although the offensive in its early stages indicated that the South Vietnamese could not stand alone, it had also shown that American air and naval power could stave off defeat in the South while imposing severe punishment upon the North. The American riposte to Hanoi's offensive not only failed to prompt a strong response in turn from North Vietnam's major allies but also indicated the limits beyond which the Soviet Union and China appeared very reluctant to go in their support. Moreover, should the North Vietnamese leadership foresee a Nixon re-election victory, it could well decide that prospects for improved terms on or off the battlefield would be even less likely after November 1972 than before.

The president on May 8 offered to withdraw all American forces from Vietnam within four months following an international ceasefire and the release of American prisoners of war. This offer did not respond to the North Vietnamese position, however, that any ceasefire was unacceptable so long as it did not at the same time provide for a coalition government in which communist and neutralist forces would share power with Saigon and from which South Vietnamese President Nguyen Van Thieu would be excluded. Whatever the validity of the charges and countercharges by all parties concerned (as well as their supporters and critics), at the root of the stalemate in the negotiations over the past year lay, as always, profound mutual distrust, diametrically opposed objectives over future leadership in South Vietnam, and a persistent expectation on both sides that time was working to their respective advantage—factors working very much against the incentives for settlement described above.

JAPAN AND WESTERN EUROPE

While a compromise settlement of the war in Vietnam would remove the chief immediate liability of the Nixon foreign policy, it would not alleviate the rising unease of many observers over other aspects of the president's effort to effect a transformation in America's world role. Particularly with respect to relations with the nation's major allies, there was widespread concern that the initiatives of the preceding year might seriously loosen the close bonds developed since World War II, while failing to substitute a viable alternative. In part, this concern arose from what was perceived as the administration's singular concentration on developing the triangular relationship with the Soviet Union and China and the methods by which it sought to develop this relationship. In part, this concern also arose from what was perceived as a new penchant for sudden and unilateral action by America in dealing with its allies and, more generally, from a disposition to view allied relationships in a competitive, as well as cooperative, light. The announcement on July 15, 1971 of the president's impending trip to Peking was seen as an example of the former; the announcement on August 15, 1971 suspending convertibility of the dollar into gold and imposing a temporary 10 percent surcharge on dutiable imports was seen as an example of the latter.

In the case of Japan, the effects of these unilateral moves—and, above all, the rapprochement with China—continued to be a matter of speculation and controversy almost a year later. For two decades Japanese policy toward China had followed the United States lead, despite the growing Japanese conviction in recent years that closer relations with China were vital to Japan. The impression could not but form that the United States either had downgraded the significance of the alliance with Japan or, more plausibly, was persuaded that the price to be paid for secrecy and abruptness would prove transitory, presumably because the Japanese had neither the will nor the incentive to alter their relationship with America substantially.

In some measure, the shock dealt to Japan was subsequently softened by the restoration of Okinawa to Japanese control in the spring of 1972, by the admission in June of Dr. Henry A. Kissinger, the president's assistant for national security affairs, that the failure to consult and to inform the Japanese prior to the July 15 move had been a mistake that would not be repeated, and by the August summit meeting in Hawaii between President Nixon and the new Japanese premier Kakuei Tanaka. But by late summer 1972, the damage done to American-Japanese relations had by no means been fully repaired.

In Western Europe as well, the credibility of the American security commitment was viewed with increasing skepticism. In part, this skepticism was the almost inevitable result of the fact that the Soviet Union had achieved nuclear equality with the United States—an equality explicitly acknowledged by the president at the Moscow summit meeting. In part, it was the result of the quite pervasive expectation that in the post-Vietnam period domestic pressures would be very great on any administration to withdraw the bulk of American forces in Europe—a withdrawal that could only reinforce doubts as to whether in the extreme situation America would be willing to sacrifice itself for Europe. In part, finally, unease over the American commitment to Western Europe was the result of juxtaposing the emerging elements of competition and rivalry in the economic relations of the Atlantic states with the emerging pattern of direct Soviet-American negotiation and accommodation.

Did the measures taken over the past year affecting the nation's major allies point, as the president stated in his 1972 report to Congress, toward a "more mature political partnership" that permitted the pursuit of "autonomous policies within a common framework of strategic goals?" Were they designed to bring into being a world of five major units—the United States, the Soviet Union, China, Western Europe, and Japan—and one in which a "stable structure of relationships" would, by replacing the old bipolar world of containment and confrontation, permit the United States a substantial measure of retrenchment, flexibility, and self-restraint? Or were they designed instead to foster, as many critics warned, a triangular world—the contours of which would be designed by this country and the two large communist powers, and to which Western Europe and Japan, now presumably downgraded in the nation's scale of interests, would be forced to adapt? And if it is a triangular world toward which the present policies were working, would not such a world require us either to maintain indefinitely our military superiority over Western Europe and Japan, or risk—through the eventual defection of our allies—the disintegration of the alliance system, with unforeseen consequences to the world power balance? These were the underlying and more far-reaching questions around which controversy over American foreign policy promised in large measure to turn in the immediate future.

THE MIDDLE EAST

In another area of major and continuing American interest—the Middle East—U.S. policy found itself effectively restrained over the past year by larger events elsewhere. A number of developments in that corner of the world, important as they were, did not impinge directly on U.S. actions and therefore fall outside the scope of this review.

The Arab-Israeli conflict, so much at the center of the world stage in the aftermath of the 1967 six-day war and the subsequent efforts to bring about some kind of lasting settlement in the area, assumed a generally quieter and less menacing stance in our survey year.

In particular, the last half of 1971 saw the final playing out of earlier diplomatic initiatives, the most significant of which had been proposals put forth by Secretary of State William P. Rogers in August 1970 looking toward a ceasefire, a full opening of the Suez Canal, and a partial Israeli withdrawal from occupied territories. These efforts simply ran out of steam by the end of the year.

This lull in U.S. policy extended into the first half of 1972 as well, as attention became riveted on the two forthcoming summit meetings. Finally, in July 1972, the U.S. suddenly found itself presented with a new challenge and uncertain opportunity when the Egyptians expelled the bulk of their Soviet advisers. U.S. caution over how to react to this unexpected turn of events was compounded, as usual in a presidential election year, by domestic political considerations (imagined or real) of how best to move while keeping in mind that segment of the public always keenly interested in any developments concerning Israel.

THE THIRD WORLD

In contrast to the attention and care given relations with the major communist powers, relations with the developing states continued to have the low priority during the past year that they have had during the entire tenure of the current administration, as well, to be sure, as of its predecessor. In part, the subordinate position to which the Third World has been relegated may be attributed to the marked penchant of the Nixon administration for a return to a more traditional and hierarchical world, in which, it is assumed, our larger interests lie outside the Third World. In part, however, the demotion of the developing states may simply be seen as a reaction to the inflated expectations and subsequent frustrations of the 1960s, a reaction given added force by the realization that the developing states have shown themselves much less vulnerable to external influence and control than previously thought.

Thus, a view that was deemed heretical a decade ago—that the Third World is not a decisive arena of international politics and shows little prospect of becoming so—appeared to have become near orthodoxy. In consequence, the leverage formerly enjoyed by the developing states suffered a marked decline, as witnessed by the general abandonment of the policy of economic appeasement to win political friends. Although the change was apparent everywhere, it was perhaps most notable in the nation's relations with the states of Latin America. An almost consistently negative assessment of the Alliance for Progress experiment appeared to have prompted the conclusion that what could not be done to develop these states through indigenous efforts and foreign private investment probably could not be done at all.

Thus, in January 1972 the president announced that the United States would no longer extend "bilateral economic benefits" to any country undertaking expropriation that did not make provision for some compensation. Primarily a reaction against the nationalization measures of the Chilean government, the president's policy was intended as a warning to other Latin American regimes that might be tempted to follow the Chilean example. Indeed, these pressures—exerted not only directly but, equally important, through such agencies as the International Monetary Fund—left no doubt that the administration was intent upon making Chile an object lesson to others in the hemisphere.

Quite apart from the marked coolness with which the government of Salvador Allende in Chile was treated from the outset, the administration was not completely indifferent to change outside the hemisphere that promised to lead either to instability or, above all, to the substantial reduction of American influence. The limits of tolerance toward political change continued to be defined largely by the expected consequences of such change.

The point was best illustrated during the year by the administration's reaction to the crisis between India and Pakistan arising from the attempt of the Pakistan government to suppress the rebellion in East Bengal, a crisis that finally led to war between the two states in November 1971. Rather than preserving a position of neutrality in a conflict in which it could not become substantially involved (given domestic restraints and a residual sense of realism), the administration chose instead to support Pakistan (thus adopting the same stance as China) in the dual hope that India would be deterred from going to war against Pakistan and the Soviet Union would be deterred from supporting India in any such war. In its actions, the administration was clearly prompted by annoyance with India over its behavior during prewar diplomatic efforts, as well, presumably, by a sense of duty to Pakistan, an ally. What was of particular significance here, however, was not the almost wholly abortive and counterproductive character of the administration's effort but the notable reluctance of the administration to accept any diminution of its (or any increase of Soviet) influence on the subcontinent.

THE CONCENTRATION OF POWER IN THE WHITE HOUSE

The drama inherent in so many of the developments in U.S. foreign policy in the year under review was emphasized by the manner in which this policy was formulated and carried out. For many observers, the policy shifts and reversals were made the more startling by being initiated by a president whose earlier career gave little hint he would move in such contradiction to his past record as he did. The president's supporters praised his moves—particularly in regard to China and the Soviet Union—as those of a man with historic vision and a finely developed sense of pragmatism. His critics called them opportunistic and an exercise in showmanship, and a minority labeled them dangerous as well.

The trend toward centralization of the most critical aspects of foreign policy formulation and implementation within the White House, under the day-to-day direction of the president's assistant for national security affairs and his hand-picked staff, continued unabated. The shift in the balance of power away from the rest of the executive branch appeared all but complete. Even the most senior officials in the Departments of State, Defense, and elsewhere found themselves in many cases as surprised as the average citizen when some of the year's most important actions or decisions were announced to an unsuspecting world.

In part, this manner of conducting foreign policy stemmed from a deep-seated concern for secrecy. Premature revelations of major shifts in policy give opponents time to muster their arguments and even torpedo such moves in advance by selective disclosure. Beyond that, the president and many of his closest policy and political advisers believed the domestic impact of such moves as the opening to China, for example, would be heightened by the very shock value inherent in the handling of the announcement.

Whatever the motivation for this particular presidential style, it was clear that the overall benefits that stemmed from the new policy initiatives were purchased at a cost to the nation's foreign policy machinery. Many experienced observers commented on a growing malaise and disillusionment over the steady dilution of the role of the career services, civilian and military, charged with implementing the new decisions emanating from the White House. Particular concern began to be expressed over the departure from the civilian services (the Foreign Service, most of all) of many of their most talented middle-level and even senior officers, at the same time that the sense of purpose among new entrants seemed to fade.

The relative balance between the White House on the one hand and the executive branch on the other was not the only one decisively upset in the course of the survey year. With all the tools at his disposal, the president was also increasingly effective in keeping the legislative branch in a position of apparently permanent uncertainty. Critics of the war in Vietnam found their position regularly undermined by announcements of new troop withdrawals, secret discussions with high-ranking North Vietnamese negotiators, and the like. Furthermore, the inability of Congress to concentrate on specific issues and maintain continuing pressure against the White House on those areas of greatest concern yielded an added advantage to the administration. In almost every instance end-the-war resolutions, for example, were consistently, even easily, turned aside through deft political maneuvering. Congress, and in particular leaders of the key committees, remained reluctant to exert the most persuasive constitutional authority—the power of the purse. Some internal debate and reforms (including action, not completed by late summer 1972, on a war powers bill that would limit the president's freedom of action in the commitment and use of U.S. military forces, and the partial devolution of authority from the chairman of the House Foreign Affairs Committee to some of his younger colleagues) suggested that Congress might seek a more active and meaningful foreign affairs role in the future. Nonetheless, at the end of our survey year few would question that the president, acting primarily through Dr. Kissinger and his staff, remained thoroughly in control of U.S. foreign policy.

The People Speak

It's hard to put into words, but I think the situation is only fair because of the war in Vietnam and the faith a lot of countries are losing in the U.S. because of it.
> a female domestic servant in Chicago

The Russians and Communists are going to sneak up on us; they're infiltrating everything.
> a homemaker in a California suburb

The peace overtures to North Vietnam, China, and Russia have shown the world we aren't warmongers.
> an elderly housewife in New York State

Most of our allies are getting away from us—like because of our dropping the value of the dollar.
> a baker's helper in Florida

Our prestige has been upheld because of our stand on the war and presidential visits. I think most countries appreciate us and think we are doing right.
> a grocery-store manager in a California suburb

We don't have many countries on our side any more.
> a retired auto worker in Detroit

In comparison to international problems, we're not putting enough emphasis on domestic problems.
> a labor representative in New York State

The continued war and spending so much money on it, when the money could be saving lives instead of destroying lives. This country is spending millions of dollars on a war that should have ended years ago.
> a female domestic servant in Chicago

I hope we're not being taken in by China and Russia.
   a black housewife in the South

Almost two-thirds of the public indicated a belief that the U.S., on balance, had made at least some progress on the world scene during the preceding year. (See Chapter I.) The composite score * on this question was 66 (on a scale of 100), four points higher than the rating given for overall domestic progress. To determine in what ways the past year's developments contributed to this generally positive assessment, we asked the American people about progress in various aspects of international life: economic affairs, ties with our allies, Vietnam, and relations with both China and the Soviet Union.

It became evident that developments on the economic front had little to do with the overall feeling of progress. When asked about the country's handling of "economic matters in the international field, such as balance of payments and foreign trade problems," the public's general assessment was that the nation had lost ground. (See Chapter IX.)

Beyond that, the public also showed an awareness of the uneven quality of recent relations with our allies, stemming from such matters as the startling economic moves made to protect our balance-of-payments situation and the rather peremptory manner in which Japan was treated at the time of the president's announcement of his forthcoming trip to Peking. When we asked about progress in "maintaining close relations with our major allies, such as Great Britain, France, West Germany, and Japan," Americans responded:

Made much progress	6	percent
Made some progress	27	
Stood still	40	
Lost some ground	14	
Lost much ground	2	
Don't know	11	
	100	percent

---

* The method by which composite scores are calculated is explained in Appendix 5.

Four out of ten respondents believed that the U.S. had stood still. Negative assessments were particularly prevalent among generally better-informed groups: the college-educated, those earning $15,000 and up, and suburbanites. (See Table A-11.) Since a larger proportion of those less inclined to pay close attention to international affairs opted for "progress," the overall composite score on this question was 56, slightly above the "stood still" point.

VIETNAM

Along with the presidential trips to Peking and Moscow, one of the most dramatic events to the great mass of Americans during the survey year was the renewed bombing of North Vietnam and the mining of its ports in response to the communist offensive in South Vietnam. Before we report on how the American people assessed developments in Vietnam, some preliminary background may be helpful.

During the long history of the Vietnam War, two tendencies—which on the surface appear somewhat in conflict, but which both spring from a desire to see American involvement in Vietnam ended—have characterized American public opinion about the war. The first has been a tendency to endorse proposals for attaining a just and honorable settlement short of capitulation to the communists; the second has been a tendency to approve most of the escalatory military steps taken by U.S. presidents from Kennedy to Nixon. (The 1971 invasion of Laos was one of the few exceptions in the latter respect. The reason this did not get a favorable reception, according to a February 1971 Gallup poll, was that the public believed the move into Laos, in contrast to most other escalatory steps, would lengthen, not shorten, the war.)

A parallel tendency, particularly evident at the time of the Tet offensive in early 1968, has been for the public to respond to communist offensives with feelings of increased belligerency. In the aftermath of Tet, for example, the Institute for International Social Research found that the public became so hawkish that more than one-half favored escalating the war in the South—25 percent by gradually broadening and intensifying U.S. military operations and no less than 28 percent by undertaking an all-out crash effort to win quickly even at the risk of bringing China or

Russia into the war. Six out of ten thought the bombing of North Vietnam, already at a high level, should be intensified as well. (The hawkish sentiment engendered by the Tet offensive proved to be short-lived, however. Four months later the Institute found that the proportion of the public favoring escalation had dropped from more than one-half to one-third, while half of the public had swung to the dovish side, in favor of discontinuing the struggle and pulling out of Vietnam or at least cutting back the American military effort.)

In view of the initial reaction to the Tet offensive, then, it would not seem surprising that widespread approval greeted President Nixon's re-escalation of the war against North Vietnam following the communists' spring 1972 offensive. According to a Harris Survey published in mid-May, six out of ten members of the public endorsed the mining of North Vietnam's ports, surely the most provocative step the U.S. had taken vis-à-vis the Soviet Union in a number of years. This public approbation represented a striking shift in opinion: just six months earlier (November 1971) Harris had found that the dominant mood favored terminating all forms of U.S. military involvement in Vietnam. By a ratio of close to three to one, the public approved "getting completely out of Vietnam" not later than May 1972 (the date, ironically enough, when the president moved to bomb and mine in the North). In the same Harris Survey, a majority of the public indicated that, even if U.S. withdrawal should mean a communist takeover, they were opposed to leaving U.S. troops in Vietnam (even in a noncombatant role) and to continuing the use of U.S. bombers and helicopters to support the South Vietnamese army.

It is clear that, at least in its immediate impact, the 1972 spring offensive accomplished something the communists may not have intended: it renewed the belligerence of the American public. This response is dramatically apparent in answers to a question about ending U.S. involvement in the war, posed first by the Institute for International Social Research in 1968, on a second occasion in the *Hopes and Fears* survey in the spring of 1971, and finally in our current survey. The question:

Suppose the United States were confronted with a choice of only the two alternatives listed on this card, which one would you rather have the United States follow?

A. *End the war by accepting the best possible compromise settlement even though it might sooner or later allow the Vietnamese Communists to take over control of South Vietnam.*

B. *Fight on until a settlement can be reached which will insure that the Communists do not get control of South Vietnam.*

	1968	1971	1972
	(in percentages)		
End war even though communists might take over sooner or later	31	55	44
Fight on until settlement insuring communists don't take over	62	36	48
Don't know	7	9	8
	100	100	100

In 1968 more than six out of ten Americans were in favor of fighting on to keep the communists out of power. By early 1971 sentiment had swung to the dovish side: by 55 percent to 36 percent the public favored ending the war even at the risk of a communist takeover. In 1972, about six weeks after the communists' renewed offensive, almost one-half of the American people (48 percent) favored fighting on, with only 44 percent wanting to end the war, come what may. Whether this mood—apparently more belligerent, possibly more hopeful of "victory" with the introduction of television- and laser-directed "smart bombs" and other highly sophisticated weaponry, and perhaps less troubled about the conflict since the U.S. is paying the price increasingly in dollars only, not in lives of American ground troops—would continue, or be followed instead by the kind of reversal that set in a few months after the Tet offensive, only time and future surveys can determine.

The shift from a majority feeling in 1971 that the U.S. should "end the war" to the predominant attitude in mid-1972 that it should "fight on" was most pronounced among people thirty to forty-nine, those with less than a college education, Republicans, manual workers, and especially men, southerners, and people living in small communities throughout the country. On the other hand, "end the war" sentiment was in the majority (although by reduced margins from 1971) among women; young people; professional, business, and white collar workers; people living in the

West and in large cities throughout the country; black Americans; and especially the college-educated.

Nevertheless, a large proportion of the American people continued to be disturbed about the way the Vietnam War has been handled, as responses to the following question indicate: *Are you satisfied or dissatisfied with the way the U.S. government has been handling the problem of Vietnam recently?*

Satisfied	46	percent
Dissatisfied	47	
Don't know	7	
	100	percent

In response to our question, the public's views about progress in dealing with "the problem of Vietnam" were marked by caution and reserve. The composite score on the question was 57, indicating a preponderant feeling that some, but not much, progress had been made during the preceding year. The breakdown was:

Made much progress	9	percent
Made some progress	43	
Stood still	20	
Lost some ground	15	
Lost much ground	9	
Don't know	4	
	100	percent

Women and young people were less sanguine about progress than men and older people. (See Table A-11.) Also less optimistic were blacks. Conversely, more positive than average were several interrelated groups: families in the top income bracket, suburbanites, and professional and business people. They were joined in this case by those who characterized themselves as moderately conservative and by Republicans, who exhibited the greatest sense of progress of any group. (Similarly, on the question about satisfaction in "handling the problem of Vietnam," discussed earlier, more than three-quarters of Republicans expressed approval of the president's policies.)

GOOD OR EVIL?

With cries of moral indignation about what the U.S. is doing in Indochina and elsewhere in the world coming from a good many

quarters, and a Harris Survey finding in November 1971 that
two-thirds of the public thought it wrong for the U.S. to be fighting in Vietnam, we wondered whether, on balance, the American
people would evaluate their country's international behavior as
beneficial or harmful. We asked: *Taking into account the well-
being of people throughout the world, do you feel, generally
speaking, that in its international actions in recent years the
United States has been a force for good in the world, or not?*

Has been	69	percent
Has not been	23	
Don't know	8	
	100	percent

Not unexpectedly, those believing the U.S. has not been a positive force were found mostly among the young, those with higher
education, professionals and businessmen, suburbanites, and
those who characterized themselves as liberals. But even among
those groups, negative feelings remained in distinctly minority
proportions, never exceeding one-third of the total. Americans, in
short, do not believe that U.S. actions in Indochina (no matter
how they may view the costs and realities of the war) and elsewhere have been so monstrous as to make their country a force for
evil on the world scene.

RELATIONS WITH CHINA AND THE SOVIET UNION

Although feelings about progress in international economics, relations with allies, and the Vietnam War were restrained, ex-
uberance was rife when it came to dealings with mainland China
and the Soviet Union. To our questions about how much progress
had been made over the past year in handling relations with these
two powers, the American people answered:

	China	Russia
	(in percentages)	
Made much progress	12	10
Made some progress	60	59
Stood still	14	18
Lost some ground	4	3
Lost much ground	1	1
Don't know	9	9
	100	100

The overall composite score on handling relations with the Chinese was a striking 72, propelled there by the fact that six out of ten saw "some" progress, and more than one in ten, "much" progress. A composite score of 70 resulted from almost equally optimistic assessments of how the U.S. had handled recent relations with the Soviet Union. (See Table A-11 for demographic breakdowns.) As expected, it appears that the president's spectacular trips to Peking and Moscow contributed most to the public's overall assessment of progress on the international front.

Two Harris Surveys released in February and May 1972 reported that almost three-quarters of the public endorsed these presidential trips. As is usual when the issue is talking things over with other nations (even adversaries), large majorities approved negotiating with both great communist powers, even though the public's expectations about results were not extravagant. In another demonstration of this trend (and in the wake of the strategic arms limitation agreements reached in Moscow), more than eight out of ten of our respondents (81 percent) indicated that they felt "the U.S. should go further in negotiating with Soviet Russia with a view toward reducing armaments on both sides."

This general support for loosening things up internationally did not extend to Cuba. When the public was asked, *"Now that President Nixon has made his trip to Communist China, do you think the U.S. should or should not establish regular diplomatic relations with Fidel Castro's government in Cuba?"* 42 percent came out in favor; 48 percent were opposed; and 10 percent said they were not sure. Majority sentiment in favor of establishing relations appeared among: the college-educated, families in the top income bracket, white collar workers, people living in the West and in the largest metropolitan areas throughout the country, suburbanites, and liberals. Opposition to establishing relations with Cuba was especially strong among those with incomes of $10,000 to $14,999 a year, the nonlabor force, residents of the Midwest and of small communities and rural areas throughout the country, and, especially, those who said they were very conservative.

INTERNATIONALISM VS. ISOLATIONISM

In our survey and several others conducted over the last two years, there has been significant decline in public concentration on dangers abroad and a growing feeling that we should now turn our energies inward and tackle urgent domestic problems. This outlook was almost certainly buttressed by the almost euphoric reactions engendered by the presidential excursions to mainland China and the Soviet Union. But does this tendency portend a return to the isolationism of pre-World War II days? To get at this matter in broad dimension, we sought reactions to a series of statements, some of which obviously conflict with one another. We asked:

Please read all the statements on this card and, when you have finished, tell me with which ones you agree and with which ones you disagree.

A. *The United States should cooperate fully with the United Nations.*

Agree	63 percent
Disagree	28
Don't know	9
	100 percent

B. *In deciding on its foreign policies, the U.S. should take into account the views of its major allies.*

Agree	80 percent
Disagree	12
Don't know	8
	100 percent

C. *Since the U.S. is the most powerful nation in the world we should go our own way in international matters, not worrying too much about whether other countries agree with us or not.*

Agree	22 percent
Disagree	72
Don't know	6
	100 percent

D. *The U.S. should come to the defense of its major European allies with military force if any of them are attacked by Soviet Russia.*

Agree	52	percent
Disagree	32	
Don't know	16	
	100	percent

E. *The U.S. should come to the defense of Japan with military force if it is attacked by Soviet Russia or Communist China.*

Agree	43	percent
Disagree	40	
Don't know	17	
	100	percent

F. *The U.S. should mind its own business internationally and let other countries get along as best they can on their own.*

Agree	35	percent
Disagree	56	
Don't know	9	
	100	percent

G. *We shouldn't think so much in* international *terms but concentrate more on our own* national *problems and building up our strength and prosperity here at home.*

Agree	73	percent
Disagree	20	
Don't know	7	
	100	percent

Most noteworthy among the answers are (1) that only slightly more than one-half of the public felt that the U.S. should come to the defense of western European allies with military force if they were attacked; (2) that this proportion dropped to just more than four in ten in the case of Japan; and (3) that almost three-quarters of the public felt we should now think less in international terms and more about domestic problems.

To determine how the population divided along internationalist-isolationist lines, we used an "international patterns" system devised by the Institute for International Social Research in 1964.

(It is described in full in Appendix 4.) To qualify as "completely internationalist" under this scheme, a respondent had to agree that the U.S. should cooperate with the U.N., take into account the views of its allies, and come to the defense of western Europe and Japan while disagreeing with the suggestions that the U.S. go its own way, mind its own business, and concentrate more on national problems. To be considered "completely isolationist," a respondent had to give precisely the opposite answers. Categories were also provided for "predominantly internationalist" (meaning he conformed to the "completely internationalist" pattern in most, but not all, respects); "predominantly isolationist" (meaning he conformed to the "completely isolationist" pattern in similar proportions); and a middle category labeled "mixed" (meaning a mixture of internationalist and isolationist patterns).

The proportions of respondents in each category were:

Completely internationalist	13	percent
Predominantly internationalist	41	
Mixed	33	
Predominantly isolationist	10	
Completely isolationist	3	
	100	percent

More than one-half of the American people were at least predominantly internationalist; one-third were in the mixed category; and only 13 percent opted for isolationism.

A composite scoring system was again used on this breakdown (ranging from 100 in the case of "completely internationalist" to zero in the case of "completely isolationist"). The average composite score was 63, midway between "mixed" and "predominantly internationalist." Tending to be less firmly internationalist than the average were: women; older people; the nonlabor occupational category (made up mostly of retired people); those with little education and low family incomes; and black Americans. On the other hand, men, families in the top income bracket, the college-educated, those in the professional and business category, westerners, and Republicans (far more than Democrats) were among those more internationalist than average. An interesting footnote: the score among those in the Midwest, formerly considered isolationist territory, was precisely the same as that for the sample as a whole.

LESSENED INTERNATIONALISM

The proportion of Americans who can currently be labeled outright isolationists was very small indeed (13 percent). There has been, nevertheless, an easing of the stalwart internationalist consensus that characterized the post-World War II years, with the change presumably attributable in large measure to disillusionment over the war in Vietnam along with growing concern about urgent domestic problems.

This lessened internationalism becomes clearer when our 1972 responses are compared with those given to the same questions asked by the Institute for International Social Research in 1964 and 1968. (To guarantee complete comparability, statements D and E in the 1972 series have been omitted from the analysis since the series in both 1964 and 1968 contained only the five remaining statements. The 1972 figures are not therefore precisely the same as those given in the preceding tabulation.)

TABLE 6   INTERNATIONALISTS AND ISOLATIONISTS
percentages

	1964	1968	1972
Completely internationalist	30	25	18
Predominantly internationalist	35	34	38
Mixed	27	32	35
Predominantly isolationist	5	6	5
Completely isolationist	3	3	4
	100	100	100

The percentage of isolationists ("predominant" and "complete") did not change. The proportion of those who were "completely internationalist," however, was almost halved between 1964 and 1972, with the "predominantly internationalist" category and, more significantly, the "mixed" category, both increasing. The American people have thus by no means become outright isolationists, but they have moderated their enthusiastic internationalism of yesteryear.

An examination of shifts in reactions to the statements from which international-isolationist behavior was derived reveals several significant trends:

- Those agreeing with the statement that the U.S. should cooperate with the U.N. dropped from 72 percent in 1964 and in 1968 to 63 percent in 1972. (In November 1971 a Gallup poll found that a majority of those with opinions on the subject believed the U.N. was doing a poor job, a viewpoint possibly strengthened by the admission of Communist China a month earlier over American opposition. And the majority view among those with opinions was that "the U.N. proved to be highly ineffective as a world organization, because it could not stop the India-Pakistan War," according to a Harris Survey released in January 1972.)

- Opposition to the statement that the U.S. should mind its own business and let other countries get along as best they can fell from 70 percent in 1964 to 66 percent in 1968, and 56 percent in 1972.

- And, in a parallel trend, agreement with the statement that we shouldn't think so much in international terms but concentrate more on national problems here at home rose from 55 percent in 1964 to 60 percent in 1968 and then to 73 percent in 1972 (a drop, it should be noted, from the high of 77 percent registered in the 1971 *Hopes and Fears* study, but still significantly higher than in the earlier years).

These figures suggest, once again, that the impression held by a number of observers is accurate: although Americans are far from the isolationism of pre-World War II days, they are, indeed, turning measurably inward. Their earlier staunchly internationalist attitudes have been somewhat vitiated. Their present outlook is well summed up by the overwhelming approval that greeted the following statement, which in highly simplistic fashion outlines the essence of the still vaguely defined Nixon Doctrine: *The U.S. should continue to play a major role internationally, but cut down on some of its responsibilities abroad.*

A remarkable 87 percent of Americans agreed with the statement, only 7 percent disagreed, and 6 percent had no opinion.

XI.
Defense and Aid

Lots of countries admire us; they envy our capabilities.
   a retired woman in Baltimore

They are sending all our money overseas.
   a Brooklyn hospital worker

I don't think we're on top like we were after World War II.
   a pharmacist's wife in an eastern city

The Record Speaks

Little that was new in military strategy appeared in the survey year; the Nixon administration had introduced its key shifts earlier. Once again, the president defined as his basic defense objective the maintenance of "sufficiency" and sought to distinguish sufficiency from the previous doctrine of "assured destruction."

"In its narrow military sense," President Nixon declared in his February 1972 report to Congress *U.S. Foreign Policy for the 1970s,* "it means enough force to inflict a level of damage on a potential aggressor sufficient to deter him from attacking. . . . In its broader political sense, sufficiency means the maintenance of forces adequate to prevent us and our allies from being coerced." Sufficiency was held up as a strategic posture with a broader political utility than its predecessor. Assured destruction left us with "only one strategic course of action"—massive attacks on Soviet cities—and was therefore useful only for deterring similarly massive initial attacks. Sufficiency, said to require a "flexible range of strategic options," presumably made nuclear weapons—and the U.S.–Soviet balance—relevant to a broader range of military and even political threats.

Despite this and similar explanations, the essential departure sufficiency represented, in contrast to assured destruction, remained both unclear and controversial.

Within the framework of this doctrinal dispute and the even larger controversy over the international role and international responsibilities the U.S. should assume, it was not surprising that Congress was especially critical of foreign economic and military aid. In a year marked by numerous disagreements between the White House and Capitol Hill, none was more surrounded by passion and partisan concern than the question of levels of U.S. support to be given to friends abroad.

THE DOCTRINE OF "SUFFICIENCY"

Sufficiency evidently encompasses the old concept of assured destruction in that sufficiency implies an ability to guarantee against nuclear attack by maintaining the capability to destroy an unacceptable (i.e., sufficient) portion of an adversary's population and industrial capacity even in the aftermath of an all-out attack on our own strategic forces. But what is the "flexible range of strategic options" sufficiency confers? More important, to what sort of threats or attacks are such responses to be available? What kind of coercion can we expect to use nuclear threats to prevent?

No reliable guidance was afforded in the president's message beyond his assertion that: "No president should be left with only one strategic course of action, particularly that of ordering the mass destruction of enemy civilians and facilities." Does this mean a capability of destroying all or some portion of an adversary's forces remaining after an attack, presumably less than all-out, on this country? If so, then the forces needed for sufficiency would appear to encompass the capability of striking first against enemy retaliatory capacity as well. Yet it has long been considered axiomatic that a capability to destroy a potential adversary's strategic forces is the greatest threat to strategic stability. Still more uncertain was the issue of how strategic forces would, by the flexibility of the targeting options they afforded a U.S. president, make it possible to resist "coercion," which could evidently take forms of military and even diplomatic pressure as well as actual nuclear attack.

Whatever the persisting uncertainty over the concept of sufficiency, the administration was reasonably clear about the strategic forces it regarded as essential (if not always equally clear about the doctrine they were to support). Quantitatively, these force requirements were defined to preclude the Soviet Union from achieving a "significant numerical advantage in overall offensive and defensive forces." Qualitatively, sufficiency was held to require a marked acceleration in efforts to modernize and strengthen the three offensive strategic weapons systems—sea-based missiles, land-based missiles, and bombers—with emphasis normally given to the further development of sea-based capabilities, but with no weakening of traditional insistence on the "triad." Along with the modernization of offensive systems, a realigned defense system against attacks by bombers and missiles was projected.

Thus, among the principal strategic force programs in the 1973 defense budget were the following:

- a marked increase in spending on the Trident submarine (the rechristened Undersea Long-Range Missile System, ULMS), which could now become operational as early as 1978;
- a continued hardening of the Minuteman ICBM silos, making them less vulnerable to attack, and a continued modernization of the land-based missiles through replacement of the single warhead Minuteman by missiles carrying multiple independently targetable warheads (MIRV) and (most controversial of all in view of its counterforce and other doctrinal implications) improvement of the accuracy of ICBM warheads;
- a notable increase in spending on a new manned bomber, the B-1, to replace the aging B-52s;
- a substantial increase of funds for a new air defense system, the airborne warning and control system (AWACS); and,
- after the strategic arms limitation talks (SALT) agreement, money for initial work on an anti-ballistic-missile system (ABM) to protect the command authority at Washington, D.C.

These requirements, administration spokesmen were careful to point out, did not portend an attempt to regain strategic superiority over the Soviet Union. On the contrary, they were described as the indispensable measures for retaining a position that, in the face of the continuing buildup of Soviet strategic forces, would insure against undue pressures being exerted either on us or our major allies.

With the exception of some shifting of the projected requirements of an ABM, the program requests for expansion and improvement of strategic weapons systems were not made conditional upon the outcome of SALT. Although the initial SALT agreements placed quantitative limitations on both defensive and offensive missiles the United States and the Soviet Union could possess, few limits were placed either on the qualitative improvements in existing missile systems or on both quantitative and qualitative changes in systems other than missiles (i.e., bombers). Indeed, the Nixon administration was quick to argue that failure to adopt its program would not only jeopardize U.S. security but also weaken the chances of future SALT agreements.

GENERAL-PURPOSE FORCES

In contrast to strategic force requirements (determined essentially by analysis of the U.S.–Soviet strategic nuclear balance), the requirements for general-purpose forces were presumably determined by a more complex set of factors, including: the implications of the emerging triangular relationship between the United States, the Soviet Union, and China; the strategic parity now accepted with the Soviet Union; the assumptions of the Nixon Doctrine; and (perhaps most important of all) the number of budget dollars available and the exigencies of domestic and alliance politics.

The triangular U.S.–China–Soviet relationship (which assumes the improbability of Sino-Soviet cooperation) has apparently been interpreted to mean that our general-purpose forces must be capable of meeting a major threat in Europe *or* Asia—not, as before, in both Europe *and* Asia at once—and of simultaneously coping with a minor contingency elsewhere—a so-called one-and-a-half-war strategy in contrast to the two-and-a-half-war strategy of the previous administration.*

Strategic parity has been said to mean that the probability has increased of challenges that take the form of less than a full-scale conventional war. This view presumably operates to limit cuts in conventional forces, but it did not block substantial reductions in conventional forces from pre-Vietnam levels.

The Nixon Doctrine, still rather ambiguous and elusive in its detailed military implications three years after its initial formulation, has been interpreted to mean at least that continued improvements in allied military capabilities (particularly in Asia) are necessary to maintain our allies' security while permitting the further reduction in American ground forces—again, primarily in Asia. These improvements, however, do not eliminate the need to maintain strong forward American air and sea deployments, and they affirmatively require the U.S. to continue to provide substantial military assistance.

The impact of practical budgetary ceilings on defense—where the role and influence of Congress and the drain of other areas of federal spending are most visible—necessarily forces choices between alternative force structures.

And finally, the political and psychological requirements of our various alliance relationships, almost as much as the purely military requirements, add another powerful intangible.

No change was projected in the 1973 defense budget for the forces assigned to protect Western Europe against conventional attack. On the contrary, all congressional proposals for a major reduction of these forces were firmly and successfully resisted by the administration. Indeed, as the idea of mutual and balanced force reductions (MBFR) appeared to be a somewhat more viable prospect than previously, the administration began increasingly to use the "bargaining chip" argument made familiar

---

* Skeptics argue that in point of fact there is little real difference in these two "strategies," since there never had been any real intention to buy the forces necessary for a two-and-a-half-war posture in the first place. The fact was, these skeptics say, that the "strategy" was simply a sop to the military leadership, not a policy given any reality through procurement of hardware and the like.

(and supposedly successfully applied) in SALT to the issue of European force levels.

In Asia, on the other hand, American ground forces were reduced considerably, primarily as a result of the continuing withdrawal from Vietnam. Even in Asia, however, the strategy of retrenchment without disengagement set forth in the Nixon Doctrine was given very cautious application, with particular restraints resulting from the continuation of the war in Vietnam.

DEFENSE SPENDING

U.S. force structures, together with projected costs of the continuing involvement in Vietnam, resulted in proposed defense expenditures for fiscal 1973 of $76.5 billion. In terms of current spending, this defense budget represented an increase of $700 million over fiscal 1972. The total obligational authority requested by the president for the Department of Defense in 1973, including authorization for programs going beyond fiscal 1973, came to $83.2 billion, an increase of approximately $5 billion over the total obligational authority for fiscal 1972. These figures were, of course, subject to change, depending upon subsequent events, not the least being congressional action. (Congress has, it should be noted, made substantial cuts in succeeding Nixon administration defense budgets.)

Certain overall trends in defense spending are apparent, though. As a percentage of both GNP and the federal budget, defense spending has decreased in the past decade. In 1964, the defense budget represented 8.3 percent of GNP and 41.8 percent of the total federal budget. In 1973 these percentages were down to 6.4 and 30 respectively. Moreover, even if, as seems inevitable barring major doctrinal change, defense spending in absolute terms will be appreciably higher in the late 1970s than today, it is still unlikely that the percentages given for 1973 will change markedly. This comes, of course, at a time of continuing debate on relative national priorities and a growth in sentiment for greater attention to domestic rather than international problems and issues.

The sharply increased costs of manpower and weapons systems almost guarantee an increase in defense spending. In the case of manpower alone, the Brookings Institution, in *Setting National Priorities: The 1973 Budget,* calculated that "two legislative decisions—the comparability pay standards for all government employees and the goal of an all-volunteer force—caused the fiscal 1973 defense budget to be $15 billion higher than it would have been at 1968 pay scales." The elimination of the savings that accompanied the old lower pay scales—which, in conjunction with conscription, were, in effect, a national manpower tax—contributed importantly to the rapid consumption of any budgetary gains realized from continuing withdrawal from Vietnam.

To the sharply rising costs in manpower must be added the almost astronomical rise in costs of weapons systems. The B-52 aircraft cost nearly $8 million apiece; the estimated cost of each B-1 bomber is at least $30 million and may go two to three times higher. The Polaris submarine, equipped with missiles, cost $100 million; the estimated cost of each new long-range missile submarine (Trident), also armed, is $1 billion. The cost of these two weapons systems alone, if carried to completion, is estimated at some $24 billion. The total cost of all new major strategic weapons systems now in either the development or procurement stage could run as high as $70 billion. Bearing in mind the cost overruns that have regularly attended the development and procurement of new weapons systems, the final costs are likely to be considerably higher.

Assuming that there will be no major reduction in force structures, that most present plans for modernization of weapons systems are completed, and that manpower costs continue to rise, the outlook is for an increase in overall defense spending that might go as high as 16 to 18 percent over a five-year period. Although this would still leave defense spending in the neighborhood of 7 percent of GNP, it would also mean a military budget of between $90 and $100 billion by fiscal 1977.

Given the strong pressures for increased spending on domestic social programs; a revenue base that, under current taxation policies, holds out little prospect of expanding to meet these pressures; the challenge to the premises on which our defense programs are based; and the persistent doubt whether we really get our money's worth, it is scarcely surprising that defense

spending has become a central and divisive political issue. Even the traditionally supportive Senate Armed Services Committee issued a report in July 1971 that was highly critical of procurement policies, weapons performance standards, overall management practices, and the like. Democratic presidential candidate Senator George McGovern sought to make discontent over this degree of spending—and the alleged militarization of U.S. society and policy that accompanied the spending—a major issue of the 1972 campaign.

THE SALT AGREEMENTS

As expected, the growing controversy over defense spending was rapidly linked to the strategic arms limitation agreements. After a period of two and a half years, during which the carefully orchestrated SALT negotiations occasionally took on the overtones of a "Perils of Pauline" melodrama, the Soviet Union and the United States completed the first major step on the long road toward comprehensive arms control. The agreement on May 26, 1972 consisted of two parts: a treaty of unlimited duration on anti-ballistic-missile systems and a five-year interim agreement freezing offensive strategic missiles pending negotiation of a permanent accord.* Both agreements provided for withdrawal by either party on six months' notice if it decided that extraordinary events related to the subject matter of the agreement jeopardized its supreme national interests.

The principal provisions of the agreements were:

- The ABM treaty limits each country to two anti-ballistic-missile sites, of 100 interceptors each, separated by a distance of at least 800 miles. One is to be for the defense of its national command authority (in effect, the capital of each state) and the other for the defense of one field of intercontinental ballistic missiles. Limits are also placed on deployment of the large radars that are essential to an effective ABM system. By the ABM agreement, the U.S. and the Soviet Union have, in

---

* The U.S., however, said that failure to replace the five-year agreement with a permanent offensive weapons treaty could serve as grounds to abrogate the "permanent" ABM treaty.

effect, accepted that defense against nuclear attack is impossible. Many regarded this agreement as the most important step in arms control since the nuclear era began—and the willingness of an administration that had made the Safeguard ABM system its prime strategic program to accept this reversal as a major testimony to the depth of its commitment to real, if cautious, arms control measures.

- The interim agreement on offensive arms covers both land- and sea-based missiles. With respect to land-based ICBMs, it limits the missiles of either party to those under construction or deployed at the time of signing. In effect, this will limit the United States to 1,054 ICBMs and the Soviet Union to approximately 1,600. In a major development, the Soviet Union accepted a freeze on its SS-9 heavy ICBM launchers, with their counterforce potential, through a provision that forbids the conversion of "light" (i.e., smaller than SS-9 sized) ICBMs into heavy missiles.

- The provisions in the interim agreement relating to sea-based missiles are more complicated. The Russians are limited to a level, agreed in the course of the Moscow summit to be treated as their current level, operational and under construction, of approximately 740 nuclear missiles in nuclear submarines. At the same time, the interim agreement permits them to build to a ceiling of 62 such submarines with no more than 950 such missiles, though only on condition that for each addition beyond agreed current levels, they dismantle an equivalent number of older land-based ICBMs or older submarine missiles. For its part, the United States is limited to a ceiling of 44 Polaris submarines and 710 missiles, with a similar requirement for dismantling older missiles. Long-range bombers and other aircraft, and medium- and intermediate-range missiles, are not included in the interim agreement, nor does the agreement prohibit many of the strategic offensive programs that the United States and the Soviet Union are presently pursuing.

Although generally well received by Congress and the public, the immediate effect of the arms control agreements—especially the offensive-weapons agreement—was to sharpen debate over the current defense budget. In addressing Congress on his return from the Moscow summit, the president declared that "the agreements forestall a major spiraling of the arms race—one which would have worked to our disadvantage, since we have no current building programs for the categories of weapons frozen and since no new building program could have produced any new weapons in those categories during the period of the freeze." To be sure, the interim agreement still left the Soviet Union with a numerical superiority in land- and sea-based missiles, and some critics severely attacked the president for thus "ratifying" a Soviet edge. Against this numerical superiority, however, the United States could weigh a substantially larger and more effective long-range bomber force, as well as forward-based systems. Of even greater importance in the strategic balance is the advantage this country enjoys, and can be expected to retain throughout the 1970s, in nuclear weapons technology—above all, in MIRV warheads. As a result of this lead, the United States possesses more than twice as many warheads today as the Soviet Union.

By limiting the quantity of land- and sea-based missiles the parties could hold, the Moscow agreements largely turned the future strategic nuclear arms race away from numbers. By not limiting the qualitative improvements the parties could make on their missile systems, the Moscow agreements accentuated the competition in the area of technology, especially warhead design.

Indeed, the president insisted that it was precisely because the Moscow agreements confined the arms race largely to the area of technology that current strategic programs—particularly the B-1 and the Trident—must be vigorously pushed. The failure to modernize in the immediate years ahead, he urged, could jeopardize the technological lead this country presently enjoys. Such failure, moreover, could remove the principal incentive the Soviet Union might have in negotiating a follow-on agreement. Thus the programs designed to modernize the country's offensive strategic forces were deemed essential by the administration not only as a safeguard to offset Soviet technological advances but as new "bargaining chips" for the next round of SALT. Many opposed B-1 and Trident on strictly military and technical grounds, arguing that a decision now on replacement of the B-52 and Poseidon systems was premature, and perhaps imprudently so.

But it was the linking of the arms control agreements with the strategic forces program that provoked the sharpest debate. In some measure, arguments against the linkage were provided by administration spokesmen themselves in discussing the significance of the ABM treaty. Both Gerard Smith, director of the Arms Control and Disarmament Agency, and Henry A. Kissinger, the president's assistant for national security affairs, declared that the effect of the ABM treaty is to make it virtually impossible for either side to defend itself against massive nuclear attack. But if this is so, critics of the B-1, Trident, and other programs noted, why was it necessary to push ahead on these programs, particularly in view of the technological advantages the United States presently enjoyed over the Soviet Union and would continue to enjoy during the period of the interim agreement? The critics found these advantages, when taken together with the ABM agreement, more than sufficient to guarantee the American capability for a devastating retaliatory strike. Although one element of the president's program—the accurate ICBM warhead—was dropped, at least temporarily, by the military committees, the president was largely successful in winning acceptance of his proposals, in no small degree because of his skillful use of the argument that SALT I required maintenance of U.S. momentum, not only for its own sake, but as an inducement to future agreements.

Whatever the pros and cons in the current controversy, the point remained that a beginning—limited perhaps, but nonetheless truly important—had been made on nuclear disarmament.

ECONOMIC AND MILITARY AID

Mounting criticism of the U.S. foreign aid program came to a head during our survey year, when, on October 29, 1971, the Senate voted down funding for the program, 41 to 27. The unexpected and unprecedented defeat was the result of both liberal and conservative opposition. Liberals opposed the bill on the ground that military rather than humanitarian considerations had come to dominate the allocation of funds, while conservatives criticized the program for failing to gain international support for U.S. policies in return for the billions of dollars spent abroad.

Two weeks later, a Senate-passed, two-bill package that separated economic and military aid along with a new House bill were sent to a conference committee where they remained deadlocked for a month over an amendment tying withdrawal of all troops from Indochina within six months to the bill. Final action on the appropriation authorization did not come until March 2, eight months into the fiscal year, when the Senate, by a vote of 45 to 36, adopted a compromise authorization bill already passed by the House.

The fiscal 1972 aid authorization totaled nearly $3.2 billion —$1.45 billion for military aid, $1.17 billion for bilateral economic aid, and $.57 billion for related international programs, including the Peace Corps and multilateral development banks. The large number of Senate votes against the bill indicated continued dissatisfaction with the foreign aid program and a likely battle over next year's appropriation.

The People Speak

I would hope to maintain our position of world leadership— without undue taxation.
> a professional man in Michigan

We are helping other countries too much when there are people in our own country that are deserving.
> a retired man in rural Illinois

I'm afraid of an invasion from another country—and we aren't prepared.
> a farmer's wife in the Midwest

There are so many allies that are unstable.
> a female teacher in a small town in Illinois

I'm fearful of the agreements that are being signed with other nations in regard to disarming, etc. We will hold to these agreements and others won't, and then there will be war.
> the wife of an air-conditioning engineer in Baltimore

We continue to excel as the No. 1 nation, promoting love and peace.
   a labor representative in New York State

We are too involved with the problems of other countries.
   a building superintendent in a New York city

That the public would like to see the United States assume a new international posture—one of influence without entanglement —is supported by trends revealed in responses to two statements presented to the public by us in mid-1972 and by the Institute for International Social Research in 1968 and, in one case, in 1964 as well.

One statement has to do with America's role as a great power; the other, with the traditional U.S. policy of containment of communism. The statements and responses follow:

The U.S. should maintain its dominant position as the world's most powerful nation at all costs, even going to the very brink of war if necessary.

	1964	1968	1972
		(in percentages)	
Agree	56	50	39
Disagree	31	40	50
Don't know	13	10	11
	100	100	100

The U.S. should take all necessary steps, including the use of armed force, to prevent the spread of communism to any other parts of the free world.

	1968	1972
	(in percentages)	
Agree	57	46
Disagree	29	43
Don't know	14	11
	100	100

In 1964 a majority of the public agreed with the thesis that the U.S. should maintain its position as the world's most powerful nation at all costs, even going to the very brink of war if necessary.

By 1972 that view was held by less than four in ten, with one-half of the public expressing disagreement. Similarly, between 1968 and 1972, the two-to-one majority sentiment for the U.S. taking all necessary steps to prevent the spread of communism had dissipated into virtual stalemate.

Associated with this changed perception of the U.S. international role are feelings about the extent to which the U.S. should continue to participate, through expenditure of funds or resources, in various international activities. We sought to explore the public's sense of international commitment through a series of questions. First, we asked: *Do you think the amount the U.S. is now contributing toward the work of the United Nations should be increased, kept at the present level, reduced, or ended altogether?*

Increased	10 percent
Kept at present level	46
Reduced	29
Ended altogether	9
Don't know	6
	100 percent

We applied our scoring system to all the support-for-international-activities questions, with "increased" rated at 100, "kept at present level" at 50, and "reduced" or "ended altogether" at zero. The composite score on this question was 36, giving it the highest ranking in the series. (See Table A-6.) Support for the United Nations was especially strong among the young and especially weak among people over fifty. U.N. scores were also high among manual workers and black Americans, perhaps reflecting sympathy for cooperation with lands in which they have ethnic or racial roots. Republicans, on the other hand, were noticeably adverse toward the U.N., as were westerners and those with little education and with low incomes.

Two questions in this series dealt with foreign aid. We asked:

Now I'd like to ask you about the foreign aid and loans the U.S. is extending to a number of backward countries to develop their economies in order to give their people a better life. Do you feel that the amount the U.S. is now devoting to this purpose should be increased, kept at the present level, reduced, or ended altogether?

Increased	7 percent
Kept at present level	33
Reduced	42
Ended altogether	13
Don't know	5
	100 percent

And what about military aid in money and equipment the U.S. is now furnishing to some of our allies, such as South Korea, the Philippines, and Brazil? Should the amount of tax money the U.S. is now providing for this purpose be increased, kept at the present level, reduced, or ended altogether?

Increased	3 percent
Kept at present level	32
Reduced	42
Ended altogether	16
Don't know	7
	100 percent

On both foreign economic and military aid, clear majorities opted for either reducing the American effort or terminating it completely. Those most in favor of economic aid included the young and those earning $15,000 and over. (See Table A-6.) Republicans, westerners, older Americans (fifty and over), and those with low incomes and little education were among the least supportive. For military aid, opposition was sharpest among women, people in the top and the bottom income brackets, easterners, and residents of our largest metropolitan areas and of rural areas. Only two groups were considerably above average in support for both kinds of aid—white collar workers and those living in cities of 50,000 to 500,000.

The last two questions in this series dealt with the U.S. military presence overseas. We asked:

As you may know, the U.S. now has substantial forces stationed in Western Europe as part of NATO's defense against the danger of Soviet aggression. Do you think America's contribution of ground troops now serving in Europe should be increased, kept at the present level, reduced, or ended altogether?

Increased	6 percent
Kept at present level	44
Reduced	30
Ended altogether	15
Don't know	5
	100 percent

As you probably know, the U.S. is now spending a large amount abroad on military bases in many parts of the world and on our military forces that are stationed there. Do you feel the amount of tax money now being devoted to these purposes should be increased, kept at the present level, reduced, or ended altogether?

Increased	5 percent
Kept at present level	45
Reduced	38
Ended altogether	8
Don't know	4
	100 percent

On the issue of maintaining U.S. forces in Europe and U.S. military bases abroad, a virtual standoff emerged between those who wanted to retain present levels and those who wanted the U.S. effort reduced or ended altogether. Reducing the U.S. military establishment in Europe was especially favored by the college-educated, the well-to-do, suburbanites, the "very liberal" group, and residents of our largest cities. (See Table A-6.) Those same groups, plus midwesterners, ruralites, older Americans, and blacks were most in favor of reducing or terminating expenditures for overseas bases as well. Least opposition to maintaining both U.S. force levels in Europe and the present network of military bases overseas appeared among those thirty to forty-nine, southerners, residents of cities of 2,500 to 500,000, and the "very conservative."

NATIONAL DEFENSE

Beyond the issues of international participation is the question
of how adequate Americans believe their nation's defense arrangements are. To get the public's assessment, we asked: *Do you,
yourself, feel that our national defense is stronger now than it
needs to be, not strong enough, or about right at the present
time?*

Stronger than necessary	14	percent
Not strong enough	27	
About right	51	
Don't know	8	
	100	percent

One-half of Americans thought that U.S. military strength was
adequate, while slightly more than one-quarter thought it was not.

But what about paying for defense? How do Americans assess
the defense budget? With defense spending developing into a
central issue of the 1972 presidential campaign, we decided to
supplement our survey with a question about defense spending.
In August 1972, again through the facilities of The Gallup
Organization, we asked the American people: *Considering the
situation today at home and abroad, do you think the amount of
money the federal government in Washington spends for national
defense and military purposes should be increased, kept at the
present level, reduced, or ended altogether?*

Increased	9	percent
Kept at present level	40	
Reduced	37	
Ended altogether	5	
Don't know	9	
	100	percent

At first glance, there appear to be inconsistencies between the
answers to this question and to the previous one. On the earlier
question, 27 percent of our respondents said that national defense
was not strong enough. When the issue was put in terms of

hard cash, though, only 9 percent thought defense expenditures should actually be increased. Conversely, although only 14 percent said our defense capability was stronger than necessary, 37 percent wanted to reduce defense outlays. A partial explanation for these results may lie in the conviction of many today that waste and inefficiency in defense spending could be reduced without a corresponding cut in military capabilities—"more bang for the buck," as it used to be called.

In their answers to this question, though, Americans were almost evenly divided on the issue of cutting defense spending: 49 percent called for the same amount as at present or more; 42 percent wanted defense spending reduced or ended altogether.

The far larger numbers of Americans who wanted the defense budget reduced rather than increased produced a composite score on this question of 32, well below the "kept at present level" figure of 50. (See Table A-6.) Support for defense spending ranked lower than that for the United Nations (36) but above support for U.S. forces in Europe (29); for U.S. military bases abroad (28); and for economic and military aid (24 and 21, respectively).

Anti-spending sentiment was especially high among young people; women; the college-educated; professionals and businessmen; people living in the East, the West, and in our largest cities; blacks; and Democrats. Conversely, the strongest support for defense spending was found among men, Republicans (of whom more than 57 percent wanted spending kept at the present level or increased), and people living in the South (a region that has always exhibited strikingly nationalistic sentiments, and where present or increased levels of defense spending were endorsed by 56 percent).

From the answers to this battery of questions, it is clear that Americans are not willing to see the U.S. go an extra mile in participation in international affairs, especially with respect to foreign economic and military aid. The public is divided on the question of maintaining or cutting back the present level of U.S. troop strength in western Europe and the present network of U.S. military bases throughout the world. And the plurality view is in favor of keeping defense spending close to the present level.

XII.
Governmental Reform and Reorganization

They aren't doing enough for the people. The country is going down the drain. There's no confidence in the president. The government is spending more than it takes in. We still haven't any leaders in sight. They will all sell us out.

　　　a cattle raiser in rural Mississippi

The president is doing the best he can, right or wrong.

　　　the wife of a school teacher in a small California city

They, the government, get going on some problem; then it's back where it started. No one is seeing to it that anything really gets done.

　　　a Detroit housewife

The Record Speaks

In American politics the eighteen months preceding a presidential election are a time for national soul-searching, as candidates and their supporters seek to identify the problems that are uppermost in the voter's mind. The year 1971–72 was certainly no exception to this rule. Each of the leading contenders for the Democratic presidential nomination—Senator Hubert H. Humphrey of Minnesota, Senator George McGovern of South Dakota, Senator Edmund S. Muskie of Maine, and Governor George Wallace of Alabama—sought to identify his cause with what he perceived to be the major concerns of the voter—the war in Vietnam, busing, pollution, inflation, unemployment, taxation, the "welfare mess," or the omnipresent issue of "crime in the streets."

The most successful of these candidates during the primary elections—McGovern and Wallace—drew many of these issues together with a theme that soon sounded a dominant note in the electoral politics of 1972: the failure of government to respond to what the voter regarded as his most pressing grievances. The dissatisfaction of the electorate with the system's inability to grapple with society's major problems was equally strong on the right and on the left of the political spectrum.

Among conservatives it expressed itself in angry attacks on courts that they believed were too lenient with criminals, or too eager to order children bused to schools distant from their own neighborhoods to provide equality of educational opportunity for whites and blacks. This cause found its champion in George Wallace. For liberals, the unresponsiveness of the system was most clearly visible in the executive branch—where they felt officials were prosecuting with mindless vigor a cruel and immoral war in Vietnam, while neglecting poverty, unemployment, environmental pollution, and other pressing urgencies at home. George McGovern became the champion of this liberal movement.

These candidates from opposite ends of the Democratic political spectrum seemed to capitalize on the same kind of public disillusionment with the political system and in some respects to have more in common with each other than with candidates of the center. Both appeared to profit from an "anti-Establishment" mood on the part of many voters.

A major theme of American politics during 1971–72 thus became "reform of the system." The Nixon administration was as alert to this feeling as its Democratic challengers. As the president said in his 1971 State of the Union message: "Most Americans today are simply fed up with government at all levels."

Reformers were concerned in part with the structure and operation of the government itself—the presidency, Congress, and the courts. But the thrust of reform was also directed at the relationship between government and the citizen and at ways in which ordinary voters might exert more effective influence over public policy. These reform movements are closely interrelated; changes in governmental machinery, for example, are often designed to increase the citizen's ability to exert political influence.

THE PRESIDENCY AND GOVERNMENTAL REFORM

When President Nixon took office in 1969, the feeling was widespread that executive power had become far too dominant in the American political system and that the time was ripe for a reassertion of the congressional role in policymaking, particularly in foreign affairs. This attitude was in large measure a product of the war in Vietnam, where America was entangled in a costly and frustrating military stalemate that seemed to result largely from successive commitments by American presidents beginning in the 1950s. One of the leading contenders for the Democratic presidential nomination in 1968, Senator Eugene McCarthy of Minnesota, attracted wide support with a campaign that openly promised to downgrade the importance of the presidency in the American governmental structure.

By the middle of 1972, however, Richard Nixon's position of leadership at the summit of the American governmental structure was as secure as any president's in recent memory. The efforts of reformers to curb the president's discretion in foreign affairs had all been beaten back or so watered down that they were no longer recognizable as serious challenges to presidential authority. In May 1972, the president took steps of escalation in the Vietnam War even more daring in their assertion of presidential prerogative than those President Lyndon B. Johnson had undertaken earlier. At the end of the survey year, only the most limited prospect remained that a war powers bill would eventually be enacted, requiring the consent of Congress for any long-range American military involvement abroad. But given the techniques of persuasion open to American presidents, it seemed unlikely that even such a measure, if adopted, would seriously limit executive authority.

President Nixon's success in protecting the president's dominant position in the American political system has been achieved not only by defeating congressional attempts to limit his authority but also by continuing to expand his influence within the executive branch itself during the past year. The executive departments, it has long been argued, are the president's natural enemies, and President Nixon, like other presidents before him, has faced strong opposition and even revolt on several occasions. This resistance has come from such varied quarters as Justice Department lawyers, who felt the administration was not vigorously enforcing civil rights legislation; foreign service officers and White House staff members opposed to the war in Vietnam; and Department of Health, Education, and Welfare (HEW) officials who disagreed with the administration's welfare policies.

One step taken by President Nixon to bring the executive apparatus under closer presidential control was to submit reorganization proposals to Congress that would reduce the number of executive departments from seven to four and thus, it was projected, simplify the task of overseeing the activities of these bodies. The Departments of HEW, Agriculture, Housing and Urban Development, Commerce, Interior, Labor, and Transportation were to be regrouped along with some now-independent agencies into four new superdepartments embracing the areas of human resources, community development, economic affairs, and natural resources. (Subsequently, the Department of Agriculture as a body was eliminated from this design, although some of its units were still subject to reassignment.)

None of the president's proposals for departmental reorganization was approved by Congress during the survey year, although eventual congressional approval of the Department of Community Development was given the best chance. These organizational innovations were strongly opposed by almost all of the large constituencies that depend on the traditional executive departments for representation and participation in governmental decisions affecting their welfare.

Far more importantly, however, President Nixon was particularly successful in tightening his grip on the executive apparatus, centering even more than his immediate predecessors the power to resolve major issues in the White House rather than in the executive departments. The use of this technique was most conspicuous in the area of foreign affairs, where Dr. Henry A. Kissinger played the leading role during the past year in planning and shaping the president's momentous trips to China and the Soviet Union (with great domestic political significance as well), and formulating

American foreign policy during the India-Pakistan War and virtually all other international crises.

As far as social and economic policies at home were concerned, the Domestic Council, established in the White House in 1970, has not, contrary to the president's hopes, become the domestic counterpart of the National Security Council. But the president still managed to keep his major domestic initiative during the past year—the establishment of a comprehensive system of wage and price controls—under direct White House supervision. Indeed, the Nixonian style of limiting the power of the bureaucrats has been one of the most distinctive characteristics of this administration.

In sum, then, it can be argued that efforts to effect major innovations in the federal executive branch through outside pressures largely failed. The changes that did occur came chiefly at the president's own instigation and were mainly designed to make the executive branch more responsive to his direction and control. The activities President Nixon himself initiated—for example, the reports and recommendations of his own Advisory Committee on Executive Organization—had far more influence in bringing about changes in the executive branch than the sporadic efforts of Congress or others to curtail the scope of presidential authority.

Proposals to streamline congressional operations have long been high on the agenda of political reform groups, as well as a small but dedicated circle within Congress itself. Both Common Cause, the national citizens' lobby headed by former HEW Secretary John Gardner, and Ralph Nader's consumer organization launched studies on ways to improve legislative operation. Thus far, changes that have actually taken place can best be described as incremental, although some observers feel they have had a significant effect. Most important perhaps was the requirement that teller votes in the House of Representatives be made a matter of public record at the request of a small number of House members—an innovation that makes it more difficult for legislators to conceal from their own constituents their real stand on major issues. The vote in the House denying funds to the supersonic transport plane (SST) was widely credited to the new system of recording teller votes. A number of other alterations in House and Senate procedures were also accomplished by the Legislative

Reorganization Act of 1970, including a modification in the seniority rule so that committee chairmen in the House are no longer automatically chosen on the basis of seniority.

There have also been frequent efforts in recent years to improve the federal judicial system so as to enable the courts to deal more effectively with their mounting caseloads. But the most highly publicized pressure for change has come from conservative groups that have long sought to restrict the power of the courts to issue orders requiring school busing to achieve racial balance. These efforts were finally crowned with success in June 1972, when Congress passed, and the president signed, a bill imposing a moratorium on any new court orders forcing school districts to bus or transfer students for the purpose of achieving desegregation. At year's end, the constitutionality of this legislation was still awaiting a test in the courts.

In the meantime, even more radical proposals for reform of the federal judiciary were under consideration in Congress, including a constitutional amendment providing for the periodic reconfirmation of federal district judges by the Senate. President Nixon's success in moving the Supreme Court toward a more conservative posture with four new appointments during his administration (two in the survey year) may have served to blunt the edge of this drive to modify the role of the courts in the American political system. In the 1930s, President Roosevelt's effort at drastic reform of the high court with a so-called court-packing scheme was also made unnecessary by the opportunity judicial vacancies provided to shift the philosophy of the Court without changing its basic structure.

STRENGTHENING THE CITIZEN'S ROLE IN GOVERNMENT

Throughout American history, the effort to devise ways and means of increasing the influence of the ordinary citizen in the affairs and decisions of government has been a continuous one. Periodically, however, it reaches high points. On these occasions the movement for citizen participation takes on the dedication and enthusiasm of a religious revival.

In the past, such high points have left a substantial institutional imprint on the structure and operation of American democracy.

The Jacksonian movement in the eighteenth century left us the long ballot, frequent elections, and a variety of opportunities for citizens to participate in government through popularly elected commissions set up to oversee state and municipal activities—such as school, library, and park boards. The populist movement in the early part of the twentieth century gave us the initiative, the referendum, the recall of elected officials, and a number of other channels through which the public at large could directly intervene in the governmental process.

Now in the latter part of the twentieth century, the drive for citizen participation in government seems to be cresting again. There are many manifestations of this revival in contemporary American politics. The growing strength of the consumer protection movement under Ralph Nader, the establishment of Common Cause as a citizens' lobby in Washington, the requirements for citizen participation in the activities and decisons of agencies set up to cope with poverty and unemployment in the inner-city ghetto areas—these are some of the ways in which a renewed interest in citizen participation in government has expressed itself in contemporary America.

All the federal agencies administering regulatory statutes have also been feeling new pressure from consumer and citizen groups. Some older agencies such as the Federal Trade Commission and the Antitrust Division of the Justice Department, have been given a new lease on life and have become much more vigorous in protecting consumers and seeking to break up business conglomerates that restrict competition. But there has also been a drive for the creation of new regulatory organizations that would act more aggressively on behalf of consumers. Proposals were before Congress in 1972 to establish two new consumer protection agencies—one to represent consumer interests before other federal agencies and the other to set standards for product safety.

Central to the traditional American belief in citizen participation has been the conviction that citizens can involve themselves most easily and effectively in the government closest to them—the state and local, rather than the national, government. Since Thomas Jefferson's day, this has remained a chief article of faith in the American democratic creed, in spite of the growth of national feeling and the erosion of traditional loyalties to states and localities. From this perspective, one of the principal ways in which citizen participation can be enhanced is by strengthening the position of state and local units of government in the American federal system.

The effort to strengthen these lower tiers of government has been frustrated many times in the past, however, by the fact that these units do not have adequate fiscal capacity to exercise much of the constitutional authority vested in their hands. During the administration of Dwight D. Eisenhower, an attempt on the part of national officials to return jurisdiction over several governmental programs to the states foundered because the activities would have added appreciably to state expenses at a time when many of the states already feared approaching insolvency. In the face of these fiscal facts of life, much of the rhetoric of American politics about returning power to the states has had a certain hollow ring. Virtually all state activities today in such areas as conservation, education, highways, and health depend upon federal subsidies in the form of grants-in-aid.

Hence, whatever its possible disadvantages, the revenue-sharing proposal by President Nixon in his 1971 State of the Union message was squarely directed at the major obstacle to reform in the American federal system—the inadequate fiscal resources of the states and localities. Under the Nixon proposal as originally put forward, a portion of federal tax revenues ($5 billion starting in fiscal 1972) would have been returned to state and local governments each year to be spent at their discretion. The president coupled this revenue-sharing proposal with a plan for six annual block grants to the states as a substitute for over 100 existing categorical aid programs—a reform that would give the states much greater leeway in deciding how to spend federal grant money. These block grants would have totaled $11 billion in 1972.

There were some groups in American society who found proposals of this sort somewhat disturbing. Lower-income groups, especially blacks, have little reason to expect benefit from an arrangement that will increase the power of the states over decisions on public expenditures, since their access to Washington has always been much better than their entree to state capitals. Other critics of revenue sharing have argued that it would reward states which now do far too little to raise money from their own citizens. Some states, for example, presently have no income tax.

It was in light of some of these concerns that the president's revenue-sharing proposal was modified while being considered by the House during the past year. A bill introduced by the House Ways and Means Committee Chairman Wilbur D. Mills (D-Ark.) would allocate the lion's share of the funds made available by revenue sharing to units of local government rather than the states. This legislation also stipulated that the amount of money a state receives under revenue sharing will be related to its effort to tax its own citizens for the support of state services. Overall, the Mills bill attached a good many strings to the money returned to the states, so much so that some observers suggested that the net effect of revenue sharing would be to increase the supremacy of the national government in the American federal system, rather than to shore up the power of the states.

Indeed, there were many plans under current consideration that would give the national government additional functions in the federal system. Witness, for example, President Nixon's suggestion of a national value-added tax to replace the local property levy as a source of fiscal support for public education in the United States. It has also been proposed that the federal government assume the burden of paying for all or most of the costs of state and local welfare programs. What all these developments portend is not so much a shift in power from one level of government to another as the growing interdependence of the federal system—with the states and localities administering and framing policies for programs that are federally funded and regulated. Symptomatic of this trend was the proposal made in connection with revenue sharing that the federal government take over the task of collecting states' income taxes so that the states could use the money thus saved for other purposes.

The reform of local government continued to move in two diametrically opposed directions during the survey year. There was pressure for the establishment of larger local jurisdictions to assist in the governance of metropolitan areas or to deal with problems that transcend the boundaries of existing jurisdictional units—environmental pollution, for example. It is this pressure that has led to the steady reduction in the number of units of local government in the United States over the past several decades. (From 1942 to 1967, the number of such units fell from around 155,000 to 81,000, largely as a result of school district consolidation.)

At the same time, there was growing feeling that many local units were too large already. The community-control movement, which has considerable strength in the nation today, has sought to introduce a new pattern of neighborhood government, under which many governmental services in urban areas would be decentralized. The task of supervising educational policy, for example, would be placed under the control of boards representing parents whose children attend schools in various parts of the city. According to the International City Management Association's *Municipal Yearbook,* at least 140 cities had established neighborhood, area, or district councils of this sort by 1972.

The simultaneous attraction of metropolitan and neighborhood government illustrated the contradictory impulses that continued to animate the governmental reform movement. But overall, as in all previous years since the 1930s, the trend in the United States was toward cooperative federalism, in which the national, state, and local units of government acted increasingly not so much as rivals for power but as potential partners in the task of governance.

The People Speak

We have no statesman who can evaluate conditions in this country and, because of this, we have poor progress. All we have is politicians.
      a retired advertising man in a Pennsylvania suburb

I'd like to see a change in the tax structure. It seems the working people bear all the tax burdens.
      a Baltimore housewife

We the people put the country's leaders in office, and they are not representing us.
      a black telephone operator in a large eastern city

The president is trying and you have to give him credit. It's the Congress and Senate that are holding us back.

　　a manual worker in a small New England town

So *many things are promised but, when people get elected, they don't do the things they promised.*

　　a black hospital worker in Brooklyn

I believe in ten years there will be a radical change. It has to be for the better; it can't be any worse.

　　a retired suburbanite in the Middle Atlantic area

The political leaders have played cat and mouse. The people have lost confidence.

　　a black electrician in the deep South

I fear an increase in the dehumanization of the governmental process.

　　an assistant superintendent of schools in a small California town

I hope we will see less corruption in government. Too many senators and representatives are on the take and are not doing much for us.

　　a pharmaceutical salesman in Grand Rapids

A good deal of public opinion poll data bears out President Nixon's estimate that: "Most Americans today are simply fed up with government at all levels." A June 1972 Harris Survey reported that one-half of the public agreed with the statement "The people running the country don't really care what happens to people like yourself." One month later another Harris Survey reported that "in both the public and private sector the establishment is under heavy attack," and went on to relate how public confidence in the leaders of both government and business had slipped in recent years. Harris had found in November 1971 that more than eight out of ten respondents concurred with the statement that "most elected officials promise one thing at election time and do something different once in office," and almost two-thirds went along with the charge that "only a few men in politics are dedicated public servants." And a Gallup poll released in February 1972 showed that 54 percent of the public was dissatisfied with the way the nation was being governed.

Our present survey shows, however, that the story is much more complicated than it appears on the surface. What we wanted to explore was not the people's attitudes about specific governmental actions, but rather their trust and confidence in the institutions of their society, especially governmental ones. This approach was based on the following reasoning: Americans recognize that they do not have enough knowledge about all the political, economic, and social issues to enable them to answer the bewilderingly complex problems currently confronting the nation at home and abroad. Primarily, the people are looking for institutions and leaders who not only have the necessary expertise to attack these problems but whose decisions about ends and means are based on values that the people share. The question is not so much one of public acceptance or rejection of specific action, but rather one of general goals and approaches demonstrating that leaders and institutions have their hearts in the right place. The more meaningful issue, we have concluded, is the general trust and confidence people have in leaders and institutions, public and private, than public approval of particular actions, propositions, stands, or developments.

We therefore asked the American people how much trust and confidence they have in governmental institutions as a whole and, to provide a basis for comparisons, in several other public and private groups as well, including business and industry, labor unions, the mass media, and political leaders in general. We begin with the nongovernmental institutions.

BUSINESS AND LABOR

It developed from answers to our questions that respondents had considerably more confidence in American business and industry than in American labor unions. We asked:

How much trust and confidence do you have in American business and industry today when it comes to operating efficiently and in the best interests of consumers: a great deal, a fair amount, not very much, or none at all?

And how much trust and confidence do you have in American labor unions as they now operate when it comes to reasonableness in making demands and consideration for the public interest?

	Business and Industry	Labor Unions
	(in percentages)	
A great deal	10	8
A fair amount	50	37
Not very much	30	36
None at all	6	14
Don't know	4	5
	100	100

Under our weighted scoring system (in which 100 represents a great deal of confidence and zero represents none at all), the average composite score* in the case of business and industry was 55—showing a slightly positive margin on the side of confidence. In contrast, the composite score for labor unions was 47, just onto the not-very-much-confidence side. (See Table A-8).

Business and industry's most favorable constituency included: women (a most important finding since they do most of the shopping); older people; those with only a grade school education and with family incomes of less than $5,000 per year; homeowners; southerners; Catholics; the professional and business group itself; those who called themselves moderately conservative; and, above all, Republicans.

The composite scores on labor unions exceeded the median point of 50 among: those of lowest educational achievement and lowest income; southerners; residents of medium-sized metropolitan areas (50,000–499,999); blacks; Democrats; liberals; and, as would be expected, labor union members and their spouses.

Neither of these overall composite scores suggests an abundance of public confidence and trust in either the labor or business institutions of our society. (This will become even more apparent in a comparison of all such institutional ratings.) In short, the American people at the time of our survey were not about to give three cheers for either business or labor.

---

* The method by which composite scores are calculated is explained in Appendix 5.

Some of the comments made by respondents demonstrate why. Said a recent college graduate: "I just have the feeling that a lot of big businesses disregard the welfare of the country and of the people." According to a California housewife, "The unions have grown too powerful and are no longer for the good of the working people." In the view of a public relations man in Florida, "Big business doesn't care about consumers and lacks concern for the public." An elderly retired man in New York State held particularly vehement views: "I'd like to see an end to all the unions. The unions are causing prices to go up through their wage demands and telling everyone what to do."

There is nothing particularly new about such attitudes. In a survey conducted by the Institute for International Social Research in 1964, large pluralities of the public thought that both labor unions and big business corporations should have less, rather than more, influence in governmental and political matters. And a majority (52 percent) felt that labor unions should be subjected to more governmental controls and regulations. Most surprisingly, in that study those who showed themselves to be conservatives by their views on substantive issues exhibited even stronger anti-big-business sentiment than liberals, apparently an expression of their distrust of any institution with excessive power and influence, whether it be government, labor unions, or big business.*

POLITICIANS AND THE MASS MEDIA

Scores accorded to Americans in political life and to the mass media were somewhat more positive than those given to business and labor. We asked:

How much trust and confidence do you have in general in men and women in political life in this country who either hold or are running for public office?

And how much trust and confidence do you have in the mass

---

* This survey is described in Lloyd A. Free and Hadley Cantril's *The Political Beliefs of Americans.*

media—such as the newspapers, TV, and radio in general—when it comes to reporting the news fully, accurately, and fairly?

	Persons in Political Life	Mass Media
	(in percentages)	
A great deal	8	17
A fair amount	60	50
Not very much	27	26
None at all	4	5
Don't know	1	2
	100	100

Considerably more respondents expressed a "great deal" of confidence in the mass media than in people in public life, with the result that the composite score for the mass media was 60 and for politicians 58—a small, but perhaps encouraging, disparity for those who cover the news. (See Table A-8.)

The highest demographic scores in favor of the mass media were found among: groups at the very bottom of our socioeconomic pyramid in terms of both education and income, midwesterners, residents of medium- but not large-sized metropolises, blacks, Democrats, and the self-designated moderately liberal. The lowest scores were found among the college-educated, white collar workers, Independents, and the "very conservative."

Before going on, we should like to round out the record by mentioning that the public's trust and confidence in today's generation of young people was greater than that in any of the other groups we asked about, private or public. The composite score of confidence in youth was a resounding 67. (See Chapter III.)

TRUST AND CONFIDENCE IN THE FEDERAL GOVERNMENT

To determine the people's faith in their governmental system, we first asked about their confidence in the federal government's international activities. Our query: *Now I'd like to ask you several questions about our governmental system. First, how much trust and confidence do you have in our federal government in Washington when it comes to handling international problems: a great deal, a fair amount, not very much, or none at all?*

A great deal	22 percent
A fair amount	55
Not very much	19
None at all	2
Don't know	2
	100 percent

A favorable assessment was given by more than three-quarters of our respondents, as compared with only a shade more than two in ten who gave an unfavorable evaluation. This balance of approval is particularly interesting in that almost one-half of our respondents expressed dissatisfaction with the way the government was handling the problem of Vietnam. (See Chapter X.) Presumably pushing aside Vietnam in the public's mind was the buoying impact of President Nixon's trips to Peking and Moscow. Whatever the causes for this evaluation, be they transient or not, the conclusion is inescapable: in its handling of foreign policy problems, the federal government enjoyed a substantial degree of public confidence.

What about the thornier domestic area, where, as we have seen, the public's evaluation of progress was less favorable than on the international scene? To answer this question, we asked: *And how much trust and confidence do you have in our federal government when it comes to handling domestic matters in general?*

A great deal	13 percent
A fair amount	58
Not very much	24
None at all	3
Don't know	2
	100 percent

The proportion of favorable answers dropped from 77 percent on international matters to 71 percent on domestic, and the total of unfavorable percentages rose from 21 percent to 27 percent. Nevertheless, more than seven out of ten respondents expressed at least a fair amount of trust and confidence in the federal government's handling of domestic problems, while less than three in ten said they had little or no confidence.

The overall composite score on the international side came to 66, and on the domestic side, to a lower but still respectable 61. (See Table A-8.) Scores on handling foreign policy matters were particularly high among families in the top-income bracket, white collar workers, Republicans, and—heartening in an election year for an incumbent administration that has not traditionally found support in these quarters—labor union households and Catholics.

The composite score on handling domestic matters was also especially high among Catholics. Their positive assessment was outranked only by the ratings among white collar workers, the "moderately conservative," and Republicans. Expressing less-than-average confidence on the handling of domestic matters were young people, the college-educated, families in the very top income bracket, manual workers (but not the labor union elite among them), and those who said they were very liberal. Black Americans indicated considerably below-average confidence in the government's handling of both international and national affairs, with composite scores of 59 and 54 respectively.

Despite such variations, our cross section of the American people certainly did not indicate a loss of faith in the federal government. Quite to the contrary, the overall composite scores clearly bespoke a substantial degree of public trust and confidence.

THE BRANCHES OF GOVERNMENT

Following these questions about the federal government's handling of international and domestic matters in general, we asked about relative degrees of trust and confidence in each of the three branches. Our questions:

As you know, our federal government is made up of three branches: an executive branch, headed by the president; a judicial branch, headed by the U.S. Supreme Court; and a legislative branch, made up of the U.S. Senate and House of Representatives. First, let me ask you how much trust and confidence you have at this time in the executive branch, headed by the president?

How much trust and confidence do you have under present conditions in the judicial branch headed by the U.S. Supreme Court?

And how much trust and confidence do you have at present in the legislative branch, consisting of the U.S. Senate and the House of Representatives?

	Executive	Judicial	Legislative
		(in percentages)	
A great deal	27	17	14
A fair amount	49	49	58
Not very much	18	23	23
None at all	5	7	2
Don't know	1	4	3
	100	100	100

Favorable replies ("a great deal" and "a fair amount") totaled more than three-quarters in the case of the executive; exceeded seven out of ten for the legislature; but were down to two-thirds for the judiciary. Reflecting this variation of opinion, composite scores on this three-part question were:

Executive branch	67
Legislative branch	62
Judicial branch	60

The sequence of this ranking is the same as that found by the Institute for International Social Research in 1964. In the interim, however, the preeminence of the executive over the legislative has become even more marked. Contrasting the unimposing record of the present Congress with the veritable flood of legislation passed by that body eight years ago during the Johnson administration, this result may not be altogether surprising. Nevertheless, the current ratings seemed to indicate public recognition, and perhaps endorsement as well, of the current primacy of the executive branch.

The demographic variations on this question are highly interesting. (See Table A-8.) Trust and confidence in the executive branch was highest among: older people (fifty and over), the nonlabor force (made up predominantly of retired people), those with only a grade school education, white collar workers, people living in small communities and rural areas, those who classified themselves as moderately conservative, and Republicans. Most of these groups traditionally have tended to be conservative. In contrast, lower-than-average scores on confidence in the executive were found among: those under fifty years of age; professional and business people; labor union households; manual workers in general; non-homeowners; city dwellers; Democrats and Independents; liberals; and, most markedly, black Americans. Most of these groups tend toward stands usually thought of as liberal.

This lineup shows a distinct reversal of the patterns found by the Institute for International Social Research in 1964. At that time, with Lyndon Johnson, a Democrat, in the White House, it was the groups with a more liberal bent that exhibited the most trust and confidence in the executive; today, with Richard Nixon, a Republican, in the White House, it is the more conservatively inclined who do.

Among several groups, composite scores for confidence in the legislative branch were equal to or even higher than those for the executive. People thirty to forty-nine years old, professionals and businessmen, manual workers, non-homeowners, residents of medium-sized metropolitan areas, Democrats, liberals, Catholics, and, above all, black Americans expressed the same, or more, trust in the legislative as in the executive branch.

The judicial branch, to be sure, fared less well than either of the other two. Nevertheless, expressions of trust and confidence toward this much maligned and, in the eyes of many, most controversial of the three branches of the federal government were definitely on the positive side. Such feelings were especially high among young people, white collar workers, city dwellers, midwesterners, the "very liberal" group, and especially black Americans, for whom the Supreme Court has forced open many doors.

STATE AND LOCAL GOVERNMENT

The American experiment in democracy was built in part on the assumption that the individual citizen had a right to be heard, that he had a special stake in his own governance. Further, that experiment called for responsive government, with institutions as close as possible to the people. How, then, did the public assess those levels of government closest to it? We asked:

How much trust and confidence do you have in the government of this state where you live when it comes to handling state problems?

And how much trust and confidence do you have in the local governments here in this area where you live when it comes to handling local problems?

	State Government	Local Government
	(in percentages)	
A great deal	18	14
A fair amount	49	50
Not very much	26	25
None at all	5	8
Don't know	2	3
	100	100

Two-thirds of our sample expressed a fair amount of trust and confidence or better in their state governments and 64 percent in their local governments. These favorable proportions, however, were slightly lower than the evaluations of the federal government in its handling of domestic problems. Conversely, negative responses were somewhat higher for state and local government than for the federal, resulting in the following composite scores:

Federal government in handling domestic problems   61
State government in handling state problems   60
Local government in handling local problems   57

There were interesting deviations from the predominant pattern of placing greatest trust and confidence in the federal government. The following groups indicated slightly more trust and confidence in state government than in the federal: young people, those with only a grade school education, manual workers, non-homeowners, westerners, blacks, Protestants, and especially people living in the South. Republicans, who have traditionally stressed the principle of local home rule, went even farther: they rated their *local* governments highest of all, not only higher than state governments, but even higher than the federal government, despite the Republican label on the present occupant of the White House.

In short, each level of government appealed to certain constituencies, although in general our respondents seemed least enchanted with the one closest to them—local government. But all three tiers of government did enjoy at least a fair degree of trust and confidence on the part of the public.

REVENUE SHARING AND TAXES

With a rather positive assessment of all levels of government, it is not surprising that the public endorsed the federal government's sharing some of its revenues with state and local governments. We asked: *It has been proposed that a certain percentage of the money Washington collects in federal income taxes—let's say about 3 percent—should be turned over automatically to state and local governments, without strings attached, for them to use as they see fit. Do you favor or oppose this idea?*

Favor	60 percent
Oppose	31
Don't know	9
	100 percent

The level of support for revenue sharing has dropped during the last four years, however. According to an Institute for International Social Research study conducted in 1968, the ratio of support to disapproval at that time was 68 to 22 percent. Approval, nonetheless, continues. Only among the white collar workers did support fall below the 50 percent mark, and even among that group it remained a plurality.

One of the alleged appeals of the revenue-sharing concept is based upon the assumption that the farther the level of government doing the taxing is from the people, the less the taxing hurts. But is this so? The answer, it would appear, is not quite that simple. To determine the public's attitude toward taxes, we first asked: *Obviously, nobody likes to pay more taxes. However, if taxes at some one level of government absolutely had to be raised, which would you rather see increased: federal taxes, state taxes, or local taxes?*

Federal taxes	39 percent
State taxes	20
Local taxes	24
Don't know	17
	100 percent

Here, of course, there is not much question—Washington is the least objectionable taxing authority. But what happens when the question is put in terms of kind of tax? To find the answer to that, we asked:

If taxes absolutely had to be raised to meet the growing needs of the country, which one of the kinds of taxes listed on this card would you rather see increased: income taxes, sales taxes, or real estate taxes?

And which one of these kinds of taxes would you be most unwilling *to see increased?*

	Most Preferred	Least Preferred
	(in percentages)	
Income taxes	29	35
Sales taxes	42	21
Real estate taxes	13	37
Don't know	16	7
	100	100

On both counts, an increase in the sales tax was considered preferable to raising either income or property taxes, and to date sales taxes are primarily state and local revenue sources. Unlike income or real estate levies, the sales tax normally appears as a few pennies here, a dollar or two there, and therefore may seem to be a less painful alternative when facing a tax increase. Or it may be that the American people believe they would have more control over their incomes with an increased sales tax since they determine what they buy—and, in some cases, whether they buy at all.

Deviating from the prevailing pattern, pluralities in several groups said they would prefer to see income taxes increased rather than sales taxes: those in the lowest income bracket (who may understand, as those slightly better off may not, that sales taxes are more regressive for the poor than are graduated income taxes); the college-educated (perhaps more aware of the nature of the tax system); those who categorized themselves as very liberal; the nonlabor force; and easterners.

Opposition to increases in real property taxes was highest among: homeowners (understandably); older people; the nonlabor force (made up predominantly of retired people, who have great difficulty keeping up with taxes on their homes); midwesterners; and Republicans.

These attitudes on tax alternatives take on particular import in relation to the continuing debate over the need for increased revenue and its possible sources. Our findings seem to point in the direction of some kind of federal sales tax. It appears that a value-added tax (VAT), a form of national sales tax now under discussion by the administration and others, would evoke less resistance from the public than most other options for taxing individuals, particularly if VAT were presented as a means of holding down real property taxes.

EVALUATIONS OF THE GOVERNMENTAL SYSTEM

Governments at federal, state, and local levels, as we have just seen, enjoyed overall a satisfactory amount of public trust and confidence. On the surface, our findings would seem to call into question the notion that people today are fed up with their governments. But what are the public's attitudes if we probe a little deeper? To do so, we asked another three-part question:

Now let's consider our governmental system as a whole in this country, federal, state, and local, from several points of view. First, if you had to rate our governmental system as a whole in terms of honesty, fairness, *and* justice, *what mark would you give the system: excellent, good, only fair, or poor?*

What mark would you give our governmental system as a whole when it comes to efficiency *in handling the problems it faces?*

And in showing consideration *for and* responsiveness *to the needs, hopes, and desires of ordinary citizens like yourself, what mark would you give to our governmental system as a whole?*

	Honesty, Fairness, and Justice	Efficiency	Consideration and Responsiveness
		(in percentages)	
Excellent	7	5	5
Good	34	33	28
Only fair	47	50	49
Poor	10	11	16
Don't know	2	1	2
	100	100	100

In each of these three important respects, large majorities gave the governmental system as a whole only a fair rating at best. The overall composite score in each instance was below the median point of 50, giving a uniformly unfavorable balance:

Honesty, fairness, justice	46
Efficiency	44
Responsiveness, consideration	41

A number of groups tended to give more favorable ratings than average on all or most of these aspects: people in the top income and lowest educational groups; white collar workers; residents of medium-sized metropolitan areas (50,000–499,999); westerners; those who classified themselves as moderately conservative; and Republicans. (See Table A-9). Not unexpectedly, the lowest marks were to be found among: young people, black Americans, and those at opposite ends of the ideological spectrum—the "very liberal" and "very conservative."

On balance, then, it appears that the public as a whole, at least in allegiance to symbols, retained a measure of trust and confidence in their governmental institutions. But this confidence did not extend in unqualified fashion to the quality of the governing that goes on in those institutions. As the governmental system impinges from day to day on citizen's lives—whether the impact be measured in terms of honesty, fairness, justice, efficiency, or especially responsiveness to their needs, hopes, and expectations—the people have clear and disturbing misgivings.

THE NEED FOR CHANGE

This mood of qualified dissatisfaction can be taken one step further. Without suggesting any revolutionary overtones, a majority of the public clearly saw a need for change in their governmental system. We asked: *Taking into account what you would want America to be like ten years from now, do you think a basic change will need to be made in the way our governmental system is now set up and organized or don't you think this will be necessary?*

Change	54 percent
No change	36
Don't know	10
	100 percent

The demographic variations on this question were, on the whole, to be expected, but they are fascinating nonetheless. (See Table A-10.) Only three groups felt so satisfied with the present system that as many, or more, of their constituent members were opposed to basic change as were in favor: families in the upper-middle income bracket ($10,000–$14,999), who generally have tended to be more conservative than those in the top income category; white collar workers; and particularly people living in the West who, as we have seen, had more trust and confidence in their state and local governments than residents of other parts of the country. (One might interpret this to mean, interestingly, that westerners are less "anti-Establishment" than easterners, even though the East is usually thought of as the seat of the Establishment.)

On the other hand, a need for basic change was indicated by at least six out of ten among groups which, throughout our study, have frequently shown themselves to be the most dissatisfied: easterners; young people; the very poor; manual workers; people living in smaller cities; Independents; the handful of respondents who characterized themselves as very liberal; and, most especially, black Americans, of whom almost seven out of ten opted for fundamental change, clearly indicating that they believe the present system is stacked against them.

The comments of several of those interviewed seemed to sum up the prevailing mood quite well. A hospital employee in Kentucky said, "We just don't have the government up there that can handle the problems that need taking care of." A female hairdresser in suburban New York commented: "We, the people, are losing control. The vote doesn't mean anything any more. A form of dictatorship may be coming. We have little to say now." A professional man in the South described his goal in these words: "Maybe there can be a development so as to get better-qualified people elected to office and have a fairer distribution of wealth, so that the rich will not be so rich and the poor will be better off." And an unemployed black woman in Detroit summed up the views of the vehemently discontented: "I am afraid that ten years from now this country may be in much worse shape unless some drastic changes are made."

XIII.
Americans' Values, Aspirations, and Fears

I'd like to have a nice home, get married, and have a nice family of two children. I want to enjoy my work; but I'd like a job so that I'd have enough time for leisure. As far as America is concerned, I'd like her to turn her priorities inward, which to my way of thinking means getting out of Vietnam and staying out of future wars.

a school teacher in a suburb of New York City

I'd like to see a black vice president; and better race relations between majority and minority groups.

a black equipment operator in Florida

I'm afraid my husband may lose his job and not be able to provide for the family.

the wife of an aircraft draftsman in Illinois

My worst fear is having to be on welfare.

a California restaurant worker

I would like to see the U.S. stay the No. 1 power on the journey toward peace.

a twenty-year-old army man stationed in Omaha, Nebraska

What I would really like to be is a filthy rich businessman.

a twenty-eight-year-old welder in Missouri

I'm afraid my children and grandchildren won't be able to walk or play in peace. I want the best things for them. Now they don't have good housing or schools and, most of all, they don't have equality.

a black domestic in Chicago

In the preceding pages we have listened as Americans expressed opinions, pronounced judgments, and made evaluations on a remarkably wide range of topics. What were the aspirations, fears, and values that motivated these views? In other words, which aspects of the public life of the United States and the personal lives of Americans are considered of crucial importance by the people, and which are not? What, in general, are Americans trying to attain, and what are they trying to avoid? In short, what are the goals and relative priorities in the minds of the American people, both personally and nationally?

In sketching our portrait of Americans today, we start with very broad strokes and then gradually fill in with the issues which Americans have most on their minds. The broad strokes we shall begin with are based on the ranking of concerns discussed in Chapter II and listed in Table 1.

Apart from Vietnam (which, with the bulk of American ground troops withdrawn and a corresponding decrease in U.S. casualties and draft calls, may be more a symbolic than a personally felt concern), the top ten subjects in that listing touch on problems that in some degree directly affect almost all Americans, no matter where they live: inflation, violence, crime and drugs, water and air pollution, solid waste disposal, health care, consumer protection, and problems of the elderly.

Below these came some problems peculiar to, or especially acute in, large metropolitan areas: unemployment, poverty, education, urban renewal, housing, mass transportation, and urban problems in general. This cluster not only ranked lower in the overall listing, but the demographic uniformity that had prevailed on the more universal problems dissipated. Both the lower ranking and the diversity of view indicated, of course, that the human considerations involved in the trials and tribulations of big-city life are not currently at the forefront of American values. This may be logical and understandable, even inevitable, but it does weaken the support for massively funded attacks to solve the problems that especially affect large urban minorities of our population.

Finally, with the exception of Vietnam, all items having to do with international and defense affairs fell in the lower half of the listing. The American people simply do not clothe such matters with the overriding importance they formerly enjoyed.

Asking people how much, in the abstract, they are concerned about this or that problem appears, to some, theoretical. Respondents may tend to give answers they consider socially or culturally acceptable, according to the norms of the time. What happens to their concern about social problems, then, when the issues are expressed in terms of money?

To get such a comparison, and, at the same time, to glimpse respondents' values on a more practical level, we asked a series of questions about governmental spending. Most of these have been mentioned in earlier chapters. We inquired about attitudes toward spending for education, public housing, urban renewal, assistance to black Americans, crime and drugs, health care, pollution, welfare, and international and defense affairs. Several of the items of high concern on our theoretical list—inflation, consumer protection, and maintaining respect for the U.S. abroad—did not lend themselves to this approach because major governmental spending in and of itself does not offer solutions.

Significantly, the ranking of issues by support for governmental spending was very similar to our listing by concern. The composite scores of all our questions on federal spending appear in Table 7. (Composite scores in this case were based upon values of 100 for increased federal spending, 50 for maintaining the present level, and zero for reducing spending or ending it altogether.)

The results confirm, even more dramatically than our earlier listing, the enormous shift in emphasis from international to domestic issues. Every single item on the domestic side (with the exception of the highly unpopular space program, if that can be considered a domestic issue) registered higher in the public's scheme of spending priorities than national defense and any of the purely international items.

In the case of domestic issues, the general pattern on spending was much the same as that for degrees of concern. High on the list were crime, problems of the elderly, drugs, water and air pollution, and health care. The only problem especially acute in big cities in the cluster of scores above the 70s was improved education for children of low-income families, which rated a

TABLE 7   SUPPORT FOR GOVERNMENTAL SPENDING ON
MAJOR NATIONAL ISSUES
composite scores

Combating crime	88
Helping the elderly	87
Coping with narcotic drugs and drug addicts	86
Cleaning up our waterways and reducing water pollution	81
Reducing air pollution	80
Improving the education of low-income children	80
Improving medical and health care for Americans generally	80
Helping low-income families pay their medical bills through medicaid	74
Making a college education possible for young people who could not otherwise afford it	72
Rebuilding run-down sections of our cities	69
Meeting the overall problems of our cities generally	68
Providing government-paid jobs for the unemployed	67
Providing better and faster mass transportation systems	66
Establishing more parks and recreation areas in our cities and countrysides	66
Providing better housing for people generally	64
Building better and safer roads, highways, and thruways	63
Helping to build low-rent public housing	62
Improving the situation of black Americans	57
Helping low-income families through welfare programs	53
Contributing to the work of the United Nations	36
Spending on our defense forces *	32
Maintaining U.S. forces in Europe	29
Maintaining U.S. military bases throughout the world	28
Spending on the space program	25
Providing economic and development loans to foreign countries	24
Providing military aid to foreign countries	21

* Asked in August 1972

composite score of 80. There was also considerable sentiment for increased spending on the medicaid program (composite score: 74) and for programs making it possible for needy young people to go to college (composite score: 72).

Once again, however, rebuilding the cities and meeting urban problems in general, giving jobs to the unemployed, providing better mass transportation systems, and erecting better housing were relatively far down the list, although support was definitely on the positive side and these items did significantly outrank all the defense and international concerns. And, ironically, providing more low-rent public housing, improving the lot of black Americans, and helping low-income families by means of welfare programs were all rated lower than establishing more parks and recreation areas and building better highways.

SPENDING PATTERNS AMONG POPULATION GROUPS

We have, in the preceding chapters, presented demographic variations to the questions about federal spending. Now it is time to pull them together. In the same way that we derived average overall levels of concern for international items as one group and domestic items as another (see Chapter II), we have established average overall levels of support for governmental spending on domestic and on international problems. The results appear in Table A-16.

The overall scores on domestic spending show some very sharp contrasts in outlook. As we have noted again and again, the young were third only to black Americans and the "very liberal" in advocating increased spending on domestic problems. Also significantly higher than average in their spending scores were white collar workers, labor union members and their spouses, non-homeowners, city dwellers in general and residents of our largest metropolitan areas in particular, and the self-designated liberals.

Again, consistent with earlier patterns, those least in favor of increased federal spending across-the-board for domestic purposes were people living in small communities and rural areas, those who labeled themselves conservatives, and Republicans.

So far we have been looking at differences *between* various population subgroups. Now, we want to take a different point of view. We want to look at the ranking of spending priorities *within* several subgroups in comparison to the overall ranking listed in Table 7. Deviations from the norm in spending patterns among segments of the population are, of course, indicative of different value systems at work within these groups.

Respondents aged fifty and over, for example, placed support for medical care and mass transportation higher on their list of spending priorities than did the total sample, presumably because the elderly are more prone to illness than younger people and more dependent on public conveyances. Similarly, people living in very small communities and rural areas, where doctors and hospitals are less readily available, put medical care higher on their list than did respondents generally. For equally clear reasons, they gave a higher-than-average ranking to highway construction and a lower-than-average ranking to urban renewal.

As would be expected, families with incomes below $5,000 per year gave a high ranking to governmental assistance in cases that present more acute problems for them than for other citizens—medical care (especially medicaid); government-paid jobs for the unemployed; and housing (particularly low-rent public housing).

Black Americans shared high priorities on all of these issues but medicaid. Blacks also gave higher-than-average ranking to education for low-income children; college opportunities for young people; urban problems in general (and particularly urban renewal); welfare programs; and, the highest of all, quite naturally, programs to improve the situation of blacks. On the other hand, blacks relegated such matters as the reduction of air and water pollution almost to the bottom of their list, obviously considering other problems to be far more pressing.

Republicans ranked such subjects as education for low-income children and college opportunities for the young markedly lower on their list than did the sample as a whole. At the same time such items as mass transportation, parks and recreation areas, and better highways were higher than average among Republican priorities.

The pattern among Democrats was much more in line with the norm than that of Republicans. Democrats, however, gave more-than-average emphasis to housing. Independents gave greater-than-average stress to highway construction; less-than-average, to medicaid.

And on it went, with these and many other group variations melding into the overall pattern of spending priorities given in

Table 7—a pattern that placed secondary emphasis on problems associated with the poor, the unemployed, blacks, inner-city residents, and other disadvantaged minorities.

Several aspects of the dominant pattern were incredibly shortsighted. For example, there was enormous concern about air pollution, but far less about providing the mass transportation systems that might help reduce it. There was more willingness to spend money to establish parks and recreation areas for people to play in than to provide adequate housing for people to live in. There was more interest in building highways and thruways than in improving the lot of black Americans.

Certainly, there was room for discouragement in the rankings we found. But there was room for encouragement, as well, with such items as educating low-income children and providing more opportunities for college training high on the list. These are the kinds of attitudes that keep open the potential of social mobility for the have-nots as well as the haves—and are so critical for our self-fulfillment as a nation.

DETERMINING HOPES AND FEARS

The lists of concerns and spending priorities emerged from the replies to a series of questions on specific domestic and international problems. In these questions, the people were specifically reminded of each issue and given a chance to think about it before answering. This systematic method, however, does not tell us what was in the respondents' minds before their attention was directed to a particular problem area. In other words, it does not tell us about the agenda of concerns that citizens carry with them as they go about their daily lives.

To determine the personally felt issues, whether abstract or concrete in form, that respondents would volunteer spontaneously, we administered at the beginning of each interview the "self-anchoring striving scale" questions described in Chapter I. We asked the people to tell in their own words the hopes and fears embodied in their concept of the best and the worst possible situations for themselves and for their nation. What they told us follows.

NATIONAL HOPES AND FEARS

To determine hopes and fears for the nation, we asked:

What are your wishes and hopes for the future of the United States? If you picture the future of the U.S. in the best possible light, how would things look, let us say, about ten years from now?

And what about your fears and worries for the future of our country? If you picture the future of the U.S. in the worst possible light, how would things look about ten years from now?

The open-ended replies we received were grouped according to theme. The wishes and hopes that were mentioned by at least 5 percent of our sample are listed in Table 8; the worries and fears, in Table 9. The same questions were asked by the Institute for International Social Research in 1959 and 1964 and for the *Hopes and Fears* survey in 1971. We have included figures from these surveys to add perspective to our analysis.

When our questions reminded respondents of such matters as health care, consumer protection, and problems of the elderly, the people expressed a very high degree of concern about them. Yet, in their own lists of national hopes and fears, not even 5 percent mentioned any one of these matters. They are not, in other words, problems that come to mind when Americans think in a national (or social) context, as one member of that polity that is the United States.

Other items that ranked high in the list of national concerns in response to specific questions, but were mentioned as national hopes or fears by very small percentages were: control of inflation (cited by 13 percent as a hope and the continuation or acceleration of inflation by an equal percentage as a fear); pollution abatement (cited by 12 percent as a hope and the growth of pollution by only 8 percent as a fear); law and order, combining the feelings toward both violence in American life and crime (mentioned by 14 percent as a hope, and its absence by 16 percent as a fear); elimination of the drug problem (cited by only 7 percent as a hope and its persistence by 9 percent as a fear); good education (indicated by only 6 percent as a hope and the inability to get good schooling by a mere 1 percent as a fear).

TABLE 8   NATIONAL HOPES
percentages *

	1959	1964	1971	1972
Peace	48	51	51	56
Employment	13	15	16	17
Law and order	—	—	11	14
Economic stability; no inflation	12	5	18	13
Solution of pollution problems	—	—	10	12
National unity and political stability (internal peace and order; absence of unrest, tensions, antagonisms)	—	9	15	11
Improved standard of living; greater national prosperity	20	28	11	10
Social justice (greater equality for all elements of the population)	—	—	—	8
Solution of drug problem	—	—	6	7
Efficient government; competent leadership	—	—	—	6
Education	—	—	—	6
Honest government	—	—	—	5
Elimination of racial discrimination and prejudice	14	15	10	5
Public morality (ethical standards, religion)	7	10	8	5
Better world (more international understanding and cooperation)	17	6	7	5

* A dash (—) indicates mention by less than 5 percent of the sample. A shift of 4 percentage points between studies is considered statistically significant.

Thus, even when the context was explicitly national, the horizons of the people in viewing their country's situation were distinctly limited. Unless prodded by interviewers, only small minorities of Americans in mid-1972 seemed preoccupied with most of the major problems that confronted the nation. Significantly, our survey failed to uncover any topic of intensely concentrated concern among Americans, with the possible exception of the war/peace theme.*

* Intense concern has appeared in similar surveys conducted worldwide. When the Institute for International Social Research asked a cross section

TABLE 9   NATIONAL FEARS
          percentages *

	1959	1964	1971	1972
War (especially nuclear war)	64	50	30	35
Lack of law and order	—	5	11	16
Economic instability; inflation; recession	18	13	17	13
National disunity and political instability (unrest, tensions, antagonisms, civil war)	—	8	26	13
Drug problem	—	—	7	9
Communism	12	29	12	8
Pollution	—	—	9	8
Lack of public morality (ethically, religiously)	—	5	6	6
Loss of democratic system; totalitarianism	—	5	5	5
Unemployment	7	6	7	5
Population growth	—	—	—	5
Threat, aggression, domination by a communist power	—	—	—	5

* A dash (—) indicates mention by less than 5 percent of the sample.
A shift of 4 percentage points between studies is considered statistically
significant.

PERSONAL HOPES AND FEARS

When, at the beginning of the survey interview, questions were
posed in the context of personal hopes and fears, of the good and
the bad life, the concerns that emerged were as diffuse as those
given for national hopes and fears. We asked:

*All of us want certain things out of life. When you think about
what really matters in your own life, what are your wishes and
hopes for the future? In other words, if you imagine your future*

of the Nigerian people about their hopes and fears for their nation in 1962,
for example, almost three-quarters of those surveyed mentioned national
disunity and political instability as a fear. These results indicated a public
truly worried about what was, indeed, a critical national problem. This case
is described in Hadley Cantril's *The Pattern of Human Concerns.*

in the best *possible light, what would your life look like then if you are to be happy?*

Taking the other side of the picture, what are your fears and worries for the future? In other words, if you imagine your future in the worst *possible light, what would your life look like then?*

The personal hopes mentioned by at least 5 percent of our respondents appear in Table 10; the corresponding list of fears, in Table 11. Comparable figures from previous surveys in which the same technique was used are included as well.

TABLE 10   PERSONAL HOPES
percentages *

	1959	1964	1971	1972
Peace in the world; no wars	9	17	19	32
Better standard of living	38	40	27	29
Good health for self	40	29	29	27
Aspirations for children (opportunities, especially education; success; happiness)	29	35	17	23
Happy family life	18	18	14	18
Own house or live in better one	24	12	11	12
Good health for family	16	25	13	12
Good job; congenial work	7	9	6	10
Wealth	—	5	7	8
Leisure time; recreation; travel	11	5	6	8
Peace of mind; emotional stability and maturity	5	9	8	7
Economic stability in general; no inflation	—	—	6	7
Safety from crime	—	—	—	7
Employment	5	8	6	6
Social justice (greater equality, elimination of discrimination)	—	—	—	6
Happy old age	10	8	6	6
Self-improvement or development	—	—	—	5
Christian revival	—	—	—	5

* A dash (—) indicates mention by less than 5 percent of the sample. A shift of 4 percentage points between studies is considered statistically significant.

TABLE 11   **PERSONAL FEARS**
            percentages *

	1959	1964	1971	1972
War	21	29	17	28
Ill health for self	40	25	28	21
Lower standard of living	23	19	18	18
Ill health for family	25	27	16	12
Unemployment	10	14	13	10
Economic instability in general; inflation	—	—	11	9
Drug problem in family	—	—	7	9
Inadequate opportunities or unhappiness for children	12	10	8	8
Crime	—	—	5	8
Pollution	—	—	7	6
Political instability (dissension, unrest, turmoil)	—	—	5	5
Social decay (spiritual, ethical, religious)	—	—	—	5

* A dash (—) indicates mention by less than 5 percent of the sample. A shift of 4 percentage points between studies is considered statistically significant.

In the answers to this question, we should be reaching the core of the people's preoccupations, not in their roles as citizens but in their lives as individuals. Understandably, most of the hopes and fears frequently mentioned had a homey atmosphere: health for self and family, opportunities for children, a happy family life, a decent home, along with the economic ability to preserve and enjoy these things, without the disruption that war would bring.

Just as in the 1971 *Hopes and Fears* survey, Americans expressed less concern than in earlier years with the material elements that have traditionally comprised the American dream. For example, mention of a better standard of living as a personal hope dropped from 38 percent in 1959 to 29 percent in 1972. During the same period hopes of having one's own home or a better place to live dropped by half, from 24 percent to 12 percent. Similarly, fear of a lower standard of living declined from 23 percent to 18 percent.

Mention of employment as a hope came to 6 percent (just

about the current rate of unemployment), and fear of unemployment was at the same low level that it had been in 1959 (10 percent), actually a shade below the 13 percent figure that emerged in the 1971 survey. Similarly, inflation was mentioned as a fear by only 9 percent of the population, despite all the attention paid to the subject.

Debate about the economic issue notwithstanding, it would appear that, in the material aspects of their lives, Americans on the whole were not hurting as much as many have frequently assumed. Pocketbook concerns ranked high in hopes and fears categories alike, to be sure, but none was mentioned as a hope or fear by even three respondents out of ten—not a proportion suggesting that economic matters are burning issues.

Variations among population groups about their fears and hopes were very small—and in some cases, surprising. An improved standard of living was mentioned as a hope by 31 percent of those in the very top income bracket and by only 29 percent of those in the very bottom category; a lower standard of living was cited as a fear by 16 percent in the top income group and by 21 percent in the bottom income group. Similarly, the well-to-do spoke of unemployment as a fear with an even higher frequency (11 percent) than those at the bottom of the economic pyramid (7 percent).

Hopes of black and white Americans for an improved standard of living were little different, although 27 percent of the blacks referred to a lower living standard as a fear, compared to only 17 percent of the whites. Blacks were also considerably more preoccupied with the problem of jobs; 11 percent mentioned employment as a hope, almost twice the proportion (6 percent) among whites. Similarly, unemployment was cited as a fear by 16 percent of the blacks, as compared to only 9 percent of the whites.

Age proved to be one of the most influential variables at work. Good health was mentioned as a hope by no less than 40 percent of older people, but only 12 percent of the young. Conversely, a happy family life as a hope was a preoccupation of more than one-third of the young, as compared to less than one in ten of the oldsters. Those in between (thirty to forty-nine) were far more concerned about children, both in terms of hopes and of fears, than either the young or the old (presumably, more of their children were still at home).

These egocentric value patterns were, of course, natural and inevitable. They also suggest that, in their day-to-day lives, most Americans' continuing concerns go little farther than their homes and families. The principal exception, it would appear, is on what is perhaps the most pervasive issue of all—peace and war.

Peace was mentioned by 32 percent of our citizens as a personal hope and by a far more imposing 56 percent as a national hope. War loomed as a personal fear for 28 percent and as a national fear for 35 percent. This marked apprehension over war, particularly on the personal side, should not come as a great surprise: war is considered by one and all as a threat on both personal and national levels, as a threat, in fact, to one's very way of life.

Interestingly enough, in comparison with preceding years, peace rose in priority as both a personal and national hope. This upward shift is especially striking in the face of the presumed reduction in international tensions resulting from the presidential trips to Peking and Moscow. One can conjecture that the American people in increasing numbers may now believe that peace is sufficiently within their grasp to be worth wishing for, even at the level of one's personal hopes, whereas before they may have taken a state of war (cold or hot) almost as a given.

Other public issues on which Americans expressed strong concern when asked specifically about the issue received but meager attention on the personal hopes and fears scale. They included: economic stability without inflation, mentioned by 7 percent as a hope, and its converse, by 9 percent as a fear (proportions relatively unchanged from 1971 but up substantially from 1959 and 1964); employment, cited by 6 percent as a hope (about the same as in earlier years), and unemployment, mentioned by 10 percent as a fear (down from 1964 and 1971 to the 1959 level); the drug problem, up from 7 percent in 1971 to a still not very high 9 percent as a fear, despite the threat it involves to children and family life; safety from crime, mentioned by 7 percent as a hope, and crime itself, moving up from 5 percent in 1971 to 8 percent as a fear; political instability, indicated by only 5 percent as a fear (unchanged from 1971 but more than double the previous years); pollution, cited by 6 percent as a fear (again, not a significant shift from the year before).

It would thus appear that, when considering their personal lives, relatively few Americans were so preoccupied with the most pressing public problems of the day that they cited them spontaneously when asked to describe the best and worst lives for themselves. Implicitly at least, the lack of consensus among volunteered concern suggests that such issues as pollution, crime, drugs, violence, unemployment, and even inflation were simply not wearing Americans as a whole down, certainly not enough for them to feel anything remotely approaching profound disillusionment or dissatisfaction. Americans in mid-1972 were not saying that they never had it so good, but they did seem to be indicating that, on the basis of their own values in the light of their own aspirations and fears, things were not all that bad either.

XIV.
State of the Nation

The president is bringing our boys home from Vietnam and is stabilizing prices. Our government is accomplishing a lot. Throughout our state and the nation things are better.
> a railroad inspector in Pennsylvania

The domestic situation is only fair. There are the unresolved problems of blacks and browns; inadequate financing for public education; inability to protect and improve the environment; failure to provide adequate housing or to solve the unemployment problem.
> a school superintendent in a small western city

Mr. Wallace was shot. Prices are going up. The drug situation is getting worse. People can't get jobs. The war is still going on.
> a Delaware housewife

It's God's country and we will pull out great. I'm not worried about the future of America.
> the wife of a salesman in a small eastern city

With every progressive program we have, we seem to lose more ground.
> a social worker in Massachusetts

I love America. No other country is as good to live in.
> a female white collar worker in an eastern city

Things are improving, but not rapidly. Most of the people I know are happy. We all have problems but things are pretty good.
> a shoe-factory worker in Massachusetts

We have come now to the final roundup of our bewildering array of proportions, percentages, and scores—to a public audit, as it were, of the state of the nation.

As we have seen, when foreign policy topics were reviewed one by one, predominant opinion was that the country had lost at least a little ground in the fields of international economics, balance of payments, and foreign trade; had made only a bit of progress in regard to Vietnam and maintaining ties with our allies; but had forged ahead in handling relations with mainland China and the Soviet Union. When we average the individual ratings of progress recorded in each of these respects, the composite foreign policy score is a moderately affirmative 60 (on our scale of 100).

Yet, when we asked respondents for an overall assessment of progress the U.S. had made in handling foreign policy problems over the past year, the composite rating rose to a considerably higher 66 (see Chapter I). In the eyes of the American people, the easing of tensions with China and the Soviet Union apparently far outweighed the drabber national performance in regard to Vietnam, our allies, and international economics.

On the domestic side, assessments of progress on various individual items were also characterized by contrasts. The public, in assigning composite scores of 60 and above, indicated a belief that considerable progress had been made during the survey year in handling problems of the elderly, medical care, and especially education, housing, and problems of black Americans. More modest estimates of progress were given for business and economic conditions generally, abatement of air and water pollution, and handling urban problems overall.

On the other hand, scores were at or around the "stood still" point of 50 in the case of mass transportation and of poverty and welfare problems. Scores in the 40s, pointing to a sense of regression, were given for unemployment and drugs. And even lower scores, in the 30s, were registered on crime and inflation, indicating that in these two fields the public felt considerable ground had been lost.

When we calculate the average of this range of scores, the composite domestic figure is 53, just above the "stood still" point. Yet, as discussed in Chapter I, when the people were asked to sum up the overall domestic situation, they registered a composite score of 62, indicating their belief that the U.S. had made measurable progress in handling domestic problems in general over the preceding year.

Thus, once again, in the eyes of the public, the whole turned out to be bigger and better than the sum of its parts. We suspect this is largely because people express concern in the abstract about lack of progress on problems we as a nation face even though those problems have not yet become painful or troublesome enough to them personally to affect their assessment of the domestic situation as a whole.

This hypothesis is borne out by the rather surprising results derived from the following question, asked almost at the end of one set of interviews: *Now let's sum things up a bit. Is it your impression that America today is a better place or a worse place to live than it was, say, ten years ago—or don't you think there is much difference one way or the other?*

Better place	38 percent
Not much difference	27
Worse place	32
Don't know	3
	100 percent

Thus, despite the widespread discussion about national decay and things going from bad to worse in this country, almost four out of ten of our respondents thought America was a better place to live today than it was ten years ago. And very close to two-thirds thought it was at least as good a place, if not better. Less than one-third—a sizeable minority, but a minority nonetheless—opted for the "worse place" alternative. (Black Americans, it should be noted, were among the most sanguine of all groups on this question; no less than 46 percent said America was a better place to live than ten years ago.) Once again, these results do not suggest that the great majority of Americans are "fed up" with their country.

From the ladder ratings and other data presented in Chapter I, the public appears to have judged, between early 1971 (when, as the *Hopes and Fears* survey showed, there was actually a sense

of national decline) and mid-1972 (when our survey was conducted), that their country had made a long night's journey into
day. But, as we shall see below, the dawn they perceived was still
rather murky.

EVALUATING DOMESTIC AND INTERNATIONAL SITUATIONS

If the people expressed a relative sense of forward movement on
the international and domestic fronts, how did they assess the
international and domestic situations in absolute terms? To find
the answers, we asked:

*How would you rate the international situation the U.S. faces in
general at the present time: excellent, good, only fair, or poor?*

And how would you rate the domestic situation in the U.S. today?

	International Situation	Domestic Situation
	(in percentages)	
Excellent	2	1
Good	33	29
Only fair	48	54
Poor	9	10
Don't know	8	6
	100	100

Close to six out of ten respondents thought the international
situation was only fair at best, and almost two-thirds judged the
domestic situation as negatively. As a result, the composite scores
on these two questions were 43 for the international situation and
only 41 for the domestic. As was the case with the composite
scores on progress described in Chapter I, the ratings given both
the international and domestic situations by various subgroups
of the population were almost unbelievably uniform. (See Tables
A-18 and A-19.)

On the international side, the only groups that were significantly
more favorable than the norm were families in the upper-middle
income bracket ($10,000–$14,999 per year), professionals and
businessmen, and white collar workers. They were joined by Republicans, whose score, the highest of any group, was still only

50, exactly at the midway point between "good" and "only fair."
On the other hand, the evaluations of black Americans and those
with only a grade school education (40 in both cases) were significantly below the lackluster overall score of 43.

There was even less variation in the ratings on the domestic
situation. The only groups giving significantly lower-than-average
ratings were blacks and Independents (both 38) and those few
respondents who categorized themselves as very liberal (37). Just
one group stood out noticeably on the favorable side: Republicans.
Their composite score was only 46, though, indicating that even
to the members of the president's own party, the country's domestic situation was tipped toward the negative.

STATE OF THE NATION

We have now reached what used to be called "the $64 question,"
the final evaluation of this public audit, the state of the nation:
*Finally, let's pull everything together. Taking into account the
situation both at home and abroad at the present time, what would
you say is the state of the nation in this year 1972: excellent, good,
only fair, or poor?*

Excellent	3 percent
Good	38
Only fair	50
Poor	7
Don't know	2
	100 percent

Almost six out of ten Americans (57 percent) described the
state of their nation as "only fair" at best. Only a shade more
than four out of ten (41 percent) said it was at least "good."

Nevertheless, this overall assessment was less unfavorable than
that of the international and domestic situations separately. The
rating given the international situation was 43 and the domestic
situation, 41; the composite score on the overall state of the nation
was a higher 46. As before, the whole was viewed as better than
the sum of its parts, but, also as before, the weight of opinion
fell on the negative side. (We suspect, incidentally, that our reference to "the state of the nation" in the final question triggered

some nationalistic "rally 'round the flag" impulses that may have edged the score up a bit.)

Once again, the assessments made by population subgroups showed remarkable uniformity. (See Table A-20.) Only four groups were significantly more sanguine than average about the state of the nation: families in the next to the bottom income bracket ($5,000–$6,999 per year); residents of cities with populations under 50,000 (who have shown themselves generally to be more conservatively inclined); those who called themselves moderately conservative; and Republicans, who turned in the highest score of any group, a 53. On the other hand, only two groups had significantly more adverse views than the rather restrained response of our sample as a whole: black Americans, with a score of 43, and those who called themselves very liberal, with a score of 42.

The two most extreme scores on the state of the nation covered a relatively limited range: from a low of 42 to a high of 53. This high degree of uniformity suggests, as have many other findings in our survey, that Americans—despite differences of opinion on a good many issues of the day and the slight variations in values, aspirations, and fears described in the preceding chapter—appear in general to hold a common system of values, goals, and social outlooks against which the national situation is judged. And this is true of Americans of almost all income groups, races, and religions, no matter what their ideological persuasion or where they live—East, West, South, North, in cities, towns, villages, or rural areas. Looking at their own and the country's situation in mid-1972 against the background of this shared value system, the American people seemed to say: *We are doing well enough in our own personal lives. The country has made some progress too, both domestically and internationally, over the past year. It is up from the rock-bottom low it hit in 1971. But, despite this improvement, the state of the nation is just "fair to middling." As a country we still have a long way to go, and to get there we will have to make some basic changes in the way we govern ourselves.*

Afterword

Throughout this book we have proceeded cautiously, trying to be as objective and factual as possible and limiting our comments and conclusions to clear implications from survey figures. We shall end this odyssey of ours, however, with a speculative flight, plotting our course more on the basis of informed judgments and intuitions than hard data.

The situation, as we now see it, boils down to this: with the notable exceptions of the very poor, blacks, and certain other minorities, the great mass of Americans has achieved the American dream of middle-class affluence aspired to by most of the world's other peoples. Against the norms of our materialistic society, most of the people seem to be saying, "We are doing quite well, thank you. Things aren't so bad at all."

But in realizing the dream—indeed, in *living* the dream—many Americans have experienced disillusionment and even ennui. They are satisfied on the whole with the material aspects of their lives: with their jobs, their homes, their neighborhoods, their children, their standard of living. But the achievement of their long-held goals, symbolized above all by vacuous suburbia, has not brought contentment.

At the same time, increasing urbanization and geographic mobility (about one-fifth of Americans change their place of residence every year) have strained or broken those social bonds which hold people together, give warmth to human relationships, and assure each individual a place and a personal identity within society. Today, many (if not most) Americans, whether consciously or not, tend to feel rootless, not deeply involved with the people who live around them. This loss of social bonds and disruption of social patterns have inevitably led to a weakening of the cultural guidelines that shape people's lives, ascribe value, and encourage stability.

The old norms have been undermined, or have become outmoded. The excitement, pleasure, and fulfillment that can come from serving a higher purpose than the material satisfaction of self and family appear to be missing. Even with a second car, a freezer of TV dinners, and an electric toothbrush, Americans seem to be saying, "Is *this* all there is to living the life of our dreams? Is *this* all we can look forward to from now on?"

Not only on the personal front but also on the national front, we discern the same feelings of emptiness and lack of direction. What has happened to America's role as defender of the democratic faith and protector of the free world, a concept that, combined with the crusade of containment of communism, rightly or wrongly gave purpose, meaning, and structure to the international life of the United States for more than two decades?

And on the domestic side, what has happened to the great American ideals of the past: democracy, equality, social justice, neighborly humanitarianism, human fellowship, and brotherhood? Why haven't we been able to achieve the goal described by a black factory worker in our sample: "I hope for a peaceful country, with all people living in harmony with all mankind, regardless of race, creed, or color. We are all God's children. Why can't we act that way?"

We don't act that way because the people of the United States have been neither inspired nor challenged to do so for some time now. Our present national mentality puts too much emphasis on defense of the status quo. Having made it into middle-class affluence, most of us have been more concerned with protecting the gains we have made than climbing new peaks of personal success or social responsibility. The dynamism, the sense of progress and perfectibility, have largely gone out of American life.

And no wonder, really. A whole new mode of national life that was introduced with the New Deal in the 1930s has been little altered in the past forty years. The 1930s liberals, and the more recent "new pragmatists," have all been problem-solvers (or, more accurately, aspiring problem-solvers). All too often, in fact, they have not dealt with the roots of the problems themselves, but with their symptoms.

And none of them, from Franklin D. Roosevelt to Richard M. Nixon, developed an encompassing system of political and social philosophy to explain and rationalize actions on the operational front of government. They have seen a problem or a symptom, and have simply moved, in varying ways and with varying degrees of enthusiasm, to alleviate it—by legislation and, above all, by massive governmental spending. We have had government by crisis, not government by plan.

Most of the fundamental economic and social problems of this country have stubbornly refused to be solved by such a pragmatic approach: the cancer in our cities; the hopeless mire of our transportation system; the blight of enduring poverty; the cruelly inadequate education of our children, especially those of blacks and other minority groups; uncontrollable and unpredictable economic forces; the terror of crime and drugs; the random violence in American life; the continuing bane of unemployment; and housing that is not only in short supply but which, particularly in our slums, is shockingly inadequate.

The public has come to feel that the solutions of the problem-solvers, particularly in the form of governmental programs costing more and more dollars, have not worked (and probably will not work) as well as hoped. Subconsciously at least, the people are looking for basic and reliable guidelines that will point the way out of the current social morass. And they are looking, in vain, we believe, at traditional American ideology, which lauds individual rights over governmental responsibilities, private action over public action, and is permeated with economic and social stereotypes and shibboleths inherited from our *laissez-faire* past. This set of credos that have served our needs well in the past appears in all too many ways simply not applicable to today's problems.

So the American people, whether they yet realize it or not, seem to us to be searching for a new political, social, and economic philosophy, one that will infuse them with new purpose. They want a philosophy that will lay out, explain, rationalize what must be done through governmental, social, and individual action to raise the quality of life in the United States, and perhaps outside it as well. They need a new ideological framework that will encompass basic changes in outlooks and approaches rather than the customary assortments of hastily-put-together programs deriving from almost total reliance on the problem-solving approach. They want a philosophy that will help provide an answer to the clear and insistent question, "Quo Vadis, America?"

Appendix I

QUESTIONS AND OVERALL RESULTS

The interviewing of the 1,806 respondents was conducted by The Gallup Organization on and between the first two weekends in June 1972. Owing to the large number of topics included in the survey, it was necessary to "split" the sample three ways. In other words, three different versions of the ballot were used, denominated "A," "B," and "C," respectively. Questions requiring the highest degree of statistical reliability were included in all three versions; less important questions were included in only two versions; and some questions were divided among the three ballots, thereby appearing in only one version.

The "A" version was administered to 669 respondents; the "B" version to 613; and the "C" version to 524. The designations (A), (B), and/or (C) following each of the questions listed below indicate in which version or versions of the ballot that particular question was included. From this one can deduce the number of interviews on which that particular set of replies was based. The composition of the total sample and its various parts is given in Appendix 6.

The subject matter covered by various sets of questions is indicated below. The questions themselves and the overall results follow.

Subject	Question Numbers
Personal and National Hopes and Fears and Ladder Ratings	1–11
International Issues	12–23
International Concerns	24

Internationalism vs. Isolationism	25–26
Progress: International	27–29
Domestic Issues	30–56
Domestic Concerns	57–58
Progress: Domestic	59–62
Taxes and Governmental Spending	63–67
Trust and Confidence in Institutions	68–84
Overall Evaluations	85–87

Ladder Ratings: Hopes and Fears

1. All of us want certain things out of life. When you think about
    what really matters in your own life, what are your wishes and
    hopes for the future? In other words, if you imagine your future
    in the best possible light, what would your life look like then
    if you are to be happy? Take your time in answering; such things
    aren't easy to put into words. (A,B)
    [Answers are given in Table 10 on page 259.]

2. Taking the other side of the picture, what are your fears and
    worries for the future? In other words, if you imagine your future
    in the worst possible light, what would your life look like then?
    Again, take your time in answering. (A,B)
    [Answers are given in Table 11 on page 260.]

3. Here is a ladder representing the "ladder of life." Let's suppose
    the top of the ladder represents the best possible life for you;
    and the bottom, the worst possible life for you. On which step of
    the ladder do you feel you personally stand at the present time?
    (A,B)

    Average Rating: 6.4

4. On which step would you say you stood five years ago? (A,B)

    Average Rating: 5.5

5. Just as your best guess, on which step do you think you will stand
    in the future, say about five years from now? (A,B)

    Average Rating: 7.6
    *[For demographic breakdowns of personal ladder ratings,
    see page 304.]*

6. Now let's consider just the past twelve months. In terms of your
    own personal happiness and satisfaction, would you say that today,
    as compared with one year ago, you are better off, about the same,
    or worse off? (A,B)

    Better off 46% About the same 41% Worse off 12% Don't know 1%

7. Now, what are your wishes and hopes for the future of the United
    States? If you picture the future of the U. S. in the best
    possible light, how would things look, let us say, about ten years
    from now? (A,B)
    [Answers are given in Table 8 on page 257 .]

8. And what about your fears and worries for the future of our
    country? If you picture the future of the U. S. in the worst
    possible light, how would things look about ten years from now?
    (A,B)
    [Answers are given in Table 9 on page 258 .]

9. Looking at the ladder again, suppose the top represents the <u>best</u>
    possible situation for our country; the bottom, the <u>worst</u> possible
    situation. Please show me on which step of the ladder you think
    the United States is at the present time. (A,B)

    Average Rating: 5.5

10. On which step would you say the United States was about <u>five years</u>
    <u>ago</u>? (A,B)

    Average Rating: 5.6

11. Just as your best guess, if things go pretty much as you now expect,
    where do you think the United States will be on the ladder, let us
    say, about <u>five years from now</u>? (A,B)

    Average Rating: 6.2
    *[For demographic breakdowns of national ladder ratings, see
    page 307.]*

International Issues

12. Turning now to some international matters, are you satisfied or
    dissatisfied with the way the United States government has been
    handling the problem of Vietnam recently? (C)

    Satisfied 46%   Dissatisfied 47%   Don't know 7%

13. Suppose the United States were confronted with a choice of only
    the two alternatives listed on this card, which one would you
    rather have the United States follow in regard to Vietnam? (C)

    A. End the war by accepting the best possible compromise
        settlement even though it might sooner or later allow
        the Vietnamese Communists to take over control of
        South Vietnam.   44%

    B. Fight on until a settlement can be reached which will
        insure that the Communists do not get control of
        South Vietnam.   48%

        Don't know   8%
                                                                        ‾‾‾‾
                                                                        100%

14. Do you, yourself, feel that our national defense is stronger now
    than it needs to be, not strong enough, or about right at the
    present time? (C)

            Stronger 14%   Not strong enough 27%   About right 51%

                        Don't know   8%

15.   As you may know, the United States now has substantial military
       forces stationed in Western Europe as part of NATO's defense
       against the danger of Soviet aggression. Do you think America's
       contribution of ground troops now serving in Europe should be
       increased, kept at the present level, reduced, or ended altogether?
       (C)

           Increased 6%   Kept at present level 44%   Reduced 30%

               Ended altogether 15%   Don't know   5%

16.   Now I'd like to ask you about the foreign aid and loans the United
       States is extending to a number of backward countries to develop
       their economies in order to give their people a better life. Do
       you feel that the amount the United States is now devoting to this
       purpose should be increased, kept at the present level, reduced,
       or ended altogether? (C)

           Increased 7%   Kept at present level 33%   Reduced 42%

               Ended altogether 13%   Don't know 5%

17.   And what about military aid in money and equipment the United
       States is now furnishing to some of our allies, such as South
       Korea, the Philippines, and Brazil? Should the amount of tax
       money the United States is now providing for this purpose be
       increased, kept at the present level, reduced, or ended
       altogether? (C)

           Increased 3%   Kept at present level 32%   Reduced 42%

               Ended altogether 16%   Don't know 7%

18.   As you probably know, the United States is now spending a large
       amount abroad on military bases in many parts of the world and on
       our military forces that are stationed there. Do you feel the
       amount of tax money now being devoted to these purposes should be
       increased, kept at the present level, reduced, or ended
       altogether? (C)

           Increased 5%   Kept at present level 45%   Reduced 38%

               Ended altogether 8%   Don't know 4%

19.   Do you think the amount the U.S. is now contributing toward the
       work of the United Nations should be increased, kept at the present
       level, reduced, or ended altogether? (C)

           Increased 10%   Kept at present level 46%   Reduced 29%

               Ended altogether 9%   Don't know 6%

       *[For demographic breakdowns of composite scores on Questions
       15-19 regarding governmental spending on international matters,
       see page 318.]*

20. Turning now to the question of foreign trade, do you think the
United States should cut down on certain kinds of imports from
foreign countries, or do you feel we should follow the principles
of free trade? (C)

Cut down on imports 43%   Support free trade 50% Don't know 7%

21. Now that President Nixon has made a trip to Communist China, do
you think the United States should or should not establish regular
diplomatic relations with Fidel Castro's government in Cuba? (C)

Should 42%   Should not 48%   Don't know 10%

22. Taking into account the wellbeing of people throughout the world,
do you feel, generally speaking, that in its international actions
in recent years the United States has been a force for good in the
world or not? (C)

Has been 69%   Has not been 23%   Don't know 8%

23. On the whole, do you think that the chances of a major world war
breaking out have increased, stayed the same, or decreased in recent times? (C)

Increased 27%   Stayed the same 31%   Decreased 39%

Don't know 3%

International Concerns

24. Now I'd like to find out how worried or concerned you are about
some of the international problems we face: a great deal, a fair
amount, not very much, or not at all. If you really aren't concerned about some of them, don't hesitate to say so. (B)

A. First, how worried or concerned are you about the problem of
Vietnam?

Great deal   70%   Not very much   5%

Fair amount 23%   Not at all   1%

Don't know 1%

B. Maintaining respect for the United States in other countries?

Great deal   46%   Not very much 12%

Fair amount 35%   Not at all   4%

Don't know 3%

C. Keeping our military and defense forces strong?

Great deal   49%   Not very much 12%

Fair amount 33%   Not at all   3%

Don't know 3%

D. Maintaining close relations with our allies and keeping our military alliances strong?

Great deal 42%   Not very much 14%

Fair amount 37%   Not at all   2%

Don't know 5%

E. Under present circumstances, how worried or concerned are you about the danger of a major world war breaking out in the near future?

Great deal 37%   Not very much 27%

Fair amount 27%   Not at all   6%

Don't know 3%

F. The problem of Communist China?

Great deal 24%   Not very much 28%

Fair amount 35%   Not at all   6%

Don't know 7%

G. The problem of Soviet Russia?

Great deal 24%   Not very much 27%

Fair amount 38%   Not at all   6%

Don't know 5%

H. The threat of communism at home and abroad?

Great deal 41%   Not very much 19%

Fair amount 29%   Not at all   7%

Don't know 4%

[For demographic breakdowns of composite scores on these questions about international worries and concerns, see page 310.]

Internationalism vs. Isolationism

25. Please read all the statements on this card and, when you have finished, tell me with which ones you agree and with which ones you disagree. (B,C)

A. The United States should cooperate fully with the United Nations.

Agree 63%   Disagree 28%   Don't know 9%

B. In deciding on its foreign policies, the United States should take into account the views of its major allies.

Agree 80%   Disagree 12%   Don't know 8%

C. Since the United States is the most powerful nation in the
    world we should go our own way in international matters,
    not worrying too much about whether other countries agree
    with us or not.

         Agree 22%   Disagree 72%   Don't know 6%

D. The United States should come to the defense of its major
    European allies with military force if any of them are
    attacked by Soviet Russia.

         Agree 52%   Disagree 32%   Don't know 16%

E. The United States should come to the defense of Japan with
    military force if it is attacked by Soviet Russia or Communist
    China.

         Agree 43%   Disagree 40%   Don't know 17%

F. The United States should mind its own business internationally
    and let other countries get along as best they can on their
    own.

         Agree 35%   Disagree 56%   Don't know 9%

G. The United States should maintain its dominant position as the
    world's most powerful nation at all costs, even going to the
    very brink of war if necessary.

         Agree 39%   Disagree 50%   Don't know 11%

H. We shouldn't think so much in international terms but concen-
    trate more on our own national problems and building up our
    strength and prosperity here at home.

         Agree 73%   Disagree 20%   Don't know 7%

    [For demographic breakdowns of International Patterns based on
    the foregoing questions, see page 316.]

26. Now, please tell me whether you agree or disagree with each of the
     statements listed on this card. (B,C)

A. The United States should take all necessary steps, including
    the use of armed force, to prevent the spread of communism
    to any other parts of the free world.

         Agree 46%   Disagree 43%   Don't know 11%

B. The United States should go further in negotiating with Soviet
    Russia with a view to reducing armaments on both sides.

         Agree 81%   Disagree 11%   Don't know 8%

C. The United States should continue to play a major role inter-
    nationally, but cut down on some of its responsibilities
    abroad.

         Agree 87%   Disagree 7%   Don't know 6%

Progress: International

27. Now I'm going to mention some problems we face in the inter-
     national field and ask whether from your own point of view the
     United States has made much progress, made some progress, stood
     still, lost some ground, or lost much ground in handling each
     of them during the last twelve months. (A,B)

     A. First, what about the problem of Vietnam?

         Made much progress 9%   Made some progress 43%
                             Stood still 20%
         Lost some ground 15%   Lost much ground 9%
                             Don't know 4%

     B. Handling relations with Communist China?

         Made much progress 12%   Made some progress 60%
                             Stood still 14%
         Lost some ground 4%   Lost much ground 1%
                             Don't know 9%

     C. And what about relations with Soviet Russia?

         Made much progress 10%   Made some progress 59%
                             Stood still 18%
         Lost some ground 3%   Lost much ground 1%
                             Don't know 9%

     D. Maintaining close relations with our major allies, such as
         Great Britain, France, West Germany, and Japan?

         Made much progress 6%   Made some progress 27%
                             Stood still 40%
         Lost some ground 14%   Lost much ground 2%
                             Don't know 11%

     E. Handling economic matters in the international field, such as
         balance of payments and foreign trade problems?

         Made much progress 1%   Made some progress 21%
                             Stood still 24%
         Lost some ground 24%   Lost much ground 6%
                             Don't know 24%

     *[For demographic breakdowns of composite scores based on the
     foregoing items regarding progress in the international field,
     see page 330.]*

28. Considering the international situation overall, do you think that
     in handling foreign policy problems in general during the last
     twelve months the U. S. has made much progress, some progress,
     stood still, lost some ground, lost much ground? (A,B,C)

         Made much progress 8%   Made some progress 56%
                             Stood still 17%
         Lost some ground 9%   Lost much ground 2%
                             Don't know 8%

     [For demographic breakdowns see page 332.]

29.   Looking at the matter a little differently, how would you rate the international situation the United States faces in general at the present time: excellent, good, only fair, or poor? (A,B,C)

Excellent 2%	Only fair 48%
Good 33%	Poor 9%

Don't know 8%

[For demographic breakdowns, see page 346.]

Domestic Issues

30.   Now I'd like to get your views about the best ways to deal with some of our domestic problems here at home. First, which two or three of the approaches listed on this card do you think would be the best ways to reduce crime? Just call out the letter in front of the two or three items you think are the most important. (C)

A.   Cleaning up social and economic conditions in our slums and ghettos that tend to breed drug addicts and criminals. 61%

B.   Getting parents to exert stricter discipline over their children.   48

C.   Putting more policemen on the job to prevent crimes and arrest more criminals.   22

D.   Reforming our courts so that persons charged with crimes can get fairer and speedier justice.   37

E.   Improving conditions in our jails and prisons so that more people convicted of crimes will be rehabilitated and not go back to a life of crime.   40

F.   Really cracking down on criminals by giving them longer prison terms to be served under the toughest possible conditions.   35

Don't know   3

31.   Now a few questions about wage and price controls by the federal government in Washington.   Is it your impression that the way the Pay Board has been controlling wages in recent months has been fair and just, or not? (C)

Yes 36%   No 51%   Don't know 13%

32.   Do you feel that the controls now being imposed by the governnent on wages should be made more strict, less strict, or kept about as they are? (C)

More strict 30% Less strict 21% Kept as they are 36%

Don't know 13%

33. And what about price controls? Is it your impression that the way
     the Price Commission has been controlling prices in recent months
     has been fair and just, or not? (C)

                    Yes 33%   No 59%   Don't know 8%

34. Do you feel that the controls now being imposed by the government
     on prices should be made more strict, less strict, or kept about
     as they are? (C)

                    More strict 55% Less strict 14% Kept as they are 24%

                              Don't know   7%

35. Turning now to the matter of education, how would you rate the
     public schools in the neighborhood or area where you live:
     excellent, good, only fair, poor? (C)

                    Excellent 15%   Only fair 24%

                    Good 42%   Poor 10%

                         Don't know 9%

36. Which one of the approaches listed on this card do you think would
     be the best way to give black children throughout the country a
     better education, while at the same time being fair to white
     children? Just call out the letter of the item you choose. (C)

     A. By requiring all public schools to become thoroughly
         integrated, mixing black and white children, and using
         enforced busing where necessary.   9%

     B. By allowing any child, with the consent of his parents,
         to pick the public school he or she wants to attend, and
         providing busing for this purpose.   18

     C. By forgetting about busing to achieve racial balance,
         and instead spending more money to provide the best
         possible education for children in whichever schools
         they now attend.   62

     D. By maintaining the school setup as it now stands
         without increased spending.   7

         Don't know   4
                                                                     ‾‾‾‾
                                                                     100%

37. Suppose more blacks were elected to public office to serve as
     mayors, congressmen, governors, or senators. Do you think this
     would be a good thing or a bad thing -- or wouldn't it make much
     difference to you, one way or the other? (C)

          Good thing 31% Bad thing 15% Wouldn't make much difference 49%
                              Don't know 5%

38. Would you be happy or unhappy to see black families of a lower
     income and education level than yourself who are now living
     elsewhere move into the neighborhood or area where you live --
     or wouldn't this make much difference to you one way or the
     other? (C)

           Happy 7%   Unhappy 40%   Wouldn't make much difference 48%
                          Don't know 5%

39. [ASKED OF WHITES ONLY] And what about black families of about
     your own income and education level who are now living elsewhere?
     Would you be happy or unhappy to see them move into the neighbor-
     hood or area where you live -- or wouldn't this make much differ-
     ence to you, one way or the other? (C)

           Happy 11%   Unhappy 24%   Wouldn't make much difference 60%
                          Don't know 5%

40. [ASKED OF WHITES ONLY] And how would you feel about white
     families of a lower income and education level than yourself
     moving into the neighborhood or area where you live? Would you
     be happy or unhappy -- or wouldn't this make much difference to
     you, one way or the other? (C)

           Happy 6%   Unhappy 37%   Wouldn't make much difference 53%
                          Don't know 4%

41. Considering the problems now faced by people living in our large
     central cities, please read the two propositions listed on this
     card and then tell me how you feel about each of them. Obviously,
     you can favor both; or favor one but not the other; or oppose both.

     A. The government should undertake huge rebuilding programs in
         our central cities to provide adequate housing and facilities
         for the people who now live there.

     B. The United States should force surrounding suburban areas to
         permit the building of more low- and medium-cost housing and
         facilities to take care of people from the central cities
         who would like to move there.

     First, would you be for or against Proposition A? (C)

              For 60%   Against 32%   Don't know 8%

     And would you support or oppose Proposition B? (C)
              Support 47%   Oppose 44%   Don't know 9%

42. Which one of the kinds of places listed on this card comes closest
     to describing the place where you now live? (A,B,C)

     A. In a city 36%   C. In a town or village 15%
     B. In the suburbs 22% D. In a rural area out in the country 18%
                          Don't know 9%

43. How satisfied are you with living in the neighborhood or locality
     where you are now located: a great deal, a fair amount, not very
     much, or not at all? (C)

               Great deal   56%   Not very much 8%
               Fair amount   32%   Not at all   2%
                              Don't know 2%

44. If you could live anywhere you wanted to, which one of the kinds
     of places listed on this card would be your very first choice?
     (A,B,C)

     A. In a city 18%   C. In a town or village 19%
     B. In the suburbs 22% D. In a rural area out in the country 38%
                              Don't know 3%

45a. Do you use an automobile regularly at the present time? (C)
                    Yes 82%   No 17%   Don't know 1%

  b. [IF YES] As you probably know, a great deal of air pollution
     comes from automobiles. How much more would you be willing to
     pay for a car to cover the cost of installing antipollution
     equipment: nothing, $5, $10, $20, $50, $100, $200, $500? (C)

          Zero- 22% $10- 3% $50- 17% $200- 10%
          $5-   5% $20- 9% $100- 17% $500- 6%
                              Don't know 11%

46. Turning now to <u>water</u> pollution, please tell me how much more in
     taxes or water rates you would be willing to pay each year to help
     clean up our waterways: nothing, $5, $10, $20, $50, $100, $200,
     $500? (C)

          Zero- 24% $10- 11% $50- 13% $200- 5%
          $5-   11% $20- 11% $100- 9% $500- 4%
                              Don't know 12%

47. As you probably know, many of our localities are having a great
     deal of trouble disposing of trash and other solid wastes. To
     help out, it has been suggested that drinks should not be sold in
     throw-away bottles or cans, but only in returnable bottles, on
     which a good-sized deposit would be charged. Would you favor or
     oppose a national law along these lines? (C)

               Favor 81%   Oppose 15%   Don't know 4%

48. Some people say the U.S. should put more emphasis on curbing
     pollution and improving the quality of life in this country by
     deliberately holding back on economic and technical growth, for
     example by prohibiting an increase in certain kinds of industrial
     activities. Others say this would result in fewer jobs and a
     lower standard of living in America. If you had to choose, would
     you favor or oppose the U.S. deliberately limiting economic and
     technical growth in this country? (C)

               Favor 27%   Oppose 60%   Don't know 13%

49. Some people say that, in order to keep pollution down and prevent overcrowding, the U.S. should deliberately try to cut down on the growth of our population through such measures as encouraging birth control and reducing tax exemptions and welfare payments for large families. Others say such matters as family size should be left to the individuals involved and their consciences. If you had to choose between these two points of view, would you favor or oppose the U.S. deliberately taking steps to limit population growth? (C)

Favor 47%   Oppose 44%   Don't know 9%

50. Let's turn now to the problem of poverty. Suppose you had to choose between the alternatives on this card, which one do you think would be the best way to handle the problem of families with little or no income? Just read off the letter of the item you choose. (C)

A. For state and local governments to continue their present systems of welfare payments, with the federal government chipping in a good part of the tax money required.   37%

B. For the federal government in Washington to guarantee every family a certain minimum income even if one or more of its members are working for very low wages, with the government making up any shortage in family income out of federal tax money.   42

C. For welfare payments to needy families to be stopped, leaving the problem of poverty to be taken care of by private charities.   9

Don't know   12
                    ‾‾‾‾
                    100%

51. When people can't find any jobs, would you be in favor of the government putting them on the payroll and finding work for them such as helping out in hospitals or cleaning public parks or would you be against this idea? (C)

Favor 89%   Oppose 8%   Don't know 3%

52. Turning to another topic, there is a lot of talk these days about discrimination against women and women's rights. Taking into account this question of discrimination and all other aspects of their lives, how would you, yourself, rate the situation of women in general in this country today: excellent, good, only fair, or poor? (C)

Excellent 21%   Only fair 20%

Good 52%   Poor 4%

Don't know 3%

53. Should mothers with school age children in families receiving welfare be required to take any job offered them, or should they be allowed to turn down a job and still keep their welfare payments? (C)

    Be required to take job 53%   Turn down job, keep welfare 36%

    Don't know 11%

54. Do you think that women with school age children should feel free to take full-time jobs if they want to, or, in your opinion, should they stay home and take care of their children? (C)

    Take full-time jobs 52%   Stay home 40%   Don't know 8%

55. Would you favor or oppose the U.S. using tax money to set up day care centers for the care of children whose mothers are working away from home? (C)

    Favor 61%   Oppose 31%   Don't know 8%

56. Which one of the health care systems listed on this card do you think would be the best way to provide adequate medical and health care for all people? Just read off the letter by the answer you choose. (C)

    A. A universal system of health insurance covering everybody
       and paid for by the federal government out of money
       raised by taxes.   22%

    B. A system of compulsory health insurance covering every-
       body who has a job and his or her family, with employers
       and employees sharing the costs, and the federal govern-
       ment providing health insurance only for people who do
       not have jobs.   40

    C. The present system of voluntary health and medical care.   30

       Don't know   8
                                                                  ────
                                                                  100%

Domestic Concerns

57. Now I'd like to find out how worried or concerned you are about a number of problems I am going to mention: a great deal, a fair amount, not very much, or not at all. If you aren't really concerned about some of these matters, don't hesitate to say so. (B)

    A. First, how worried or concerned are you about crime in this
       country?
                          Great deal   71%   Not very much   3%
                          Fair amount   24%   Not at all   1%
                             Don't know 1%

B. And the problem of drug addicts and narcotic drugs?

    Great deal   74%   Not very much 5%
    Fair amount 18%   Not at all 1%
                Don't know 2%

C. The amount of violence in American life?

    Great deal   75%   Not very much 4%
    Fair amount 19%   Not at all 1%
                Don't know 1%

D. Providing adequate housing for all the people?

    Great deal   29%   Not very much 15%
    Fair amount 49%   Not at all 4%
                Don't know 3%

E. Protecting consumers against misleading advertising, dangerous
    products, and unsafe foods and drugs?

    Great deal   58%   Not very much 10%
    Fair amount 29%   Not at all 1%
                Don't know 2%

F. Improving our education system?

    Great deal   48%   Not very much 13%
    Fair amount 35%   Not at all 2%
                Don't know 2%

G. Reducing poverty in this country?

    Great deal   45%   Not very much 12%
    Fair amount 40%   Not at all 1%
                Don't know 2%

H. And how worried or concerned are you about rising prices and
    the cost of living?

    Great deal   76%   Not very much 5%
    Fair amount 18%   Not at all *
                Don't know 1%

I. Unemployment in this country?

    Great deal   47%   Not very much 10%
    Fair amount 39%   Not at all 2%
                Don't know 2%

J. And economic and business conditions generally?

        Great deal 31%   Not very much 15%

        Fair amount 48%   Not at all 2%

              Don't know 4%

58. Now I'm going to ask you how worried or concerned you are about some more problems of a different kind: a great deal, a fair amount, not very much, or not at all. (B)

A. First, how worried or concerned are you about insuring that Americans in general, including the poor and the elderly, get adequate medical and health care?

        Great deal 55%   Not very much 5%

        Fair amount 37%   Not at all 1%

              Don't know 2%

B. Cleaning up our waterways and reducing water pollution?

        Great deal 61%   Not very much 7%

        Fair amount 29%   Not at all 1%

              Don't know 2%

C. Reducing air pollution?

        Great deal 60%   Not very much 9%

        Fair amount 28%   Not at all 1%

              Don't know 2%

D. Collecting and disposing of garbage, trash, and other solid wastes?

        Great deal 53%   Not very much 10%

        Fair amount 34%   Not at all 1%

              Don't know 2%

E. Rebuilding run-down sections of our cities?

        Great deal 39%   Not very much 14%

        Fair amount 41%   Not at all 4%

              Don't know 2%

F. And how worried or concerned are you about the problem of black Americans?

        Great deal 32%   Not very much 22%

        Fair amount 35%   Not at all 7%

              Don't know 4%

G. Improving mass transportation systems, such as buses, trains, and, in some cities, subways?

Great deal	20%	Not very much	31%
Fair amount	35%	Not at all	9%

Don't know 5%

H. The problems of our elderly "senior citizens?"

Great deal	47%	Not very much	11%
Fair amount	37%	Not at all	2%

Don't know 3%

I. The problems of our cities in general?

Great deal	33%	Not very much	13%
Fair amount	46%	Not at all	4%

Don't know 4%

[For demographic breakdowns of composite scores derived from Questions 57 and 58 concerning domestic worries and concerns, see page 313.]

Progress: Domestic

59. Now I'm going to mention some <u>domestic</u> problems here at home and ask whether, in your eyes, we as a nation have made much progress, made some progress, stood still, lost some ground, or lost much ground in handling each of them during the last twelve months. (A,B)

A. First, what about rising prices and the cost of living?

Made much progress	3%	Made some progress	20%

Stood still 17%

Lost some ground	36%	Lost much ground	22%

Don't know   2%

B. Handling the problem of unemployment?

Made much progress	1%	Made some progress	27%

Stood still 30%

Lost some ground	24%	Lost much ground	12%

Don't know   6%

C. And what about economic and business conditions generally -- that is, the overall prosperity of the country?

Made much progress	4%	Made some progress	42%

Stood still 24%

Lost some ground	17%	Lost much ground	5%

Don't know   8%

D. And what would you say about combating crime?

    Made much progress 1%   Made some progress 19%

    Stood still 26%

    Lost some ground   32%   Lost much ground   19%

    Don't know   3%

E. Coping with the problem of narcotic drugs and drug addicts?

    Made much progress 3%   Made some progress 31%

    Stood still 21%

    Lost some ground   23%   Lost much ground   18%

    Don't know   4%

F. Providing adequate medical and health care for all our
    citizens, including the poor and the elderly?

    Made much progress 7%   Made some progress 51%

    Stood still 23%

    Lost some ground   11%   Lost much ground   4%

    Don't know   4%

G. And what about the way we have handled poverty and welfare
    problems during the last year?

    Made much progress 3%   Made some progress 31%

    Stood still 26%

    Lost some ground   22%   Lost much ground   11%

    Don't know   7%

H. How have we done in the field of mass transportation within
    and between metropolitan areas by bus, train, or, in some
    cities, subways?

    Made much progress 4%   Made some progress 27%

    Stood still 27%

    Lost some ground   16%   Lost much ground   8%

    Don't know   18%

I. And what about problems of the elderly -- that is, of our
    "senior citizens ?"

    Made much progress 5%   Made some progress 44%

    Stood still 29%

    Lost some ground   9%   Lost much ground   5%

    Don't know   8%

60. Now let's consider a few more domestic problems of a different kind. (A,B)

A. First, when it comes to handling the problem of black Americans in general do you, yourself, feel that we as a nation have made much progress, some progress, stood still, lost some ground, or lost much ground over the last twelve months?

Made much progress 12%   Made some progress 51%

Stood still 17%

Lost some ground   10%   Lost much ground   5%

Don't know   5%

B. How have we done, in your opinion, in providing adequate education for young people as a whole, both white and non-white, throughout the country?

Made much progress 14%   Made some progress 50%

Stood still 15%

Lost some ground   12%   Lost much ground   4%

Don't know   5%

C. Providing adequate housing for the American people as a whole, both white and nonwhite?

Made much progress 8%   Made some progress 52%

Stood still 21%

Lost some ground   9%   Lost much ground   4%

Don't know   6%

D. And what about cleaning up our waterways and reducing water pollution throughout the country?

Made much progress 4%   Made some progress 45%

Stood still 23%

Lost some ground 12%   Lost much ground   8%

Don't know   8%

E. And reducing air pollution?

Made much progress 3%   Made some progress 46%

Stood still 25%

Lost some ground   11%   Lost much ground   7%

Don't know   8%

F. Finally, how much progress, if any, do you feel we have made in handling the overall problems of our cities generally?

Made much progress 2%   Made some progress 42%

Stood still 26%

Lost some ground   14%   Lost much ground   4%

Don't know   12%

[For demographic breakdowns of composite scores, see page 334.]

61. Summing up the overall domestic situation here in the United
     States today, do you think that in handling domestic problems
     generally we as a nation have made much progress, some progress,
     stood still, lost some ground, or lost much ground during the
     last twelve months? (A,B,C)

           Made much progress 4%   Made some progress 54%
                             Stood still 22%
           Lost some ground   12%   Lost much ground   3%
                             Don't know   5%
           [For demographic breakdowns, see page 337.]

62. Looking at the matter a little differently, how would you rate the
     domestic situation in the United States today in general:
     excellent, good, only fair, or poor? (A,B,C)

                Excellent 1%   Only fair 54%
                Good 29%   Poor 10%
                             Don't know 6%
           [For demographic breakdowns, see page 348.]

                Taxes and Government Spending

63. Now I have a couple of questions about taxes. Obviously, nobody
     likes to pay more taxes. However, if taxes absolutely had to be
     raised to meet the growing needs of our country, which one of the
     kinds of taxes listed on this card would you rather see increased:
     income taxes, sales taxes, or real estate taxes? (A)

           Income taxes 29%   Sales taxes 42%   Real estate taxes 13%
                             Don't know 16%

64. And which one of these kinds of taxes would you be most unwilling
     to see increased: income taxes, sales taxes, or real estate
     taxes? (A)
           Income taxes 35%   Sales taxes 21%   Real estate taxes 37%
                             Don't know   7%

65. Looking at this matter from a somewhat different point of view,
     if taxes at some one level of government absolutely had to be
     raised, which would you rather see increased: federal taxes,
     state taxes, or local taxes? (A)
           Federal taxes 39%   State taxes 20%   Local taxes 24%
                             Don't know 17%

66. Now I'm going to read off the names of some programs the federal
     government in Washington is helping to finance. As I mention
     each program, please tell me whether you feel the amount of tax
     money now being spent for each should be increased, kept at the
     present level, reduced, or ended altogether. (A)

A. First, what about the federal program to help build low-rent public housing?

Increased 40%   Reduced 12%

Kept at present level 40%   Ended altogether 4%

Don't know 4%

B. Federal programs to improve the education of children from low-income families?

Increased 62%   Reduced 3%

Kept at present level 28%   Ended altogether 2%

Don't know 5%

C. Federal programs to make a college education possible for young people who could not otherwise afford it?

Increased 54%   Reduced 7%

Kept at present level 32%   Ended altogether 4%

Don't know 3%

D. The program to build better and safer roads, highways, and thruways throughout the country?

Increased 37%   Reduced 10%

Kept at present level 49%   Ended altogether 1%

Don't know 3%

E. Programs to rebuild run-down sections of our cities?

Increased 51%   Reduced 11%

Kept at present level 29%   Ended altogether 5%

Don't know 4%

F. The medicaid program to help low-income families pay their medical bills?

Increased 52%   Reduced 6%

Kept at present level 35%   Ended altogether 2%

Don't know 5%

G. Programs to clean up our waterways and reduce water pollution?

Increased 64%   Reduced 4%

Kept at present level 26%   Ended altogether 1%

Don't know 5%

H. Programs to reduce air pollution?

Increased 61%   Reduced 4%

Kept at present level 28%   Ended altogether 1%

Don't know 6%

I. Programs to provide better housing for people generally?

  Increased 37%   Reduced 7%

  Kept at present level 48% Ended altogether 3%

    Don't know 5%

J. Federal programs to help elderly people, for example, by increasing the social security payments they receive?

  Increased 74%   Reduced 2%

  Kept at present level 21% Ended altogether *

    Don't know 3%

67. Now, again, let me read off the names of some other programs the federal government in Washington is helping to finance and ask whether you think the amount of tax money now being spent for each of these purposes should be increased, kept at the present level, reduced, or ended altogether? (A)

A. Programs to help improve the situation of black Americans?

  Increased 33%   Reduced 11%

  Kept at present level 43% Ended altogether 7%

    Don't know 6%

B. Programs to provide better and faster mass transportation systems in and between metropolitan areas, such as buses, trains, and, in some cities, subways?

  Increased 41%   Reduced 9%

  Kept at present level 39% Ended altogether 3%

    Don't know 8%

C. Welfare programs to help low-income families?

  Increased 30%   Reduced 18%

  Kept at present level 41% Ended altogether 6%

    Don't know 5%

D. Improving medical and health care for Americans generally.

  Increased 62%   Reduced 2%

  Kept at present level 32% Ended altogether 2%

    Don't know 2%

E. Programs to combat crime?

  Increased 77%   Reduced 1%

  Kept at present level 18% Ended altogether 1%

    Don't know 3%

F. Coping with the problem of narcotic drugs and drug addicts?

    Increased 74%   Reduced 2%

    Kept at present level 20%   Ended altogether 1%

             Don't know 3%

G. Programs to provide government-paid jobs for the unemployed?

    Increased 48%   Reduced 10%

    Kept at present level 31%   Ended altogether 5%

             Don't know 6%

H. Establishing more parks and recreation areas in our cities
    and countrysides?

    Increased 41%   Reduced 7%

    Kept at present level 47%   Ended altogether 2%

             Don't know 3%

I. Meeting the overall problems of our cities generally?

    Increased 41%   Reduced 6%

    Kept at present level 44%   Ended altogether 1%

             Don't know 8%

J. The space program for exploring the moon and other planets?

    Increased 12%   Reduced 32%

    Kept at present level 25%   Ended altogether 27%

             Don't know 4%

*[For demographic breakdowns of composite scores on these
questions regarding government spending, see page 320.]*

Trust and Confidence in Institutions

68. Now I'd like to ask you several questions about our governmental
system. First, how much trust and confidence do you have in our
federal government in Washington when it comes to handling international problems: a great deal, a fair amount, not very much,
or none at all? (C)

    Great deal   22%   Not very much 19%

    Fair amount 55%   None at all   2%

           Don't know 2%

69. And how much trust and confidence do you have in our federal
     government when it comes to handling domestic problems in general:
     a great deal, a fair amount, not very much, or none at all? (C)

              Great deal   13%   Not very much 24%

              Fair amount   58%   None at all   3%

                         Don't know 2%

70. As you know, our federal government is made up of three branches:
     an executive branch, headed by the president; a judicial branch,
     headed by the U.S. Supreme Court; and a legislative branch, made
     up of the U.S. Senate and House of Representatives. First, let me
     ask you how much trust and confidence you have at this time in the
     executive branch, headed by the president: a great deal, a fair
     amount, not very much, or none at all? (C)

              Great deal   27%   Not very much 18%

              Fair amount   49%   None at all   57%

                         Don't know 1%

71. How much trust and confidence do you have under present conditions
     in the judicial branch, headed by the U.S. Supreme Court: a
     great deal, a fair amount, not very much, or none at all? (C)

              Great deal   17%   Not very much 23%

              Fair amount   49%   None at all   7%

                         Don't know 4%

72. And how much trust and confidence do you have at present in the
     legislative branch, consisting of the U.S. Senate and House of
     Representatives: a great deal, a fair amount, not very much, or
     none at all? (C)

              Great deal   14%   Not very much 23%

              Fair amount   58%   None at all   2%

                         Don't know 3%

73. How much trust and confidence do you have in the government of
     this state where you live when it comes to handling state problems:
     a great deal, a fair amount, not very much, or none at all? (C)

              Great deal   18%   Not very much 26%

              Fair amount   49%   None at all   5%

                         Don't know 2%

74. And how much trust and confidence do you have in the local govern-
     ments here in this area where you live when it comes to handling
     local problems? (C)

              Great deal   14%   Not very much 25%

              Fair amount   50%   None at all   8%

                         Don't know 3%

     *[For demographic breakdowns of composite scores on these
     questions regarding trust and confidence in federal, state,
     and local governments, see page 323 .]*

75. It has been proposed that a certain percentage of the money
     Washington collects in federal income taxes -- let's say about
     three percent -- should be turned over automatically to state
     and local governments, without strings attached, for them to use
     as they see fit. Do you favor or oppose this idea? (C)

                  Favor 60%   Oppose 31%   Don't know 9%

76. Now let's consider our governmental system as a whole in this
     country, federal, state, and local, from several different points
     of view. First, if you had to rate our governmental system as a
     whole in terms of honesty, fairness, and justice, what mark would
     you give the system: excellent, good, only fair, or poor? (C)

                  Excellent 7%   Only fair 47%

                  Good 34%   Poor 10%
                            Don't know 2%

77. What mark would you give our governmental system as a whole when
     it comes to efficiency in handling the problems that face us:
     excellent, good, only fair, or poor? (C)

                  Excellent 5%   Only fair 50%

                  Good 33%   Poor 11%

                            Don't know 1%

78. And in showing consideration for and responsiveness to the needs,
     hopes, and desires of ordinary citizens like yourself, what mark
     would you give our governmental system as a whole: excellent,
     good, only fair, or poor? (C)

                  Excellent 5%   Only fair 49%

                  Good 28%   Poor 16%

                            Don't know 2%

     *[For demographic breakdowns of composite scores on these
     questions regarding our governmental system as a whole,
     see page 326.]*

79. Taking into account what you would want America to be like ten
     years from now, do you think a basic change will need to be made
     in the way our governmental system is now set up and organized
     or don't you think this will be necessary? (C)

                  Yes 54%   No 36%   Don't know 10%

     [For demographic breakdowns, see page 328.]

80. Turning to another subject, how much trust and confidence do you
     have in American business and industry today when it comes to
     operating efficiently and in the best interests of consumers:
     a great deal, a fair amount, not very much, or none at all? (C)

                  Great deal   10%   Not very much 30%
                  Fair amount 50%   None at all   6%
                            Don't know 4%

81.   And how much trust and confidence do you have in American labor
        unions as they now operate when it comes to reasonableness in
        making demands and consideration for the public interest: a great
        deal, a fair amount, not very much, or none at all? (C)

                Great deal   8%   Not very much 36%

                Fair amount 37%   None at all 14%

                        Don't know 5%

82.   Now let's consider young people as a whole today -- that is, those
        in their teens and early twenties. How much trust and confidence
        do you have in the young in general when it comes to facing up to
        their own and the country's problems in a responsible way: a
        great deal, a fair amount, not very much, or none at all? (C)

                Great deal 27%   Not very much 17%

                Fair amount 49%   None at all 4%

                        Don't know 3%

83.   And how much trust and confidence do you have in the mass media --
        such as the newspapers, TV, and radio in general -- when it comes
        to reporting the news fully, accurately, and fairly: a great deal,
        a fair amount, not very much, or none at all? (C)

                Great deal 17%   Not very much 26%

                Fair amount 50%   None at all 5%

                        Don't know 2%

84.   Finally, how much trust and confidence do you have in general in
        men and women in political life in this country who either hold
        or are running for public office: a great deal, a fair amount,
        not very much, or none at all? (C)

                Great deal   8%   Not very much 27%

                Fair amount 60%   None at all 4%

                        Don't know 1%

        *[For demographic breakdowns of composite scores on these
        further questions about trust and confidence, see page 323.]*

Overall Evaluations

85.   Now let's sum things up a bit. Is it your impression that
        America today is a better place or a worse place to live than it
        was, say, ten years ago -- or don't you think there is much
        difference one way or the other? (C)

                Better place 38%   Worse place 32%   Not much difference 27%

                        Don't know 3%

86. Now that you have had a chance to review our overall situation
     today at home and abroad, is it your considered opinion that,
     in general, we as a nation have made much progress, some progress,
     stood still, lost some ground, or lost much ground during the
     past twelve months? (A,B,C)

              Made much progress 7%   Made some progress 60%

                        Stood still 17%

          Lost some ground 10%   Lost much ground 2%

                      Don't know 4%

     [For demographic breakdowns, see page 339.]

87. Finally, let's pull everything together. Taking into account the
     situation both at home and abroad at the present time, what would
     you say is the state of the nation in this year 1972:   excellent,
     good, only fair, or poor? (A,B,C)

                   Excellent 3%   Only fair 50%

                   Good 38%   Poor 7%

                        Don't know 2%

     [For demographic breakdowns, see page 350.]

Appendix 2

TABLES GIVING DEMOGRAPHIC BREAKDOWNS

Because of limitations of space, only selected demographic breakdowns are given in the tables that follow. Most of the demographic categories used in the breakdowns are perfectly clear; a few, however, need a word of explanation.

In the case of the breakdown by *education,* "college" includes those who have had some college education as well as those who have graduated; the same is true for "high school" and "grade school" (in fact, the latter also includes those few, mostly oldsters, who have had no education at all). *Income* is based on the total earnings of the family as a whole (that is, those members living together in the dwelling where the interview was conducted).

The *occupation* categories are clear except for "nonlabor," which consists primarily of households headed by retired people, or, to a lesser extent, by students, housewives, or the physically handicapped. One of the characteristics of this category is a heavy predominance of older people. Unfortunately, the figures for "farmers" could not be given in the tables that follow because they now represent such a small proportion of our total population that too few were drawn into our sample (67) to provide any degree of statistical reliability. The same is true in the case of the "Jewish" category under *religion.* Only 45 respondents in our sample were Jewish. Under *union membership,* "union households" includes not only people who themselves belong to labor unions but also the spouses of such union members.

The different areas under *region* included the following states: EAST: Connecticut, Delaware, District of Columbia, Maine, Maryland, Massachusetts, New Hampshire, New Jersey, New York, Pennsylvania, Rhode Island, Vermont, and West Virginia.

MIDWEST: Illinois, Indiana, Iowa, Kansas, Michigan, Minnesota, Missouri, Nebraska, North Dakota, Ohio, South Dakota, and Wisconsin.

SOUTH: Alabama, Arkansas, Florida, Georgia, Kentucky, Louisiana, Mississippi, North Carolina, Oklahoma, South Carolina, Tennessee, Texas, and Virginia.

WEST: Alaska, Arizona, California, Colorado, Hawaii, Idaho, Montana, Nevada, New Mexico, Oregon, Utah, Washington, and Wyoming.

Type of place categories are based on respondents' own answers to a question asking whether they live in a city, in the suburbs, in a town or village, or in a rural area. The reason for handling the matter this way, rather than basing such differentiations on objective data, is the enormous difficulty in defining what is and what is not a "suburb." After struggling with this problem for some time, we finally concluded that the most meaningful definition is a psychological one: if a person feels that he is a "suburbanite," then he ought to be classified as such; otherwise, not.

The *liberal-conservative* categories are also based upon respondents' own self-designation as very liberal, moderately liberal, middle of the road, moderately conservative, or very conservative. The categories under *politics* derive from the question, "In politics as of today, do you consider yourself a Republican, Democrat, or Independent?"

The percentages that came out of the computer were rounded to the nearest one-tenth of a point. To make them easier to comprehend, however, in the following tables we have rounded them to the nearest whole number. The composite scores given in the tables, on the other hand, were computed on the more precise basis of tenths of points. Hence, if one takes the rounded percentages given in the tables and multiplies and divides manually to derive composite scores, the results may vary in some cases by about a point in either direction from the scores given in the tables. The latter, however, are obviously the more accurate.

In the following tables, an asterisk (*) indicates a figure less than one-half of one percent; a hyphen (-) signifies zero.

TABLE A-1   AVERAGE PERSONAL LADDER RATINGS

Here is a ladder representing the "ladder of life." Let's suppose the top of the ladder represents the best possible life for you; and the bottom, the worst possible life for you. On which step of the ladder do you feel you personally stand at the present time? (A,B)

On which step would you say you stood five years ago? (A,B)

Just as your best guess, on which step do you think you will stand in the future, say about five years from now? (A,B)

[NOTE: For a description of the method used in computing average ladder ratings, see page 352.]

	Past	Present	Future	Shift: Past to Present	Shift: Present to Future
NATIONAL TOTALS	5.5	6.4	7.6	+ 0.9	+ 1.2
SEX					
Men	5.4	6.2	7.4	+ 0.8	+ 1.2
Women	5.6	6.6	7.7	+ 1.0	+ 1.1
AGE					
18-29	4.7	6.1	8.1	+ 1.4	+ 2.0
30-49	5.3	6.4	7.8	+ 1.1	+ 1.4
50 & over	6.3	6.6	6.9	+ 0.3	+ 0.3
EDUCATION					
College	5.6	6.8	8.0	+ 1.2	+ 1.2
High School	5.4	6.3	7.7	+ 0.9	+ 1.4
Grade School	5.9	6.4	6.7	+ 0.5	+ 0.3
FAMILY INCOME					
$15,000 & over	5.4	7.0	8.2	+ 1.6	+ 1.2
$10,000 - $14,999	5.7	6.9	7.9	+ 1.2	+ 1.0
$ 7,000 - $ 9,999	5.3	6.2	7.5	+ 0.9	+ 1.3
$ 5,000 - $ 6,999	5.4	6.0	7.5	+ 0.6	+ 1.5
Under $5,000	5.6	5.8	6.8	+ 0.2	+ 1.0

TABLE A-1 (cont'd)

	Past	Present	Future	Shift: Past to Present	Shift: Present to Future
OCCUPATION					
Professional & Business	5.5	6.8	8.0	+ 1.3	+ 1.2
White Collar	5.6	6.4	7.7	+ 0.8	+ 1.3
Manual	5.0	6.2	7.7	+ 1.2	+ 1.5
Non-labor	6.4	6.5	6.8	+ 0.1	+ 0.3
UNION MEMBERSHIP					
Union Households	5.4	6.4	7.5	+ 1.0	+ 1.1
Non-union Households	5.6	6.4	7.6	+ 0.8	+ 1.2
HOME OWNERSHIP					
Home Owners	5.8	6.7	7.6	+ 0.9	+ 0.9
Non-owners	5.0	5.8	7.5	+ 0.8	+ 1.7
REGION					
East	5.5	6.3	7.4	+ 0.8	+ 1.1
Midwest	5.5	6.3	7.5	+ 0.8	+ 1.2
South	5.5	6.5	7.7	+ 1.0	+ 1.2
West	5.7	6.7	7.6	+ 1.0	+ 0.9
COMMUNITY SIZE					
500,000 & over	5.5	6.2	7.5	+ 0.7	+ 1.3
50,000 - 499,999	5.4	6.5	7.6	+ 1.1	+ 1.1
2,500 - 49,999	5.5	6.4	7.7	+ 0.9	+ 1.3
Under 2,500 & rural	5.6	6.5	7.6	+ 0.9	+ 1.1
TYPE OF PLACE					
City	5.5	6.1	7.2	+ 0.6	+ 1.1
Suburb	5.6	6.9	7.9	+ 1.3	+ 1.0
Town or village	5.5	6.5	7.9	+ 1.0	+ 1.4
Rural	5.5	6.4	7.5	+ 0.9	+ 1.1
RACE					
White	5.6	6.5	7.6	+ 0.9	+ 1.1
Black	4.8	5.5	7.3	+ 0.7	+ 1.8

TABLE A-1 (cont'd)

	Past	Present	Future	Shift: Past to Present	Shift: Present to Future
RELIGION					
Protestant	5.6	6.4	7.6	+ 0.8	+ 1.2
Catholic	5.4	6.6	7.6	+ 1.2	+ 1.0
POLITICS					
Republican	6.0	6.8	7.6	+ 0.8	+ 0.8
Democrat	5.3	6.3	7.5	+ 1.0	+ 1.2
Independent	5.5	6.4	7.7	+ 0.9	+ 1.3
LIBERAL - CONSERVATIVE					
Very liberal	5.4	6.7	8.0	+ 1.3	+ 1.3
Moderately liberal	5.4	6.4	7.7	+ 1.0	+ 1.3
Middle of the road	5.6	6.3	7.6	+ 0.7	+ 1.3
Moderately conservative	5.7	6.6	7.4	+ 0.9	+ 0.8
Very conservative	5.5	6.4	7.8	+ 0.9	+ 1.4

TABLE A-2   AVERAGE NATIONAL LADDER RATINGS

Looking at the ladder again, suppose the top represents the best possible situation for our country; the bottom the worst possible situation. Please show me on which step of the ladder you think the United States is at the present time. (A,B)

On which step would you say the United States was about five years ago? (A,B)

Just as your best guess, if things go pretty much as you now expect, where do you think the United States will be on the ladder, let us say, five years from now? (A,B)

[NOTE: For a description of the method used in computing average ladder ratings, see page 352.]

	Past	Present	Future	Shift: Past to Present	Shift: Present to Future
NATIONAL TOTALS	5.6	5.5	6.2	- 0.1	+ 0.7
SEX					
Men	5.7	5.7	6.3	-	+ 0.6
Women	5.6	5.3	6.1	- 0.3	+ 0.8
AGE					
18-29	5.3	5.2	6.0	- 0.1	+ 0.8
30-49	5.7	5.5	6.2	- 0.2	+ 0.7
50 & over	5.8	5.6	6.4	- 0.2	+ 0.8
EDUCATION					
College	5.6	5.4	6.0	- 0.2	+ 0.6
High School	5.6	5.4	6.3	- 0.2	+ 0.9
Grade School	5.9	5.9	6.3	-	+ 0.4
FAMILY INCOME					
$15,000 & over	5.7	5.5	6.1	- 0.2	+ 0.6
$10,000 - $14,999	5.6	5.3	6.1	- 0.3	+ 0.8
$7,000 - $9,999	5.5	5.4	6.2	- 0.1	+ 0.8
$5,000 - $6,999	5.7	5.6	6.3	- 0.1	+ 0.7
Under $5,000	5.7	5.5	6.3	- 0.2	+ 0.8

TABLE A-2 (cont'd)

	Past	Present	Future	Shift: Past to Present	Shift: Present to Future
OCCUPATION					
Professional & Business	5.6	5.4	6.0	- 0.2	+ 0.6
White Collar	5.7	5.4	6.6	- 0.3	+ 1.2
Manual	5.7	5.5	6.1	- 0.2	+ 0.6
Non-labor	5.7	5.5	6.3	- 0.2	+ 0.8
UNION MEMBERSHIP					
Union Households	5.7	5.4	6.1	- 0.3	+ 0.7
Non-union Households	5.6	5.5	6.2	- 0.1	+ 0.7
HOME OWNERSHIP					
Home Owners	5.7	5.5	6.2	- 0.2	+ 0.7
Non-owners	5.6	5.4	6.2	- 0.2	+ 0.8
REGION					
East	5.6	5.3	6.0	- 0.3	+ 0.7
Midwest	5.7	5.4	6.3	- 0.3	+ 0.9
South	5.6	5.7	6.4	+ 0.1	+ 0.7
West	5.7	5.4	6.1	- 0.3	+ 0.7
COMMUNITY SIZE					
500,000 & over	5.7	5.4	6.3	- 0.3	+ 0.9
50,000 - 499,999	5.8	5.7	6.3	- 0.1	+ 0.6
2,500 - 49,999	5.7	5.6	6.5	- 0.1	+ 0.9
Under 2,500 & rural	5.5	5.3	5.9	- 0.2	+ 0.6
TYPE OF PLACE					
City	5.7	5.5	6.4	- 0.2	+ 0.9
Suburb	5.6	5.4	6.3	- 0.2	+ 0.9
Town or village	5.7	5.4	5.9	- 0.3	+ 0.5
Rural	5.4	5.4	6.1	-	+ 0.7
RACE					
White	5.7	5.4	6.2	- 0.3	+ 0.8
Black	5.4	5.6	6.3	- 0.2	+ 0.7

TABLE A-2 (cont'd)

	Past	Present	Future	Shift: Past to Present	Shift: Present to Future
RELIGION					
Protestant	5.7	5.6	6.2	- 0.1	+ 0.6
Catholic	5.7	5.5	6.4	- 0.2	+ 0.9
POLITICS					
Republican	5.7	5.8	6.6	+ 0.1	+ 0.8
Democrat	5.8	5.4	6.3	- 0.4	+ 0.9
Independent	5.6	5.3	6.0	- 0.3	+ 0.7
LIBERAL - CONSERVATIVE					
Very liberal	5.5	5.4	6.7	- 0.1	+ 1.3
Moderately liberal	5.5	5.3	6.1	- 0.2	+ 0.8
Middle of the road	5.8	5.4	6.2	- 0.4	+ 0.8
Moderately conservative	5.8	5.7	6.3	- 0.1	+ 0.6
Very conservative	5.6	5.4	5.6	- 0.2	+ 0.2

TABLE A-3   WORRIES AND CONCERNS: INTERNATIONAL

Composite Scores

[NOTE: For the wording of the questions involved, see Question 24 on page 279. The method used in computing the composite scores given below is described on page 355.]

	Vietnam	Respect for U.S.	National Defense	Relations with Allies	Danger of War	Communist China	Soviet Russia	Threat of Communism
NATIONAL TOTALS	88	76	77	75	66	61	61	69
SEX								
Men	87	75	79	75	59	55	58	67
Women	88	76	75	75	72	65	64	72
AGE								
18-29	91	68	67	71	68	58	59	62
30-49	88	79	79	77	64	59	60	71
50 & over	85	79	83	77	65	64	65	74
EDUCATION								
College	85	66	70	71	53	52	56	58
High School	90	79	78	76	69	63	62	72
Grade School	86	79	84	79	72	66	69	79
FAMILY INCOME								
$15,000 & over	90	73	73	75	58	57	58	63
$10,000 - $14,999	86	81	80	76	61	64	64	74
$7,000 - $9,999	90	76	79	76	62	54	57	68
$5,000 - $6,999	88	78	79	76	73	66	64	70
Under $ 5,000	87	74	77	74	74	63	63	73
OCCUPATION								
Professional & Business	88	73	71	73	60	59	58	65
White Collar	87	69	74	75	62	56	56	66
Manual	90	81	83	76	71	64	65	72
Non-labor	85	73	77	76	62	58	61	67

TABLE A-3 (cont'd)

WORRIES AND CONCERNS: INTERNATIONAL

	Vietnam	Respect for U.S.	National Defense	Relations with Allies	Danger of War	Communist China	Soviet Russia	Threat of Communism
UNION MEMBERSHIP								
Union Households	90	78	80	79	69	64	68	72
Non-union Households	88	75	76	74	65	60	60	69
HOME OWNERSHIP								
Home Owners	88	78	79	76	64	61	62	72
Non-owners	88	70	71	73	70	60	59	65
REGION								
East	90	74	70	71	65	57	57	59
Midwest	88	73	75	73	62	60	62	68
South	88	81	85	81	71	63	64	79
West	84	73	78	76	65	64	63	72
COMMUNITY SIZE								
500,000 & over	89	72	74	74	65	58	60	64
50,000 - 499,999	86	79	77	74	68	62	65	68
2,500 - 49,999	88	75	78	74	63	61	61	70
Under 2,500 & rural	88	77	80	78	66	62	61	76
TYPE OF PLACE								
City	86	71	74	73	66	60	61	65
Suburb	89	82	82	79	65	62	64	71
Town or village	88	78	79	76	65	57	59	76
Rural	89	75	77	76	69	62	61	76
RACE								
White	88	76	78	76	64	61	62	70
Black	86	72	74	70	78	62	61	65

TABLE A-3 (cont'd)

WORRIES AND CONCERNS: INTERNATIONAL

	Vietnam	Respect for U.S.	National Defense	Relations with Allies	Danger of War	Communist China	Communist Soviet Russia	Threat of Communism
RELIGION								
Protestant	87	76	80	77	64	61	61	72
Catholic	89	80	77	75	70	63	64	69
POLITICS								
Republican	79	75	82	76	54	56	59	72
Democrat	90	77	77	74	70	63	64	67
Independent	92	76	76	77	69	63	62	72
LIBERAL - CONSERVATIVE								
Very liberal	94	72	68	66	58	52	52	51
Moderately liberal	91	72	72	75	65	57	60	60
Middle of the road	87	79	77	77	70	65	63	73
Moderately conservative	84	74	82	75	58	60	65	76
Very conservative	88	82	79	79	74	61	60	80

TABLE A-4

WORRIES AND CONCERNS: DOMESTIC

Composite Scores

[NOTE: For the wording of the questions involved, see Questions 57 and 58 on page 288. The method used in computing the composite scores given below is described on page 355.]

	Crime	Drugs & Addicts	Violence	Housing	Consumer Protection	Education	Poverty	Inflation	Unemployment	Business Conditions	Medical Care	Water Pollution	Air Pollution	Solid Wastes	Urban Renewal	Black Americans	Mass Transportation	Senior Citizens	Urban Problems
NATIONAL TOTALS	89	89	90	69	82	77	77	90	77	71	83	84	83	80	72	65	56	78	71
SEX																			
Men	87	88	90	68	80	77	75	88	75	71	82	85	83	81	70	63	58	76	70
Women	91	91	91	69	83	77	78	93	80	71	84	83	82	80	74	67	55	79	72
AGE																			
18-29	88	83	87	72	84	85	82	90	79	73	83	86	86	83	77	69	55	75	73
30-49	90	93	92	69	84	80	76	90	76	73	82	85	84	80	72	65	57	76	73
50 & over	90	91	91	66	79	69	74	91	77	68	84	82	80	79	69	62	57	82	67
EDUCATION																			
College	87	87	86	68	80	81	77	85	77	70	81	87	86	79	72	68	61	73	76
High School	90	90	92	70	84	78	78	91	78	72	84	84	83	82	73	63	54	78	70
Grade School	88	91	90	66	80	68	74	95	77	71	83	80	78	77	70	65	57	83	67
FAMILY INCOME																			
$15,000 & over	90	93	91	72	80	81	76	85	76	73	82	87	87	83	75	75	58	79	80
$10,000 - $14,999	90	88	91	61	85	79	75	94	76	72	81	86	85	80	68	57	54	73	67
$7,000 - $9,999	90	90	89	66	85	77	78	90	75	70	83	84	82	79	74	61	59	79	72
$5,000 - $6,999	90	88	89	74	79	78	77	90	78	72	83	84	82	80	77	66	60	77	72
Under $5,000	87	89	91	71	81	72	77	92	79	69	85	80	80	79	70	65	55	82	68

TABLE A-4 (cont'd)

WORRIES AND CONCERNS: DOMESTIC

	Crime	Drugs & Addicts	Violence	Housing	Consumer Protection	Education	Poverty	Inflation	Unemployment	Business Conditions	Medical Care	Water Pollution	Air Pollution	Solid Wastes	Urban Renewal	Black Americans	Mass Transportation	Senior Citizens	Urban Problems
OCCUPATION																			
Professional & Business	87	87	90	71	80	82	76	89	78	72	79	87	87	82	74	69	60	74	71
White Collar	88	90	90	72	80	75	74	84	78	76	84	82	83	75	73	61	53	75	75
Manual	91	91	90	67	85	81	81	92	79	72	86	87	84	83	74	66	58	80	73
Non-labor	89	90	91	68	80	68	73	91	74	66	81	79	78	78	67	61	53	78	67
UNION MEMBERSHIP																			
Union Households	92	92	92	69	90	82	78	94	81	76	86	86	84	81	74	66	58	80	74
Non-union Households	89	90	90	69	80	76	76	89	76	70	82	84	83	80	72	65	57	78	70
HOME OWNERSHIP																			
Home Owners	90	92	91	66	82	76	75	90	77	71	82	85	83	79	70	65	56	78	70
Non-owners	89	85	88	75	83	80	81	92	80	72	84	83	82	83	78	67	58	79	74
REGION																			
East	88	89	90	72	80	74	80	89	78	70	80	81	81	80	75	68	57	78	76
Midwest	90	91	91	67	83	78	74	91	76	72	83	84	83	82	73	64	54	78	71
South	90	90	90	66	81	80	75	92	75	70	84	82	81	78	68	63	55	77	64
West	88	87	88	69	84	78	80	90	83	74	86	93	90	82	73	64	63	79	74
COMMUNITY SIZE																			
500,000 & over	91	90	92	76	83	81	83	91	83	75	86	86	86	82	79	69	65	81	78
50,000 - 499,999	87	88	89	69	81	81	78	90	79	75	83	86	84	80	74	68	58	78	74
2,500 - 49,999	90	91	91	63	84	74	76	90	72	66	82	87	86	81	73	62	56	74	70
Under 2,500 & rural	88	89	88	64	80	72	70	90	74	67	81	78	77	78	64	60	46	77	62

TABLE A-4 (cont'd)

WORRIES AND CONCERNS: DOMESTIC

	Crime	Drugs & Addicts	Violence	Housing	Consumer Protection	Education	Poverty	Inflation	Unemployment	Business Conditions	Medical Care	Water Pollution	Air Pollution	Solid Wastes	Urban Renewal	Black Americans	Mass Transportation	Senior Citizens	Urban Problems
TYPE OF PLACE																			
City	89	89	90	73	82	81	82	90	81	73	85	85	86	81	78	70	62	80	74
Suburb	91	91	91	70	85	79	76	89	78	74	82	89	86	84	74	63	62	77	77
Town or village	89	91	91	63	80	68	72	92	72	68	81	87	84	78	69	63	51	79	65
Rural	88	89	89	63	80	72	70	90	74	66	80	77	75	76	60	60	47	77	61
RACE																			
White	89	90	90	66	82	76	75	90	76	70	82	84	83	80	71	62	55	77	70
Black	90	88	91	87	82	86	90	92	90	80	87	80	80	81	86	90	70	84	83
RELIGION																			
Protestant	89	89	90	67	80	76	74	89	76	69	82	82	81	78	70	63	55	77	68
Catholic	92	94	91	72	85	79	82	93	80	75	84	88	86	85	76	67	58	81	73
POLITICS																			
Republican	89	90	88	62	78	70	69	88	71	64	78	82	81	75	66	61	53	73	68
Democrat	89	90	91	72	82	80	80	92	84	76	85	83	82	80	75	70	59	80	71
Independent	90	89	90	69	84	79	77	90	75	72	84	86	86	83	71	62	58	79	72
LIBERAL - CONSERVATIVE																			
Very liberal	86	88	90	80	80	87	89	89	86	74	93	88	84	80	79	85	64	88	77
Moderately liberal	89	91	92	76	86	83	84	89	79	77	88	90	87	84	79	75	63	80	79
Middle of the road	88	88	89	66	82	77	76	93	77	70	80	82	81	80	70	60	54	74	68
Moderately conservative	90	90	89	64	79	70	69	87	74	68	77	80	80	76	66	60	54	77	68
Very conservative	97	96	97	53	82	75	66	89	74	67	85	81	85	82	69	54	58	81	66

TABLE A-5

INTERNATIONAL PATTERNS

[NOTE: The method employed in categorizing respondents as "Completely Internationalist", "Predominantly Internationalist", "Mixed", "Predominantly Isolationist", and "Completely Isolationist" is described on page 353.]

	Compl. Inter.	Pred. Inter.	Mixed	Pred. Isol.	Compl. Isol.	Composite Scores
NATIONAL TOTALS	13%	41%	33%	10%	3%	63
SEX						
Men	15	48	27	8	2	66
Women	11	35	40	11	3	60
AGE						
18-29	11	45	35	8	1	64
30-49	16	46	30	7	1	67
50 & over	12	34	36	13	5	59
EDUCATION						
College	15	48	29	7	1	67
High School	14	40	34	10	2	64
Grade School	8	35	37	13	7	56
FAMILY INCOME						
$15,000 & over	19	49	27	4	1	70
$10,000 - $14,999	11	44	31	11	3	62
$7,000 - $9,999	12	43	32	9	4	62
$5,000 - $6,999	13	39	36	10	2	63
Under $5,000	9	33	41	14	3	58
OCCUPATION						
Professional & Business	15	46	31	7	1	67
White Collar	14	44	31	10	1	65
Manual	13	41	35	9	2	64
Non-labor	11	35	36	13	5	58
UNION MEMBERSHIP						
Union Households	13	40	33	11	3	62
Non-union Households	13	41	34	9	3	63
HOME OWNERSHIP						
Home Owners	13	40	34	10	3	62
Non-owners	13	46	32	8	1	66
REGION						
East	15	35	35	13	2	62
Midwest	12	43	35	6	4	63
South	10	45	31	12	2	62
West	16	43	33	7	1	66
COMMUNITY SIZE						
500,000 & over	14	37	35	13	1	62
50,000 - 499,999	15	41	32	9	3	64
2,500 - 49,999	11	49	24	13	3	63
Under 2,500 & rural	11	42	38	5	4	63

TABLE A-5   (cont'd)

INTERNATIONAL PATTERNS

	Compl. Inter.	Pred. Inter.	Mixed	Pred. Isol.	Compl. Isol.	Composite Scores
TYPE OF PLACE						
City	13%	39%	33%	13%	2%	62
Suburb	14	41	35	8	2	64
Town or village	14	44	32	10	*	66
Rural	10	46	33	5	6	62
RACE						
White	14	43	32	9	2	64
Black	6	32	40	18	4	54
RELIGION						
Protestant	14	42	32	9	3	64
Catholic	12	39	34	12	3	61
POLITICS						
Republican	23	39	30	7	1	69
Democrat	10	41	34	12	3	61
Independent	11	45	35	6	3	64
LIBERAL - CONSERVATIVE						
Very liberal	10	45	34	9	2	63
Moderately liberal	12	40	36	11	1	63
Middle of the road	13	42	34	9	2	64
Moderately conservative	17	41	29	8	5	64
Very conservative	11	33	42	12	2	60

TABLE A-6

GOVERNMENT SPENDING: INTERNATIONAL AND DEFENSE

Composite Scores

[NOTE: For the wording of the questions involved, see Questions 15
through 19 on page 278. The method used in computing the
composite scores given below is described on page 355.]

	United Nations Activities	Economic Aid	Military Aid	U.S. Forces in Europe	Military Bases Abroad	National Defense *
NATIONAL TOTALS	36	24	21	29	28	32
SEX						
Men	35	24	24	31	30	35
Women	37	24	18	28	28	28
AGE						
18-29	46	31	20	26	29	28
30-49	34	23	22	35	32	33
50 & over	30	20	21	27	25	33
EDUCATION						
College	37	28	21	24	25	26
High School	38	23	21	31	29	34
Grade School	27	20	22	35	31	33
FAMILY INCOME						
$15,000 & over	40	31	17	24	23	29
$10,000 - $14,999	32	23	20	28	28	32
$7,000 - $9,999	37	21	22	35	30	34
$5,000 - $6,999	36	24	25	27	35	31
Under $5,000	31	20	18	31	26	34
OCCUPATION						
Professional & Business	35	26	19	28	27	27
White Collar	30	29	25	32	29	34
Manual	41	25	24	29	31	34
Non-labor	30	17	16	26	25	30
UNION MEMBERSHIP						
Union Households	40	24	24	29	31	-
Non-union Households	34	24	20	30	27	-
HOME OWNERSHIP						
Home Owners	33	23	19	28	28	-
Non-home Owners	40	27	24	35	30	-
REGION						
East	35	28	17	30	29	28
Midwest	37	23	22	26	24	30
South	39	25	26	36	34	40
West	30	19	19	26	26	28

TABLE A-6 (cont'd)

GOVERNMENT SPENDING: INTERNATIONAL AND DEFENSE

	United Nations Activities	Economic Aid	Military Aid	U.S. Forces in Europe	Military Bases Abroad	National Defense*
COMMUNITY SIZE						
500,000 & over	38	24	18	21	22	27
50,000 - 499,999	35	30	27	37	32	35
2,500 - 49,999	39	19	22	35	42	32
Under 2,500 & rural	32	22	18	32	27	33
TYPE OF PLACE						
City	40	24	22	29	30	-
Suburb	33	25	22	24	25	-
Town or village	36	19	19	35	31	-
Rural	31	24	19	33	25	-
RACE						
White	34	24	21	30	29	32
Black	45	26	20	27	25	27
RELIGION						
Protestant	35	23	22	30	28	35
Catholic	37	26	20	27	32	28
POLITICS						
Republican	28	19	22	27	28	38
Democrat	41	27	21	29	27	28
Independent	33	23	19	31	29	31
LIBERAL - CONSERVATIVE						
Very liberal	40	27	19	19	20	-
Moderately liberal	40	28	23	26	30	-
Middle of the road	34	22	20	32	29	-
Mod. conservative	32	26	24	30	26	-
Very conservative	36	24	24	44	36	-

*Figures on defense spending were derived from a supplementary question posed to a standard national sample by The Gallup Organization in August 1972. Several demographic tabulations are absent since they are not normally included in the Gallup survey. See page 221 for a further discussion of this question and its results.

TABLE A-7

GOVERNMENT SPENDING: DOMESTIC

Composite Scores

[NOTE: For the wording of the questions involved, see Questions 66 and 67 on page 294. The method used in computing the composite scores given below is described on page 355.]

	Public Housing	Housing in General	Educating Low-Income Children	Higher Education	Highways	Urban Renew.	Water Pollution	Air Pollution	Sr. Citizens	Medicaid	Black Americans	Mass Transportation	Welfare	Medical Care	Crime	Drugs & Addicts	Jobs for Unemployed	Public Parks	Urban Problems	Space Program
NATIONAL TOTALS	62	64	80	72	63	69	81	80	87	74	57	66	53	80	88	86	67	66	68	25
SEX																				
Men	61	63	80	73	64	66	78	78	84	72	56	66	51	78	88	87	64	65	66	30
Women	63	65	80	72	62	71	83	82	89	75	59	66	55	82	89	86	70	68	70	21
AGE																				
18-29	70	72	89	79	67	81	90	89	87	74	67	62	59	82	89	86	76	72	79	24
30-49	58	60	78	74	59	65	80	80	83	68	53	63	47	76	90	87	61	67	67	28
50 & over	59	62	74	67	64	63	75	73	90	78	54	71	54	81	87	86	65	62	61	24
EDUCATION																				
College	65	63	84	71	58	65	83	82	85	73	64	69	52	80	88	87	61	69	68	29
High School	64	64	81	75	65	72	84	82	87	74	56	64	52	79	89	86	68	67	71	26
Grade School	54	66	70	67	64	64	66	70	89	74	55	65	57	83	87	87	72	62	60	16
FAMILY INCOME																				
$15,000 & over	62	59	83	74	60	70	85	85	86	70	57	67	46	75	88	87	56	66	71	31
$10,000 - $14,999	63	65	78	69	64	68	87	85	83	67	52	69	45	80	91	88	64	68	69	33
$7,000 - $9,999	62	68	76	74	66	70	81	77	87	77	58	68	54	77	87	86	71	73	66	21
$5,000 - $6,999	60	62	81	75	64	63	76	79	84	76	57	53	55	80	85	83	69	64	66	19
Under $5,000	64	68	79	72	62	71	73	73	91	80	63	65	64	85	88	86	78	62	64	19

TABLE A-7 (cont'd)

GOVERNMENT SPENDING: DOMESTIC

	Public Housing	Housing in General	Low-Income Children Education	Higher Education	Highways	Urban Renewal	Water Pollution	Air Pollution	Sr. Citizens	Medicaid	Black Americans	Mass Transportation	Welfare	Medical Care	Crime	Drugs & Addicts	Jobs for Unemployed	Public Parks	Urban Problems	Space Program
OCCUPATION																				
Professional & Business	61	59	81	73	59	68	84	82	83	74	57	64	49	76	89	88	60	68	69	27
White Collar	66	68	88	80	68	73	86	86	87	78	57	70	56	83	87	89	68	75	74	30
Manual	63	69	81	74	67	72	82	83	88	72	60	66	54	82	89	86	71	67	71	25
Non-labor	60	62	72	65	60	62	72	69	90	75	55	69	55	80	90	85	66	62	58	21
UNION MEMBERSHIP																				
Union Households	65	64	83	77	67	71	83	84	87	74	54	69	55	82	89	87	73	70	71	28
Non-union Households	61	64	78	71	62	68	80	78	87	73	59	64	52	79	88	86	65	65	68	24
HOME OWNERSHIP																				
Home Owners	59	59	75	70	64	66	80	79	85	71	54	67	49	78	89	86	64	64	66	27
Non-owners	70	75	88	77	62	74	82	81	89	78	66	65	62	84	88	88	75	71	72	23
REGION																				
East	64	71	77	72	62	77	83	80	88	75	60	69	48	88	88	87	67	68	69	27
Midwest	63	63	79	71	66	66	80	81	82	70	59	65	55	76	91	88	70	62	68	22
South	57	58	78	74	66	64	84	77	90	76	53	64	57	76	86	87	63	68	66	25
West	66	64	87	73	50	68	88	83	90	73	56	63	53	78	88	82	69	67	71	27
COMMUNITY SIZE																				
500,000 & over	66	71	83	76	60	76	86	85	90	76	62	71	54	84	88	85	72	72	74	25
50,000 - 499,999	65	64	78	71	65	69	81	83	87	73	60	66	54	77	87	87	66	66	70	26
2,500 - 49,999	64	63	83	73	66	69	79	76	87	79	61	70	61	80	91	83	66	63	67	25
Under 2,500 & rural	54	57	75	69	65	59	74	74	83	68	48	57	47	77	88	89	64	62	60	25

TABLE A-7 (cont'd)

GOVERNMENT SPENDING: DOMESTIC

	Public Housing	Housing in General	Educating Low-Income Children	Higher Education	Highways	Urban Renewal	Water Pollution	Air Pollution	Sr. Citizens	Medicaid	Black Americans	Mass Transportation	Welfare	Medical Care	Crime	Drugs & Addicts	Jobs for Unemployed	Public Parks	Urban Problems	Space Program
TYPE OF PLACE																				
City	70	68	83	75	62	72	82	80	91	80	66	70	60	84	89	85	69	66	69	23
Suburb	59	68	81	72	60	70	85	85	87	71	54	66	48	77	87	85	65	72	72	28
Town or village	62	59	79	76	63	68	79	76	83	76	58	65	55	77	88	82	64	64	69	26
Rural	54	57	77	68	66	58	75	77	86	66	45	58	45	77	92	93	68	62	60	26
RACE																				
White	60	61	78	70	63	66	81	81	86	72	53	65	49	78	88	86	65	65	66	26
Black	83	88	91	89	65	88	76	75	95	84	95	73	81	91	88	88	85	78	85	14
RELIGION																				
Protestant	62	62	80	73	63	66	79	77	87	73	56	65	53	79	89	87	66	65	66	23
Catholic	58	66	78	73	64	74	84	85	86	73	55	66	52	79	90	85	72	69	72	31
POLITICS																				
Republican	56	56	72	58	59	62	82	78	85	76	52	68	43	75	91	86	54	62	65	28
Democrat	64	69	80	78	62	71	79	78	88	75	63	65	58	82	86	87	71	68	68	26
Independent	63	63	83	73	68	70	82	82	86	69	56	66	50	79	90	86	70	66	70	23
LIBERAL – CONSERVATIVE																				
Very liberal	77	82	96	89	61	86	83	87	94	90	73	84	75	86	79	90	77	78	72	33
Moderately liberal	65	68	85	79	64	74	82	80	91	79	63	71	57	81	88	86	68	72	70	24
Middle of the road	62	63	80	68	64	68	80	82	86	72	57	62	50	79	89	85	69	62	68	28
Moderately conservative	55	57	73	69	59	62	80	77	80	68	47	59	42	76	86	85	60	61	65	25
Very conservative	58	62	67	64	52	56	88	81	89	64	48	65	49	76	86	75	62	70	66	12

TABLE A-8

TRUST AND CONFIDENCE

Composite Scores

[NOTE: For the wording of the questions involved, see Questions 68 through 74 on page 297 and Questions 80 through 84 on page 299. The method used in computing the composite scores given below is described on page 355.]

	Federal Gov't. International	Federal Gov't. Domestic	Executive Branch	Judicial Branch	Legislative Branch	State Government	Local Governments	Business & Industry	Labor Unions	Young People	Mass Media	Politicians
NATIONAL TOTALS	66	61	67	60	62	60	57	55	47	67	60	58
SEX												
Men	66	58	67	60	60	59	57	53	46	66	58	58
Women	66	63	67	60	64	61	58	58	48	68	62	57
AGE												
18-29	64	58	64	63	61	60	56	50	48	69	61	56
30-49	67	60	63	60	65	59	55	53	47	67	59	57
50 & over	67	63	73	56	60	62	60	62	47	65	61	60
EDUCATION												
College	64	58	65	62	62	59	55	53	40	70	55	55
High School	67	62	66	59	62	59	58	56	49	68	62	59
Grade School	67	62	72	56	60	65	60	58	51	59	64	60
FAMILY INCOME												
$15,000 & over	70	58	68	62	62	59	55	54	44	72	58	57
$10,000 - $14,999	65	61	67	59	60	57	61	55	50	71	59	56
$7,000 - $9,999	66	63	64	57	63	59	60	53	46	67	57	56
$5,000 - $6,999	65	62	68	62	61	63	55	57	47	67	65	61
Under $5,000	65	62	67	58	62	62	57	58	52	60	66	60

TABLE A-8 (cont'd)

TRUST AND CONFIDENCE

	Federal Gov't. International	Federal Gov't. Domestic	Executive Branch	Judicial Branch	Legislative Branch	State Government	Local Governments	Business & Industry	Labor Unions	Young People	Mass Media	Politicians
OCCUPATION												
Professional & Business	65	59	64	60	64	57	56	58	43	70	61	55
White Collar	71	66	76	63	67	63	54	57	45	64	52	63
Manual	64	58	61	59	61	60	58	51	49	69	62	57
Non-labor	69	63	74	57	61	64	60	62	50	61	60	59
UNION MEMBERSHIP												
Union Households	69	62	64	61	62	62	56	50	56	65	63	59
Non-union Households	65	60	68	59	62	60	58	58	44	68	59	58
HOME OWNERS												
Home Owners	67	61	69	59	62	59	57	58	48	67	59	57
Non-owners	65	59	62	62	62	63	56	51	48	67	64	59
REGION												
East	66	60	65	59	62	53	54	53	47	64	59	56
Midwest	66	60	67	63	58	60	59	59	46	68	64	56
South	67	61	68	55	66	66	58	59	53	68	60	60
West	66	62	68	60	61	64	60	53	41	69	57	60
COMMUNITY SIZE												
500,000 & over	66	59	64	60	62	57	56	53	46	68	59	55
50,000 - 499,999	66	61	63	60	63	61	55	56	54	66	64	62
2,500 - 49,999	68	63	70	58	61	61	58	56	46	65	60	60
Under 2,500 & rural	66	61	71	60	62	63	61	57	43	68	59	57

TABLE A-8 (cont'd)

TRUST AND CONFIDENCE

	Federal Gov't. International	Federal Gov't. Domestic	Executive Branch	Judicial Branch	Legislative Branch	State Government	Local Governments	Business & Industry	Labor Unions	Young People	Mass Media	Politicians
TYPE OF PLACE												
City	66	60	63	63	62	62	54	55	50	66	60	59
Suburb	68	62	70	57	64	57	60	56	48	69	63	57
Town or village	68	63	69	59	62	65	60	58	41	63	58	62
Rural	65	61	70	59	63	60	62	56	47	70	59	56
RACE												
White	67	62	68	59	62	61	58	56	46	67	59	58
Black	59	54	55	65	63	56	51	53	57	66	65	53
RELIGION												
Protestant	67	61	69	58	61	63	59	56	47	66	59	59
Catholic	69	64	66	62	66	59	57	58	48	68	61	58
POLITICS												
Republican	72	67	82	62	62	67	69	64	41	67	61	63
Democrat	65	60	62	61	63	58	54	55	53	68	64	57
Independent	65	59	63	58	62	58	58	50	41	67	56	56
LIBERAL – CONSERVATIVE												
Very liberal	55	48	48	63	57	54	60	46	59	70	62	50
Moderately liberal	65	62	63	61	70	61	57	56	53	66	66	60
Middle of the road	67	60	68	58	58	58	58	54	43	67	58	58
Moderately conservative	70	65	75	61	63	63	56	63	44	70	59	58
Very conservative	59	60	67	55	60	69	52	55	39	61	46	56

TABLE A-9

EVALUATIONS OF GOVERNMENTAL SYSTEM
Composite Scores

[NOTE: For the wording of the questions involved, see Questions 76 through 78 on page 299 . The method used in computing the composite scores given below is described on page 355 .]

	Honesty, Fairness, Justice	Efficiency	Responsiveness
NATIONAL TOTALS	46	44	41
SEX			
Men	47	43	41
Women	46	45	40
AGE			
18-29	45	41	36
30-49	47	45	40
50 & over	47	44	44
EDUCATION			
College	49	40	39
High School	46	44	40
Grade School	45	49	44
FAMILY INCOME			
$15,000 & over	50	44	45
$10,000 - $14,999	47	40	41
$7,000 - $9,999	44	43	38
$5,000 - $6,999	44	46	39
Under $ 5,000	47	47	42
OCCUPATION			
Professional & Business	46	42	42
White Collar	50	46	50
Manual	45	43	37
Non-labor	50	45	42
UNION MEMBERSHIP			
Union Households	46	45	41
Non-union Households	46	43	41
HOME OWNERSHIP			
Home Owners	46	44	42
Non-owners	47	44	39
REGION			
East	47	41	40
Midwest	44	44	38
South	46	45	42
West	49	47	46
COMMUNITY SIZE			
500,000 & over	46	40	38
50,000 - 499,999	49	47	42
2,500 - 49,999	50	45	43
Under 2,500 & rural	44	45	43

TABLE A-9 (cont'd)

EVALUATIONS OF GOVERNMENTAL SYSTEM

	Honesty, Fairness, Justice	Efficiency	Responsiveness
TYPE OF PLACE			
City	47	45	40
Suburb	48	42	41
Town or village	47	44	42
Rural	45	44	43
RACE			
White	47	44	42
Black	40	40	32
RELIGION			
Protestant	48	44	43
Catholic	47	46	42
POLITICS			
Republican	57	46	53
Democrat	44	45	39
Independent	44	40	38
LIBERAL - CONSERVATIVE			
Very liberal	36	30	32
Moderately liberal	47	41	40
Middle of the road	46	47	42
Moderately conservative	51	45	44
Very conservative	41	35	26

TABLE A-10

NEED FOR CHANGE IN GOVERNMENTAL SYSTEM

Taking into account what you would want America to be like ten years from now, do you think a basic change will need to be made in the way our governmental system is now set up and organized or don't you think this will be necessary?

	Yes	No	Don't Know
NATIONAL TOTALS	54%	36%	10%
SEX			
Men	52	40	8
Women	57	32	11
AGE			
18-29	63	31	6
30-49	49	42	9
50 & over	53	35	12
EDUCATION			
College	49	45	6
High School	58	32	10
Grade School	52	36	12
FAMILY INCOME			
$15,000 & over	55	37	8
$10,000 - $14,999	45	45	10
$7,000 - $9,999	55	39	6
$5,000 - $6,999	44	41	15
Under $5,000	65	24	11
OCCUPATION			
Professional & Business	48	43	9
White Collar	43	50	7
Manual	60	30	10
Non-labor	57	38	5
UNION MEMBERSHIP			
Union Households	56	38	6
Non-union Households	54	35	11
HOME OWNERSHIP			
Home Owners	55	35	10
Non-owners	56	36	8
REGION			
East	60	31	9
Midwest	59	34	7
South	57	30	13
West	34	57	9
COMMUNITY SIZE			
500,000 & over	52	36	12
50,000 - 499,999	58	35	7
2,500 - 49,999	66	29	5
Under 2,500 & rural	48	40	12

TABLE A-10   (cont'd)

NEED FOR CHANGE IN GOVERNMENTAL SYSTEM

	Yes	No	Don't Know
TYPE OF PLACE			
City	59%	31%	10%
Suburb	49	42	9
Town or village	47	44	9
Rural	53	37	10
RACE			
White	53	39	8
Black	69	16	15
RELIGION			
Protestant	54	38	8
Catholic	56	33	11
POLITICS			
Republican	48	44	8
Democrat	56	33	11
Independent	60	34	6
LIBERAL - CONSERVATIVE			
Very liberal	61	30	9
Moderately liberal	55	34	11
Middle of the road	55	39	6
Moderately conservative	47	42	11
Very conservative	59	29	12

TABLE A-11

PROGRESS: INTERNATIONAL PROBLEM AREAS

Composite Scores

[NOTE: For the wording of the questions involved, see Question 27
on page 282. The method used in computing the composite
scores given below is described on page 355.]

	Vietnam	Communist China	Soviet Russia	Relations with Allies	International Economics
NATIONAL TOTALS	57	72	70	56	46
SEX					
Men	59	73	72	54	44
Women	55	70	69	57	48
AGE					
18-29	54	72	71	53	45
30-49	57	73	71	55	46
50 & over	59	70	69	58	46
EDUCATION					
College	56	76	73	50	42
High School	57	72	71	56	46
Grade School	58	65	65	61	51
FAMILY INCOME					
$15,000 & over	61	77	74	52	43
$10,000 - $14,999	58	72	70	53	47
$7,000 - $9,999	55	70	71	57	45
$5,000 - $6,999	55	70	70	61	49
Under $5,000	54	68	67	58	47
OCCUPATION					
Professional & Business	60	76	72	51	48
White Collar	58	74	72	54	44
Manual	55	70	70	57	45
Non-labor	56	68	68	58	43
UNION MEMBERSHIP					
Union Households	58	70	70	55	45
Non-union Households	57	72	71	56	46
HOME OWNERSHIP					
Home Owners	59	73	71	56	47
Non-owners	54	70	70	54	44
REGION					
East	56	72	72	55	45
Midwest	58	72	72	57	45
South	57	70	68	58	52
West	55	73	70	51	40

TABLE A-11 (cont'd)

PROGRESS: INTERNATIONAL PROBLEM AREAS

	Vietnam	Communist China	Soviet Russia	Relations with Allies	International Economics
COMMUNITY SIZE					
500,000 & over	57	72	71	55	43
50,000 - 499,999	55	72	70	55	45
2,500 - 49,999	59	71	71	56	49
Under 2,500 & rural	57	71	70	56	48
TYPE OF PLACE					
City	54	70	69	56	44
Suburb	61	74	72	52	44
Town or village	60	70	69	57	49
Rural	57	72	72	57	48
RACE					
White	58	72	71	55	45
Black	50	68	67	63	54
RELIGION					
Protestant	60	72	70	55	47
Catholic	56	71	70	58	46
POLITICS					
Republican	70	76	72	57	52
Democrat	52	70	70	57	46
Independent	55	71	70	53	42
LIBERAL - CONSERVATIVE					
Very liberal	47	75	74	59	39
Moderately liberal	55	74	72	52	46
Middle of the road	57	70	70	56	47
Moderately conservative	64	72	70	56	44
Very conservative	50	63	64	60	52

TABLE A-12

PROGRESS: FOREIGN POLICY MATTERS IN GENERAL

Considering the international situation overall, do you think that in handling foreign policy problems in general during the last twelve months the United States has made much progress, made some progress, stood still, lost some ground, or lost much ground? (A,B,C)

[NOTE: For a description of the method used in calculating the composite scores in the far right hand column below, see page 355.]

	Made Much Progress	Made Some Progress	Stood Still	Lost Some Ground	Lost Much Ground	Don't Know	Composite Scores
NATIONAL TOTALS	8%	56%	17%	9%	2%	8%	66
SEX							
Men	9	58	17	9	2	5	67
Women	6	55	17	10	2	10	65
AGE							
18-29	8	54	20	11	2	5	64
30-49	7	60	17	9	1	6	67
50 & over	8	55	15	9	3	10	66
EDUCATION							
College	9	59	15	12	2	3	66
High School	8	58	18	8	2	6	66
Grade School	6	50	17	9	2	16	65
FAMILY INCOME							
$15,000 & over	8	65	15	8	1	3	68
$10,000 - $14,999	9	58	18	9	2	4	66
$7,000 - $9,999	6	57	21	9	3	4	64
$5,000 - $6,999	9	57	15	9	1	9	68
Under $5,000	6	47	17	12	3	15	62
OCCUPATION							
Professional & Business	9	64	14	8	1	4	69
White Collar	11	51	18	11	4	5	64
Manual	6	57	18	10	2	7	65
Non-labor	8	48	18	9	3	14	64
UNION MEMBERSHIP							
Union Households	8	54	19	10	2	7	65
Non-union Households	8	58	16	9	2	7	66
HOME OWNERSHIP							
Home Owners	7	60	15	10	2	6	66
Non-owners	8	52	19	8	3	10	65
REGION							
East	8	58	15	8	2	9	67
Midwest	6	58	18	9	1	8	66
South	8	55	17	11	3	6	64
West	10	54	17	10	3	6	65

TABLE A-12   (cont'd)

PROGRESS: FOREIGN POLICY MATTERS IN GENERAL

	Made Much Progress	Made Some Progress	Stood Still	Lost Some Ground	Lost Much Ground	Don't Know	Composite Scores
COMMUNITY SIZE							
500,000 & over	6%	55%	17%	8%	3%	11%	65
50,000 - 499,999	10	52	19	11	1	7	66
2,500 - 49,999	7	62	16	9	1	5	67
Under 2,500 & rural	7	59	15	10	3	6	65
TYPE OF PLACE							
City	8	55	15	10	2	10	66
Suburb	8	58	21	7	2	4	66
Town or village	7	57	18	10	2	6	65
Rural	8	59	15	9	2	7	67
RACE							
White	8	58	17	9	2	6	66
Black	4	48	13	11	4	20	62
RELIGION							
Protestant	8	57	16	10	2	7	66
Catholic	7	61	17	6	2	7	67
POLITICS							
Republican	14	66	10	5	1	4	73
Democrat	6	54	18	10	2	10	64
Independent	5	56	20	11	3	5	63
LIBERAL - CONSERVATIVE							
Very liberal	10	56	11	12	4	7	65
Moderately liberal	10	57	16	10	2	5	66
Middle of the road	5	60	19	9	2	5	65
Moderately conservative	10	56	17	8	2	7	67
Very conservative	8	49	17	10	5	11	63

TABLE A-13   PROGRESS: DOMESTIC PROBLEM AREAS

Composite Scores

[NOTE: For the wording of the questions involved, see Questions 59 and 60 on page 291. The method used in computing the composite scores given below is described on page 355.]

	Inflation	Unemployment	Business Conditions	Crime	Drugs & Addicts	Medical Care	Poverty & Welfare	Mass Transport	Senior Citizens	Black Americans	Education	Housing	Water Pollution	Air Pollution	Urban Problems
NATIONAL TOTALS	36	45	56	37	44	61	48	51	60	64	65	64	57	58	57
SEX															
Men	39	46	57	39	44	62	47	50	59	64	66	63	58	59	56
Women	34	44	54	36	44	61	49	52	61	65	65	65	57	56	58
AGE															
18-29	38	43	55	42	49	60	48	54	56	63	63	61	53	54	56
30-49	36	45	56	35	43	62	49	51	61	64	64	65	57	58	55
50 & over	35	46	56	36	41	62	48	49	62	66	68	65	60	60	59
EDUCATION															
College	38	42	54	38	46	58	43	48	54	62	63	59	56	55	50
High School	36	46	56	39	45	62	49	52	60	64	65	65	56	58	59
Grade School	36	47	58	33	39	63	52	54	64	67	68	67	62	62	60
FAMILY INCOME															
$15,000 & over	37	45	57	38	47	60	46	49	57	63	65	62	56	55	53
$10,000 - $14,999	37	44	56	35	46	62	46	51	60	64	64	65	57	58	55
$7,000 - $9,999	42	47	58	39	41	61	46	55	63	65	68	65	56	59	59
$5,000 - $6,999	33	47	57	38	45	63	54	52	62	62	66	65	57	58	61
Under $5,000	33	43	52	37	42	62	50	50	59	66	64	63	59	58	58

TABLE A-13 (cont'd)   PROGRESS: DOMESTIC PROBLEM AREAS

	Inflation	Unemployment	Business Conditions	Crime	Drugs & Addicts	Medical Care	Poverty & Welfare	Mass Transport	Senior Citizens	Black Americans	Education	Housing	Water Pollution	Air Pollution	Urban Problems
OCCUPATION															
Professional & Business	39	46	58	39	48	60	44	51	58	62	63	63	58	58	54
White Collar	38	46	55	40	44	59	48	53	58	64	63	64	56	56	55
Manual	36	43	54	38	43	62	50	53	60	64	67	65	56	58	58
Non-labor	34	45	55	34	42	63	49	45	60	66	64	63	57	56	58
UNION MEMBERSHIP															
Union Households	36	41	50	36	41	60	48	50	60	64	63	63	54	55	55
Non-union Households	36	47	58	38	45	62	48	52	60	64	66	64	59	59	58
HOME OWNERSHIP															
Home Owners	38	46	56	38	44	62	47	51	61	64	66	66	59	59	56
Non-owners	34	43	54	37	44	60	49	51	56	65	62	59	53	55	57
REGION															
East	34	39	52	37	41	61	45	48	58	67	67	60	53	55	52
Midwest	38	46	54	36	46	60	49	50	61	61	66	64	60	62	58
South	38	51	62	40	46	64	54	58	64	63	66	71	59	59	61
West	34	45	54	36	44	58	42	51	55	66	60	61	56	52	56
COMMUNITY SIZE															
500,000 & over	35	41	50	37	42	61	46	49	57	67	62	58	55	54	52
50,000 - 499,999	37	43	57	37	47	60	48	53	59	62	63	63	57	58	59
2,500 - 49,999	40	51	63	38	44	61	52	51	63	66	68	70	58	60	62
Under 2,500 & rural	35	48	57	38	44	63	48	54	61	62	68	69	60	60	58

TABLE A-13 (cont'd)

PROGRESS: DOMESTIC PROBLEM AREAS

	Inflation	Unemployment	Business Conditions	Crime	Drugs & Addicts	Medical Care	Poverty & Welfare	Mass Transport	Senior Citizens	Black Americans	Education	Housing	Water Pollution	Air Pollution	Urban Problems
TYPE OF PLACE															
City	34	42	54	36	43	60	48	51	59	63	63	60	57	56	57
Suburb	41	44	54	39	47	63	49	52	59	66	66	64	54	56	55
Town or village	32	48	62	37	44	62	47	50	60	68	67	69	57	60	58
Rural	37	49	58	39	45	63	51	55	62	64	68	69	63	64	59
RACE															
White	36	45	56	37	44	61	47	51	59	64	65	64	57	57	56
Black	35	42	53	39	42	65	56	58	67	66	66	63	60	59	59
RELIGION															
Protestant	37	48	58	39	44	62	49	53	61	64	66	66	58	59	58
Catholic	34	40	53	36	44	62	48	51	60	67	66	62	55	56	57
POLITICS															
Republican	41	51	60	38	45	63	47	51	62	69	67	65	61	60	58
Democrat	34	44	54	38	45	62	50	53	61	64	65	64	58	58	58
Independent	36	44	55	37	45	60	48	49	57	63	65	64	54	56	54
LIBERAL - CONSERVATIVE															
Very liberal	31	35	49	38	48	55	39	42	52	52	62	56	50	50	54
Moderately liberal	37	44	55	36	46	61	46	53	57	65	61	62	54	56	54
Middle of the road	37	46	54	38	45	63	52	52	62	65	66	65	59	59	58
Moderately conservative	36	47	60	39	42	62	46	52	61	66	68	66	60	58	56
Very conservative	34	45	63	34	38	62	49	53	62	58	72	69	54	59	63

TABLE A-14

PROGRESS: DOMESTIC PROBLEMS IN GENERAL

Summing up the overall domestic situation here in the United States today, do you think that in handling domestic problems generally we as a nation have made much progress, some progress, stood still, lost some ground, or lost much ground during the last twelve months?   (A,B,C)

[NOTE: *For a description of the method used in calculating the composite scores in the far right hand column below, see page 355.*]

	Made Much Progress	Made Some Progress	Stood Still	Lost Some Ground	Lost Much Ground	Don't Know	Composite Scores
NATIONAL TOTALS	4%	54%	22%	12%	3%	5%	62
SEX							
Men	3	53	23	13	3	5	61
Women	4	55	22	11	2	6	63
AGE							
18-29	4	50	25	14	3	4	60
30-49	3	55	20	14	4	4	60
50 & over	3	57	22	8	3	7	63
EDUCATION							
College	2	49	24	17	5	3	57
High School	4	56	22	11	3	4	62
Grade School	3	55	24	7	1	10	64
FAMILY INCOME							
$15,000 & over	3	54	21	16	3	3	60
$10,000 - $14,999	3	59	19	11	5	3	61
$7,000 - $9,999	3	54	26	12	3	2	61
$5,000 - $6,999	3	52	24	12	2	7	61
Under $5,000	5	51	23	10	2	9	63
OCCUPATION							
Professional & Business	4	53	23	13	4	3	60
White Collar	2	56	20	15	2	5	61
Manual	4	53	21	13	3	6	61
Non-labor	4	55	24	8	2	7	64
UNION MEMBERSHIP							
Union Households	2	53	23	13	3	6	60
Non-union Households	4	55	22	11	3	5	62
HOME OWNERSHIP							
Home Owners	3	55	23	11	3	5	62
Non-owners	3	52	22	13	3	7	61
REGION							
East	4	51	23	11	4	7	61
Midwest	3	53	25	13	2	4	61
South	4	58	19	9	4	6	63
West	2	54	23	15	3	3	60

TABLE A-14 (cont'd)

PROGRESS: DOMESTIC PROBLEMS IN GENERAL

	Made Much Progress	Made Some Progress	Stood Still	Lost Some Ground	Lost Much Ground	Don't Know	Composite Scores
COMMUNITY SIZE							
500,000 & over	3%	50%	24%	12%	4%	7%	60
50,000 - 499,999	4	56	21	12	4	3	61
2,500 - 49,999	4	60	18	11	2	5	64
Under 2,500 & rural	3	54	24	12	1	6	62
TYPE OF PLACE							
City	3	56	22	10	4	5	62
Suburb	4	54	24	13	3	2	61
Town or village	5	51	22	13	2	7	62
Rural	4	57	22	10	2	5	63
RACE							
White	4	54	23	12	3	4	61
Black	3	55	19	12	3	8	62
RELIGION							
Protestant	4	56	21	12	2	5	63
Catholic	4	55	23	11	3	4	62
POLITICS							
Republican	5	61	19	8	2	5	66
Democrat	3	52	22	14	3	6	60
Independent	3	54	24	11	4	4	61
LIBERAL - CONSERVATIVE							
Very liberal	4	44	20	19	9	4	54
Moderately liberal	4	52	23	15	3	3	60
Middle of the road	3	56	21	11	3	6	62
Moderately conservative	2	58	26	10	1	3	63
Very conservative	7	62	17	6	6	2	65

TABLE A-15

PROGRESS: OVERALL SITUATION AT HOME AND ABROAD

Now that you have had a chance to review our overall situation today
at home and abroad, is it your considered opinion that, in general, we as
a nation have made much progress, some progress, stood still, lost some
ground, or lost much ground during the last twelve months? (A,B,C)

[NOTE: For a description of the method used in calculating the com-
posite scores in the far right hand column see page 355.]

	Made Much Progress	Made Some Progress	Stood Still	Lost Some Ground	Lost Much Ground	Don't Know	Composite Scores
NATIONAL TOTALS	7%	60%	17%	10%	2%	4%	66
SEX							
Men	7	62	17	9	2	3	66
Women	7	59	18	11	2	3	65
AGE							
18-29	6	62	18	10	2	2	65
30-49	7	60	18	10	2	3	65
50 & over	8	59	16	10	2	5	66
EDUCATION							
College	5	59	19	11	3	3	63
High School	7	61	16	11	2	3	65
Grade School	8	60	17	8	1	6	68
FAMILY INCOME							
$15,000 & over	5	64	18	10	2	1	65
$10,000 - $14,999	8	59	16	13	2	2	65
$7,000 - $9,999	7	62	16	11	3	1	65
$5,000 - $6,999	8	60	16	11	3	2	65
Under $5,000	7	57	19	8	1	8	67
OCCUPATION							
Professional & Business	7	60	19	11	2	1	65
White Collar	8	62	16	10	*	4	68
Manual	6	61	17	11	2	3	65
Non-labor	8	59	16	9	2	6	66
UNION MEMBERSHIP							
Union Households	7	57	18	13	3	2	63
Non-union Households	7	62	17	9	2	3	66
HOME OWNERSHIP							
Home Owners	7	62	18	10	1	2	66
Non-owners	8	57	16	11	4	4	64

TABLE A-15 (cont'd)

PROGRESS: OVERALL SITUATION AT HOME AND ABROAD

	Made Much Progress	Made Some Progress	Stood Still	Lost Some Ground	Lost Much Ground	Don't Know	Composite Scores
REGION							
East	6%	58%	17%	12%	2%	5%	64
Midwest	6	61	19	12	*	2	66
South	9	62	16	7	3	3	67
West	7	59	18	10	4	2	64
COMMUNITY SIZE							
500,000 & over	5	59	19	12	2	3	64
50,000 - 499,999	9	56	17	11	3	4	65
2,500 - 49,999	10	65	13	7	1	4	70
Under 2,500 & rural	5	63	18	10	1	3	66
TYPE OF PLACE							
City	7	61	14	11	3	4	65
Suburb	7	56	22	12	2	1	64
Town or village	6	62	21	8	2	1	66
Rural	7	62	15	10	1	5	67
RACE							
White	7	60	18	10	2	3	65
Black	6	62	15	11	1	5	66
RELIGION							
Protestant	7	63	16	9	2	3	66
Catholic	7	57	18	12	2	4	64
POLITICS							
Republican	10	70	12	5	2	1	70
Democrat	7	58	18	11	2	4	65
Independent	4	58	19	14	2	3	62
LIBERAL - CONSERVATIVE							
Very liberal	4	60	11	17	2	6	63
Moderately liberal	8	60	15	11	4	2	65
Middle of the road	7	61	19	9	1	3	66
Moderately conservative	9	60	17	11	1	2	67
Very conservative	5	59	16	11	4	5	63

TABLE A-16

OVERALL COMPOSITE SCORES: CONCERNS AND GOVERNMENT SPENDING

[*The first two columns below give overall composite scores on degrees of concern obtained by averaging across-the-board the scores on inter- national and domestic concerns, respectively, listed individually in Tables A-3 and A-4. In the two columns at the right are composite scores on government spending obtained by averaging the individual scores on international and domestic spending, respectively, in Tables A-6 and A-7.*]

	Internat'l Concerns	Domestic Concerns	Government Spending - Internat'l*	Government Spending - Domestic
NATIONAL TOTALS	72	78	28	69
SEX				
Men	69	77	29	68
Women	73	79	27	70
AGE				
18-29	68	79	30	75
30-49	72	79	29	67
50 & over	74	77	25	67
EDUCATION				
College	64	78	27	70
High School	74	79	28	70
Grade School	77	77	27	66
FAMILY INCOME				
$15,000 & over	68	80	27	69
$10,000 - $14,999	73	77	26	69
$7,000 - $9,999	70	78	29	70
$5,000 - $6,999	74	79	29	68
Under $5,000	73	77	25	70
OCCUPATION				
Professional & Business	68	79	27	69
White Collar	68	77	29	73
Manual	75	80	30	71
Non-labor	70	75	23	66
UNION MEMBERSHIP				
Union Households	75	81	30	72
Non-union Households	71	78	27	69
HOME OWNERSHIP				
Home Owners	72	78	26	68
Non-owners	69	79	31	73
REGION				
East	68	78	28	71
Midwest	70	78	26	69
South	76	77	32	68
West	72	80	24	70

TABLE A-16   (cont'd)

OVERALL COMPOSITE SCORES: CONCERNS AND GOVERNMENT SPENDING

	Internat'l Concerns	Domestic Concerns	Government Spending - Internat'l*	Government Spending - Domestic
COMMUNITY SIZE				
500,000 & over	69	82	25	73
50,000 - 499,999	72	79	32	70
2,500 - 49,999	71	77	31	70
Under 2,500 & rural	73	74	26	65
TYPE OF PLACE				
City	69	81	29	72
Suburb	74	80	26	70
Town or village	72	76	28	68
Rural	73	73	26	65
RACE				
White	72	77	28	68
Black	71	85	29	81
RELIGION				
Protestant	72	77	28	69
Catholic	73	81	28	71
POLITICS				
Republican	69	74	25	65
Democrat	73	80	29	71
Independent	73	79	27	70
LIBERAL - CONSERVATIVE				
Very liberal	64	83	25	80
Moderately liberal	69	83	29	72
Middle of the road	74	77	27	69
Moderately conservative	72	75	28	64
Very conservative	75	77	33	64

*These composite figures were derived by averaging the scores for
spending on: United Nations activities; economic aid; military aid;
U.S. forces in Europe; and military bases abroad.   They do not include scores on defense spending, since that question was posed to a
separate sample by The Gallup Organization in August 1972.
Composite scores for these five items and defense spending appear in
Table A-6.

TABLE A-17

OVERALL COMPOSITE SCORES: PROGRESS AND CONFIDENCE

[The first column gives overall composite scores on progress obtained by averaging across-the-board the individual scores on progress with respect to various facets of the international situation listed individually in Table A-11. The third column does the same thing with the individual scores on domestic items listed in Table A-13. The second and fourth columns simply repeat for purposes of comparison the scores on progress on foreign policy matters in general and on domestic problems in general given in Tables A-12 and A-14. The fifth column gives composite scores on trust and confidence obtained by averaging the individual scores on trust and confidence in the federal government when it comes to handling domestic matters with those on state and local governments, respectively, given in Table A-8.]

	Progress - Internat'l Problem Areas	Progress - Internat'l in General	Progress - Domestic Problem Areas	Progress - Domestic Problems in General	Trust & Confidence Federal, State, Local Governments
NATIONAL TOTALS	60	66	53	62	59
SEX					
Men	60	67	54	61	58
Women	60	65	53	63	61
AGE					
18-29	59	64	53	60	58
30-49	60	67	53	60	58
50 & over	60	66	54	63	62
EDUCATION					
College	59	66	51	57	57
High School	60	66	54	62	60
Grade School	60	65	55	64	62

TABLE A-17 (cont'd)

OVERALL COMPOSITE SCORES: PROGRESS AND CONFIDENCE

	Progress - Internat'l Problem Areas	Progress - Internat'l in General	Progress - Domestic Problem Areas	Progress - Domestic Problems in General	Trust & Confidence Federal, State, Local Governments
FAMILY INCOME					
$15,000 & over	61	68	53	60	57
$10,000 - $14,999	60	66	53	61	60
$7,000 - $9,999	60	64	55	61	61
$5,000 - $6,999	61	68	55	61	60
Under $5,000	59	62	53	63	60
OCCUPATION					
Professional & Business	61	69	53	60	57
White Collar	60	64	53	61	61
Manual	59	65	54	61	59
Non-labor	59	64	53	64	62
UNION MEMBERSHIP					
Union Households	60	65	52	60	60
Non-union Households	60	66	54	62	59
HOME OWNERSHIP					
Home Owners	61	66	54	62	59
Non-owners	58	65	52	61	59
REGION					
East	60	67	51	61	56
Midwest	61	66	54	61	60
South	61	64	57	63	62
West	58	65	51	60	62

TABLE A-17 (cont'd)   OVERALL COMPOSITE SCORES: PROGRESS AND CONFIDENCE

	Progress - Internat'l Problem Areas	Progress - Internat'l in General	Progress - Domestic Problem Areas	Progress - Domestic Problems in General	Trust & Confidence Federal, State, Local Governments
COMMUNITY SIZE					
500,000 & over	60	65	51	60	57
50,000 - 499,999	59	66	53	61	59
2,500 - 49,999	61	67	56	64	61
Under 2,500 & rural	60	65	55	62	62
TYPE OF PLACE					
City	59	66	52	62	59
Suburb	61	66	54	61	60
Town or village	61	65	55	62	63
Rural	61	67	56	63	61
RACE					
White	60	66	53	61	60
Black	60	62	55	62	54
RELIGION					
Protestant	61	66	55	63	61
Catholic	60	67	53	62	60
POLITICS					
Republican	65	73	56	66	68
Democrat	59	64	54	60	57
Independent	58	63	52	61	58
LIBERAL - CONSERVATIVE					
Very liberal	59	65	48	54	54
Moderately liberal	60	66	52	60	60
Middle of the road	60	65	55	62	59
Moderately conservative	61	67	55	63	61
Very conservative	58	63	54	65	60

TABLE A-18

EVALUATION OF INTERNATIONAL SITUATION IN GENERAL

Looking at the matter a little differently, how would you rate the international situation the United States faces in general at the present time: excellent, good, only fair, or poor? (A,B,C)

[NOTE: For a description of the method used in calculating the composite scores in the far right hand column below, see page 355.]

	Excellent	Good	Only Fair	Poor	Don't Know	Composite Scores
NATIONAL TOTALS	2%	33%	48%	9%	8%	43
SEX						
Men	2	37	47	9	5	45
Women	2	29	49	9	11	42
AGE						
18-29	1	35	48	9	7	43
30-49	1	33	50	8	8	43
50 & over	4	31	46	9	10	44
EDUCATION						
College	2	34	50	10	4	43
High School	1	36	49	8	6	44
Grade School	3	23	43	12	19	40
FAMILY INCOME						
$15,000 & over	3	34	48	9	6	44
$10,000 - $14,999	2	38	52	6	2	46
$7,000 - $9,999	1	34	49	10	6	42
$5,000 - $6,999	2	35	43	13	7	43
Under $5,000	2	27	47	8	16	42
OCCUPATION						
Professional & Business	4	35	49	7	5	46
White Collar	4	39	41	9	7	47
Manual	1	32	51	9	7	42
Non-labor	1	29	46	11	13	41
UNION MEMBERSHIP						
Union Households	1	33	48	9	9	43
Non-union Households	2	33	48	9	8	43
HOME OWNERSHIP						
Home Owners	2	34	49	8	7	44
Non-owners	1	31	45	11	12	42
REGION						
East	2	33	47	6	12	45
Midwest	2	31	50	9	8	43
South	2	36	45	11	6	44
West	1	32	50	12	5	41
COMMUNITY SIZE						
500,000 & over	1	31	47	8	13	43
50,000 - 499,999	4	34	44	11	7	44
2,500 - 49,999	1	34	51	9	5	43
Under 2,500 & rural	2	33	50	8	7	44

TABLE A-18   (cont'd)

EVALUATION OF INTERNATIONAL SITUATION IN GENERAL

	Excellent	Good	Only Fair	Poor	Don't Know	Composite Scores
TYPE OF PLACE						
City	2%	31%	46%	10%	11%	43
Suburb	3	33	51	8	5	44
Town or village	1	33	49	11	6	42
Rural	1	35	50	6	8	45
RACE						
White	2	34	48	9	7	44
Black	1	22	44	8	25	40
RELIGION						
Protestant	2	33	49	8	8	44
Catholic	2	34	49	7	8	44
POLITICS						
Republican	4	45	42	4	5	50
Democrat	1	30	48	9	12	42
Independent	2	30	52	11	5	41
LIBERAL - CONSERVATIVE						
Very liberal	1	33	39	13	14	42
Moderately liberal	2	33	51	8	6	44
Middle of the road	2	34	49	8	7	44
Moderately conservative	2	34	51	7	6	44
Very conservative	3	32	39	15	11	42

TABLE A-19

EVALUATION OF DOMESTIC SITUATION IN GENERAL

Looking at the matter a little differently, how would you rate the domestic situation in the United States today in general: excellent, good, only fair, or poor? (A,B,C)

[NOTE: For a description of the method used in calculating the composite scores in the far right hand column below, see page 355.]

	Excellent	Good	Only Fair	Poor	Don't Know	Composite Scores
NATIONAL TOTALS	1%	29%	54%	10%	6%	41
SEX						
Men	2	29	54	11	4	41
Women	1	29	54	10	6	41
AGE						
18-29	1	29	57	10	3	40
30-49	1	29	53	13	4	40
50 & over	2	29	53	8	8	42
EDUCATION						
College	*	30	55	13	2	39
High School	1	30	54	10	5	41
Grade School	2	25	52	9	12	41
FAMILY INCOME						
$15,000 & over	*	29	59	9	3	40
$10,000 - $14,999	2	31	54	11	2	41
$7,000 - $9,999	1	30	55	11	3	40
$5,000 - $6,999	2	32	46	11	9	42
Under $5,000	1	26	54	10	9	40
OCCUPATION						
Professional & Business	1	29	59	8	3	41
White Collar	2	33	50	11	4	42
Manual	1	29	53	12	5	40
Non-labor	2	28	53	10	7	41
UNION MEMBERSHIP						
Union Households	*	29	52	13	6	39
Non-union Households	2	29	55	9	5	42
HOME OWNERSHIP						
Home Owners	1	30	55	9	5	41
Non-owners	1	27	53	12	7	39
REGION						
East	1	27	52	12	8	39
Midwest	1	28	57	10	4	40
South	2	30	53	9	6	42
West	1	33	53	9	4	42
COMMUNITY SIZE						
500,000 & over	1	25	56	12	6	39
50,000 - 499,999	2	28	51	14	5	40
2,500 - 49,999	2	29	57	5	7	43
Under 2,500 & rural	1	34	53	8	4	43

TABLE A-19   (cont'd)

EVALUATION OF DOMESTIC SITUATION IN GENERAL

	Excellent	Good	Only Fair	Poor	Don't Know	Composite Scores
TYPE OF PLACE						
City	1%	27%	54%	12%	6%	39
Suburb	1	28	56	9	6	41
Town or village	1	32	57	6	4	43
Rural	1	33	53	10	3	42
RACE						
White	1	30	54	10	5	41
Black	1	22	55	12	10	38
RELIGION						
Protestant	1	31	53	9	6	42
Catholic	1	28	57	9	5	41
POLITICS						
Republican	1	37	53	4	5	46
Democrat	2	28	53	12	6	41
Independent	*	27	57	12	4	38
LIBERAL - CONSERVATIVE						
Very liberal	1	24	50	15	10	37
Moderately liberal	1	25	59	11	4	39
Middle of the road	1	32	53	9	5	42
Moderately conservative	2	30	56	9	3	42
Very conservative	2	37	40	16	5	42

TABLE A-20

EVALUATION OF OVERALL STATE OF THE NATION

Finally, let's pull everything together. Taking into account the situation both at home and abroad at the present time, what would you say is the state of the nation in this year 1972: excellent, good, only fair, or poor? (A,B,C)

[NOTE: For a description of the method used in calculating the composite scores in the far right hand column below, see page 355.]

	Excellent	Good	Only Fair	Poor	Don't Know	Composite Scores
NATIONAL TOTALS	3%	38%	50%	7%	2%	46
SEX						
Men	4	39	50	6	1	47
Women	2	37	49	8	4	45
AGE						
18-29	2	39	48	10	1	44
30-49	4	38	51	7	*	46
50 & over	4	39	49	6	2	47
EDUCATION						
College	2	40	51	7	*	46
High School	4	38	50	7	1	46
Grade School	5	37	47	7	4	47
FAMILY INCOME						
$15,000 & over	2	41	51	6	*	46
$10,000 - $14,999	3	37	52	8	*	45
$7,000 - $9,999	5	38	48	8	1	47
$5,000 - $6,999	4	44	42	7	3	49
Under $5,000	4	33	52	7	4	45
OCCUPATION						
Professional & Business	2	40	52	6	*	46
White Collar	4	37	51	5	3	47
Manual	3	38	49	8	2	46
Non-labor	5	37	47	7	4	47
UNION MEMBERSHIP						
Union Households	3	37	49	10	1	44
Non-union Households	3	39	50	6	2	47
HOME OWNERSHIP						
Home Owners	3	39	50	6	2	47
Non-owners	4	37	49	9	1	45
REGION						
East	3	37	50	7	3	46
Midwest	3	36	53	5	3	46
South	4	41	46	8	1	47
West	3	39	50	8	*	46
COMMUNITY SIZE						
500,000 & over	2	36	52	9	1	44
50,000 - 499,999	5	37	47	8	3	47
2,500 - 49,999	5	39	50	4	2	49
Under 2,500 & rural	2	42	49	6	1	47

TABLE A-20 (cont'd)

EVALUATION OF OVERALL STATE OF THE NATION

	Excellent	Good	Only Fair	Poor	Don't Know	Composite Scores
TYPE OF PLACE						
City	4%	37%	49%	8%	2%	46
Suburb	2	38	51	8	1	45
Town or village	3	37	54	4	2	47
Rural	4	39	50	6	1	47
RACE						
White	3	39	49	7	2	46
Black	2	30	55	7	6	43
RELIGION						
Protestant	4	40	48	6	2	48
Catholic	3	40	50	5	2	47
POLITICS						
Republican	4	53	39	3	1	53
Democrat	3	35	51	8	3	45
Independent	2	35	54	8	1	44
LIBERAL - CONSERVATIVE						
Very liberal	4	32	48	15	1	42
Moderately liberal	4	36	52	7	1	46
Middle of the road	3	38	51	7	1	46
Moderately conservative	3	44	47	4	2	49
Very conservative	6	35	48	6	5	48

Appendix 3

COMPUTING PERSONAL AND NATIONAL LADDER RATINGS

Average personal and national ladder ratings for the "self-anchoring striving scale" technique explained in Chapter I are computed as follows:

1. The number of respondents pointing to a specific step on the ladder is multiplied by the number (zero through 10) of that step. For example, if 162 respondents named step 7, 162 is multiplied by 7 to yield 1,134. If the step indicated was zero, the total would, of course, be zero.
2. The yields from all of these multiplications are then added for a grand total.
3. This grand total is divided by the total number of respondents who gave ladder ratings, excluding those who replied "don't know" or did not answer.

It goes without saying that under this system the highest possible average rating would be a theoretical 10; the lowest, zero.

Appendix 4

INTERNATIONAL PATTERNS

Our system of international patterns is based on reactions to the following seven statements:

1. The U.S. should cooperate fully with the United Nations.
2. In deciding its foreign policies, the U.S. should take into account the views of its major allies.
3. Since the U.S. is the most powerful nation in the world, we should go our own way in international matters, not worrying too much about whether other countries agree with us or not.
4. The U.S. should come to the defense of its major European allies with military force if any of them are attacked by Soviet Russia.
5. The U.S. should come to the defense of Japan with military force if it is attacked by Soviet Russia or Communist China.
6. The U.S. should mind its own business internationally and let other countries get along as best they can on their own.
7. We shouldn't think so much in international terms but concentrate more on our own national problems and building up our strength and prosperity here at home.

Interviews in which respondents answered "don't know" on three or more of these items were eliminated in tabulating. The remaining cases were then divided into five categories ranging from "completely internationalist" to "completely isolationist." To qualify as "completely internationalist," a respondent had to react—either to all seven of the statements, or to six (with one "don't know"), or to five (with two "don't knows")—by

353

agreeing that the U.S. should cooperate with the U.N., take into account the views of its allies, and come to the defense of its Western European allies and Japan, while disagreeing that the U.S. should go its own way, mind its own business, and concentrate more on national problems. Those termed "predominantly internationalist" conformed to this pattern in at least five cases if they reacted to all seven statements, or in at least four cases if they answered five or six of the questions (with one or two "don't knows").

The "completely isolationist" category was exactly the opposite of the "completely internationalist" one. The "predominantly isolationist" respondents conformed to the "completely isolationist" pattern to the same degree that the "predominantly internationalist" group conformed to the "completely internationalist" pattern.

The remaining interviews showing greater deviation from both the "completely internationalist" and the "completely isolationist" patterns were put into a so-called mixed category.

The method used in computing composite scores from the results is described in Appendix 5.

Appendix 5

COMPUTING COMPOSITE SCORES

To simplify presentation and facilitate comprehension, several scoring systems were used on various sets of questions so that single composite scores could be substituted for complicated arrays of percentages. The range of each of these scoring systems was from a minimum of zero to a maximum of 100. Among other advantages, this system makes it easy to put results from related questions in rank order from the highest composite score to the lowest. The various procedures involved are described below.

PROGRESS

Answers to questions asking whether the country had made progress, stood still, or lost ground in various respects during the past year were scored as follows:

"Made much progress"	100 points
"Made some progress"	75 points
"Stood still"	50 points
"Lost some ground"	25 points
"Lost much ground"	0 points

The grand total of these categorical scores was then divided by the total number of respondents who expressed an opinion, excluding those who replied "don't know" or gave no answer.

The median of the scoring range being 50, any composite scores in the neighborhood of 50 indicate a preponderance of opinion that the country virtually stood still during the preceding year in the particular respect asked about. On the other hand, scores in the neighborhood of 75 indicate a predominantly favorable view that the country made at least some progress; and scores in the top range approaching 100, that the county made a great deal of progress. Conversely, scores near 25 are indicative of a generally unfavorable feeling that the country lost at least some ground; and those in the bottom range approaching zero, that it lost a great deal of ground.

WORRIES AND CONCERNS

In scoring answers to questions about how worried or concerned respondents were about various problems, "a great deal" was rated at 100, "a fair amount" at two-thirds of 100, "not very much" at one-third of 100, and "not at all" at zero. With the median of the scoring range again being 50, scores in the upper range indicate a tendency toward considerable-to-great concern, and scores in the lower range, relatively little concern.

INTERNATIONAL PATTERNS

Under the system of international patterns described in Appendix 4, the various categories were scored as follows:

Completely internationalist	100 points
Predominantly internationalist	75 points
Mixed	50 points
Predominantly isolationist	25 points
Completely isolationist	0 points

Thus, scores above the median of 50 indicate a tendency toward internationalist views, and those in the lower range, a tendency toward isolationism.

GOVERNMENTAL SPENDING

Answers to questions about whether governmental spending for various purposes should be increased, kept at the present level, reduced, or ended altogether were scored as follows:

"Increased"   100 points
"Kept at present level"   50 points
"Reduced" or "Ended"   0 points

With the median of the scoring range 50, composite scores in that neighborhood indicate a preponderance of opinion that governmental spending for the particular program or programs asked about should be kept at about the present level. On the other hand, scores in the upper range show a predominant view that spending should be increased; and in the lower range, that the programs should be reduced or even ended altogether.

EVALUATIONS OF THE SITUATION AND OF OUR GOVERNMENTAL SYSTEM

In scoring answers to questions about the general domestic and international situations, the overall state of the nation, and our governmental system as a whole, "excellent" was rated at 100, "good" at two-thirds of 100, "only fair" at one-third of 100, and "poor" at zero.

With 50 being the median of the scoring range, composite scores above that level indicate a predominantly favorable evaluation, from good to excellent, depending upon the particular score, while scores at the lower level are indicative of a prevailingly unfavorable view, from fair to poor.

TRUST AND CONFIDENCE

In scoring answers as to how much trust and confidence respondents had in various institutions, "a great deal" was rated at 100, "a fair amount" at two-thirds of 100, "not very much" at one-third of 100, and "none at all" at zero. With the median of the scoring range being 50, scores in the upper range indicate a tendency toward considerable-to-great trust and confidence, and scores in the lower range, relatively little trust and confidence.

Appendix 6

DESIGN AND COMPOSITION OF THE SAMPLE

The Gallup Organization, which designed the sample upon which this study is based, maintains a national probability sample of interviewing areas that is used for all of its National Opinion Trends surveys, such as our present survey. The sampling procedure is designed to produce an approximation of the total adult civilian population, eighteen years of age and older, living in the United States, except those persons in institutions such as prisons or hospitals.

The design of the sample was that of a replicated, probability sample, down to the block level in the case of urban areas and to segments of townships in the case of rural areas. Approximately three hundred sampling points—clusters of blocks or rural segments—were used in this survey.

The sample design included stratification by the following seven size-of-community strata: central cities with a population of 1,000,000 and over; of 250,000 to 999,999; of 50,000 to 249,999; the urbanized fringe areas of all of these central cities as a single stratum; cities 2,500 to 49,999; rural villages; and rural open areas. Each of these strata was further stratified into seven geographic regions. Within each city-size regional stratum, the population was geographically ordered and zoned into equal sized groups of sampling units. A pair of localities were then randomly drawn in each zone with the probability of selection proportional to population size, thus producing two replications.

Within the localities selected for which population data were available, subdivisions were drawn with the probability of selection proportional to size of population. In all other localities small definable geographic areas were selected with equal probability. Within each subdivision selected for which block statistics were available, a sample of blocks was drawn with probability of selection proportional to the number of dwelling units. In all other subdivisions or areas, blocks or segments were drawn at random.

In each cluster of selected blocks or segments, a randomly selected starting point was designated on the interviewer's map of the area. Starting at this point, the interviewer followed a specified direction in the selection of households until he completed his assignment. Interviewing was conducted at times when adults in general were most likely to be at home—on weekends and weekdays after 4:00 P.M. for women and after 6:00 P.M. for men.

The prestratification by regions was supplemented by fitting each obtained sample to the latest available Census Bureau estimates of the regional distribution of the population. Also, minor adjustments of the sample were made by educational attainment (for men and women separately), derived from the Census Bureau's Current Population Survey.

In order to obtain enough interviews with black Americans to afford a reasonable degree of statistical reliability for breakdowns on the basis of race, nonwhites were systematically oversampled. This was done by instructing interviewers to obtain two extra supplemental interviews with nonwhites each time one of them was drawn into the interviewer's assigned quota in the regular sample. This produced an unusually high total for a study of this kind of 373 interviews with blacks, properly distributed geographically. Needless to say, in calculating overall figures for the sample as a whole, the interviews with blacks were then weighted down to their proper proportion of the total adult population as shown by the Census Bureau figures.

The composition of the sample in demographic terms is shown in the following table. Definitions of the breakdowns employed are given at the beginning of Appendix 2.

TABLE A-21

COMPOSITION OF THE SAMPLE

	"A" Version	"B" Version	"C" Version	Total Sample	
	Number of Interviews	Number of Interviews	Number of Interviews	Number of Interviews	% of Sample (Weighted)
NATIONAL TOTALS	669	613	524	1806	
SEX					
Men	340	229	274	913	47.9
Women	329	314	250	893	52.1
AGE					
18-29	187	166	147	500	28.6
30-49	199	211	184	594	32.3
50 & over	276	230	186	692	38.6
Undesignated	7	6	7	20	.5
EDUCATION					
College	180	178	155	513	24.5
High School	371	330	279	980	56.2
Grade School	114	105	85	304	19.1
Undesignated	4	-	5	9	.2
FAMILY INCOME					
$15,000 & over	165	120	133	418	23.1
$10,000 - $14,999	138	122	91	351	19.3
$7,000 - $9,999	110	98	82	290	15.8
$5,000 - $6,999	80	103	77	260	15.1
Under $5,000	164	155	123	442	24.4
Undesignated	12	15	18	45	2.3

TABLE A-21 (cont'd)

COMPOSITION OF THE SAMPLE

	"A" Version Number of Interviews	"B" Version Number of Interviews	"C" Version Number of Interviews	Total Sample Number of Interviews	Total Sample % of Sample (Weighted)
OCCUPATION					
Professional & Business	174	149	132	455	24.1
White Collar	68	70	54	192	10.7
Manual	256	215	207	678	37.8
Farmers	24	23	20	67	4.1
Non-labor	118	126	95	339	19.6
Undesignated	29	30	17	76	3.7
UNION MEMBERSHIP					
Union Households	172	150	139	461	25.0
Non-union Households	477	425	371	1273	71.5
Undesignated	20	38	14	72	3.5
HOME OWNERSHIP					
Home Owners	421	398	342	1161	65.3
Non-owners	213	195	156	564	30.4
Undesignated	35	20	26	81	4.3
REGION					
East	198	179	155	532	28.4
Midwest	181	168	142	491	28.1
South	188	175	149	512	26.7
West	102	91	78	271	16.8
COMMUNITY SIZE					
500,000 & over	239	217	199	655	33.7
50,000 - 499,999	150	139	124	413	22.2
2,500 - 49,999	105	94	70	269	15.6
Under 2,500 & rural	175	162	131	468	28.5

TABLE A-21 (cont'd)

COMPOSITION OF THE SAMPLE

	"A" Version Number of Interviews	"B" Version Number of Interviews	"C" Version Number of Interviews	Total Sample Number of Interviews	Total Sample % of Sample (Weighted)
TYPE OF PLACE					
City	260	245	204	709	36.3
Suburb	138	128	114	380	22.1
Town or village	95	82	73	250	15.1
Rural	117	105	92	314	18.4
Undesignated	59	53	41	153	8.1
RACE					
White	538	495	400	1433	88.0
Black	124	116	119	359	12.0
RELIGION					
Protestant	419	393	328	1140	61.0
Catholic	176	148	132	456	27.0
Jewish	21	14	10	45	2.7
Others	53	58	54	165	9.3
POLITICS					
Republican	118	128	91	337	19.8
Democrat	318	257	249	824	43.2
Independent	197	199	146	542	31.0
All others	36	29	38	103	6.0
LIBERAL – CONSERVATIVE					
Very liberal	36	56	44	136	6.2
Moderately liberal	178	143	143	464	25.5
Middle of the road	226	197	180	603	36.0
Moderately conservative	147	135	103	385	20.9
Very conservative	35	31	24	90	4.8
Undesignated	47	51	30	128	6.6